GW00646422

Edited and designed
by David Dew

Contributors

Richard Birch	Paul Kealy	Tom Segal
Scott Burton	Lawrie Kelsey	Brian Sheerin
Tom Collins	Andrew King	Martin Stevens
Graham Dench	David Milnes	Alan Sweetman
Dave Edwards	Justin O'Hanlon	Simon Turner
Nicholas Godfrey	Dave Orton	Nick Watts
Pietro Innocenzi	Lewis Porteous	Robbie Wilders
David Jennings	Peter Scargill	

Cover artwork by Jay Vincent

Published in 2020 by Racing Post Books, Raceform, 27 Kingfisher Court, Hambridge Road, Newbury, RG14 5SJ

ISBN: 978-1-83950-041-1

Printed by Buxton Press Limited

RACING POST

THE TRAINERS

THE EXPERTS

THE KEY HORSES

THE STATS

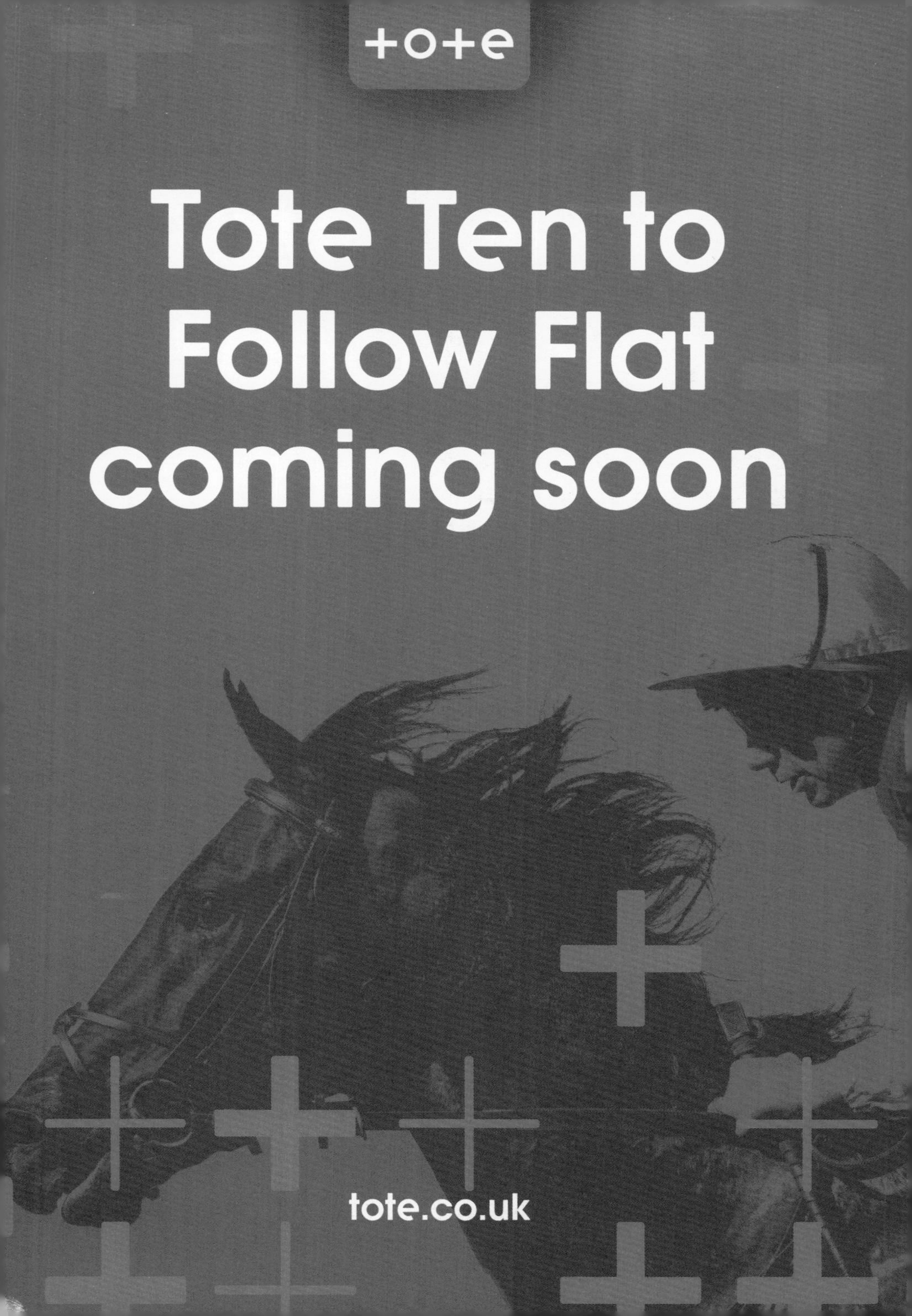
tote
Tote Ten to Follow Flat coming soon
tote.co.uk

ANDREW BALDING

Ready to build on best season yet with squad of quality ammunition

FOLLOWING a career-best year with 126 winners on the board and over £3.6 million in prize-money, Andrew Balding is looking forward to another successful and profitable summer with around 200 horses in his care at the historic Park House Stables in Kingsclere near Newbury.

The trainer says: " We have a strong team of older horses in the four- and five-year-old bracket backed up by some three-year-olds with a good number of juveniles waiting in the wings. For the past couple of seasons we've been lucky to have a very welcome influx of well-bred horses owned by King Power Racing which is the case again."

Looking ahead to the turf season, Balding is optimistic that **Kameko**, who landed the rescheduled Group 1 Vertem Futurity at Newcastle after the abandonment of Doncaster last September, can make his presence felt in the early season Classics.

Balding says: "He was a very good two-year-old who always had the physical make-up of a horse destined to do well at three. I

DID YOU KNOW?

As a big Southampton fan Balding idolised his now fellow trainer Mick Channon – who is something of a club legend with 185 goals in 510 appearances across two spells as a striker with the club. During that first spell he also led the line for England, netting 21 goals in 46 appearances

WINNERS IN LAST FIVE YEARS 126, 123, 93, 107, 95

'I don't think he's short of speed and we'll definitely be taking a look at the 2,000 Guineas'

don't think he's short of speed and we'll definitely be taking a look at the 2,000 Guineas with him.

"My feeling is that a mile and a quarter will be his optimum trip over the summer months, but he's entered at Epsom, there's only one Derby and we might well consider letting him take his chance."

Balding has high hopes that **Dashing Willoughby**, who took the Queen's Vase at Royal Ascot last year, can make up into a top staying horse this time and he says: "He's got all the qualities to win lots of nice races this year. He looks the part and there's every possibility he could develop into a Cup horse.

"The ideal plan will be to start him off in something like the Group 3 John Porter Stakes at Newbury and if he passes that examination we'd have to start thinking in terms of the Ascot Gold Cup as we know he acts well around the course."

An issue early last spring meant **Fox Tal** had a truncated season 12 months ago but

Dashing Willoughby leads the pack at Royal Ascot

Balding is confident the best is still to come from the relatively unexposed four-year-old who has seen racecourse duty just half a dozen times.

The trainer says: "He was off until September but showed a lovely turn of foot to win on his comeback at Doncaster before going on to run an absolute blinder in the Champion Stakes at Ascot just over a month later, when he was beaten only just over three lengths by Magical on softish ground.

"I'm hopeful he'll stay a mile and a half at some stage but the logical target in the mid-summer months of the season is probably the Eclipse at Sandown. He'll have to show he deserves his place in the line-up for a race like that but I'm very much looking forward to seeing him run again."

Another King Power-owned inmate who is held in high regard by Balding is **Fox**

Chairman who the trainer feels was a bit unlucky in the Group 3 Hampton Court at Royal Ascot last June, which is something of an understatement as the son of Kingman had something of a nightmare run throughout the race.

Balding says: "Nothing went his way in the Royal Ascot race and he did very well to finish second as he was buffeted around at critical points of the race and never got going until it was as good as over.

"However, he gained some compensation when winning in Listed company at Newbury next time. His overall form reads very well and he has a lot of potential for this season."

Although **Shine So Bright** proved good enough to beat Laurens in the Group 2 City Of York on the Knavesmire over seven furlongs last August, Balding is very much toying with the idea of dropping him back to sprint distances this summer.

He reasons: "He's not short of speed and I think six furlongs might be ideal and perhaps the Golden Jubilee at Royal Ascot might be the aim. He goes very well fresh so we might just go straight there."

Plenty of options for King's

King's Lynn, owned and bred by The Queen, ran only twice last term when second at Windsor before collecting a very valuable pot at Doncaster when landing the £300,000 Weatherbys Racing Bank Stakes, and Balding is certain that there is more to come from the speedy individual.

He says: "He did nothing wrong in just a couple of tries but I think he's a six- to seven-

Fox Chairman: Newbury winner has more to give

Balding has a 14% strike-rate with juveniles since the start of January 2016 – giving a profit of £65.01

ANDREW BALDING
KINGSCLERE, HAMPSHIRE

	Number of horses	Races run	1st	2nd	3rd	Unpl	Per cent	£1 level stake
2yo	51	129	21	18	12	78	16.3	+17.14
3yo	88	446	73	70	61	242	16.4	-91.56
4yo+	52	277	32	29	29	187	11.6	-84.17
Totals	**191**	**852**	**126**	**117**	**102**	**507**	**14.8**	**-158.59**
2018	183	772	123	105	106	437	15.9	-55.35
2017	160	677	93	100	71	411	13.7	-67.39

BY MONTH

2yo	W-R	Per cent	£1 level stake	3yo	W-R	Per cent	£1 level stake
Jan	0-0	0.0	0.00	Jan	5-21	23.8	-3.14
Feb	0-0	0.0	0.00	Feb	1-11	9.1	-8.25
Mar	0-0	0.0	0.00	Mar	9-19	47.4	+24.11
Apr	0-0	0.0	0.00	Apr	12-57	21.1	-17.24
May	1-6	16.7	-1.50	May	12-81	14.8	-20.87
June	2-8	25.0	+4.80	June	8-65	12.3	-26.91
July	4-15	26.7	+11.00	July	7-53	13.2	-23.32
Aug	6-27	22.2	-4.20	Aug	7-56	12.5	-28.05
Sep	6-34	17.6	+35.04	Sep	7-37	18.9	+18.61
Oct	1-25	4.0	-20.50	Oct	5-35	14.3	+4.50
Nov	1-8	12.5	-1.50	Nov	0-9	0.0	-9.00
Dec	0-6	0.0	-6.00	Dec	0-2	0.0	-2.00

4yo+	W-R	Per cent	£1 level stake	Totals	W-R	Per cent	£1 level stake
Jan	1-19	5.3	-16.00	Jan	6-40	15.0	-19.14
Feb	1-14	7.1	-11.00	Feb	2-25	8.0	-19.25
Mar	3-14	21.4	+7.00	Mar	12-33	36.4	+31.11
Apr	3-24	12.5	-15.50	Apr	15-81	18.5	-32.74
May	7-56	12.5	-16.17	May	20-143	14.0	-38.54
June	4-38	10.5	-19.63	June	14-111	12.6	-41.74
July	4-30	13.3	-3.00	July	15-98	15.3	-15.32
Aug	1-32	3.1	-25.50	Aug	14-115	12.2	-57.75
Sep	5-31	16.1	-14.38	Sep	18-102	17.6	+39.27
Oct	3-15	20.0	+34.00	Oct	9-75	12.0	+18.00
Nov	0-1	0.0	-1.00	Nov	1-18	5.6	-10.00
Dec	0-3	0.0	-3.00	Dec	0-11	0.0	-5.00

DISTANCE

2yo	W-R	Per cent	£1 level stake	3yo	W-R	Per cent	£1 level stake
5f-6f	8-48	16.7	+3.22	5f-6f	4-40	10.0	-24.64
7f-8f	12-77	15.6	+15.17	7f-8f	34-157	21.7	+12.97
9f-13f	1-4	25.0	-1.25	9f-13f	32-219	14.6	-78.89
14f+	0-0	0.0	0.00	14f+	3-30	10.0	-1.00

4yo+	W-R	Per cent	£1 level stake	Totals	W-R	Per cent	£1 level stake
5f-6f	6-53	11.3	+3.88	5f-6f	18-141	12.8	-17.54
7f-8f	13-98	13.3	-34.17	7f-8f	59-332	17.8	-6.03
9f-13f	9-91	9.9	-48.88	9f-13f	42-314	13.4	-129.02
14f+	4-35	11.4	-5.00	14f+	7-65	10.8	-6.00

TYPE OF RACE

	NON-HANDICAPS				HANDICAPS		
	W-R	Per cent	£1 level stake		W-R	Per cent	£1 level stake
2yo	21-122	17.2	+24.14	2yo	0-7	0.0	-7.00
3yo	41-199	20.6	-19.95	3yo	32-247	13.0	-71.60
4yo+	11-80	13.8	-11.88	4yo+	21-197	10.7	-72.29

Statistics relate to all runners in Britain from January 1, 2019 to December 31, 2019

furlong horse as I'm not sure he'll get any further. There are plenty of options for him going into the spring and summer and he remains anything but exposed."

Balding is also very keen on **Chil Chil**, who landed three races from just four starts following wind surgery last summer. This half-sister to the ill-fated but very smart Beat The Bank is at her best on fast ground, so the trainer wants the rain to stay away over the summer.

He says: "She kept improving and I'm hopeful there might be a bit more to come when she has quick going. The likelihood is we'll start her off in handicaps as she has a mark in the mid-80s and then it will be a case of taking it from there with her."

Two who can step up

When asked for a couple of darker types to keep an eye on, Balding is keen on the chances of **Berlin Tango** and **Khalifa Sat**, both of whom are sure to pay their way during the turf season.

He says: "Berlin Tango bolted up in an ordinary race at Ffos Las but finished the year with solid placed efforts in Listed company. I think he'll thrive on fast ground at up to a mile and a quarter and there are plenty of races in him over the spring and summer.

"Khalifa Sat is a big, scopey sort who stays very well. He won despite the very soft ground at Goodwood last September and he's always given the impression he was going to make into a better horse at three."

Tactical can strike early

Like many other trainers in Britain, Balding says the very wet winter has left him behind with many of his two-year-olds but says one youngster is nevertheless catching the eye.

He says: "I like the look of one called **Tactical**. He's the type to do well in the early part of the season because he's quite sharp already. But as far as the majority of the young horses are concerned it's going to be wait and see as we've not done a lot with them."

REPORTING BY ANDREW KING

Andrew Balding keeps an eye on his string as they work towards the new season

RALPH BECKETT

Max leads way with talent set to shine

ON OCTOBER 12 last year Ralph Beckett dominated the day with five winners across cards at Newmarket and York. In many ways, it was a day that encapsulated the Classic-winning trainer's season.

Those wins showcased the talent in his yard, highlighted the potential he has to work with this season and added to the flow of success the stable had enjoyed in the closing months of the Flat season.

But it was not all plain sailing in 2019.

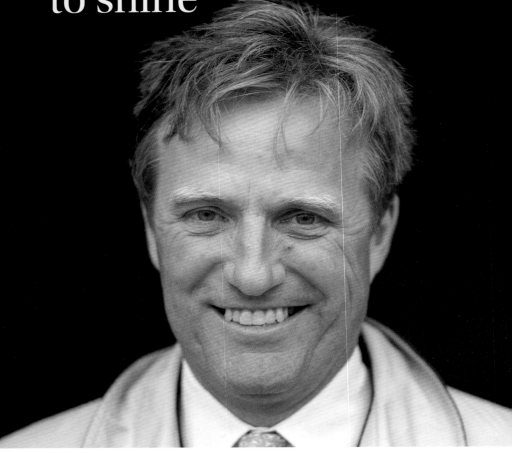

WINNERS IN LAST FIVE YEARS 82, 88, 66, 101, 80

Last year started achingly slowly for Beckett, with no winner between mid-February and the end of April. Things picked up through June, topped by the Royal Ascot victory of **Biometric** in the Britannia Stakes – the race in which the Frankie Dettori express was derailed – before the arrival of a difficult July.

However, with the horses put right, Beckett and his team finished the season with a flourish, although the trainer does not recommend such an up-and-down year as the ideal model.

"The end of the year was really where we justified our presence, if you like," he says. "I wouldn't recommend it as a way to go about your year but we did it in the end."

The star of the show on that memorable October afternoon for Beckett was **Max Vega,** who powered up the Rowley Mile to capture the Group 3 Zetland Stakes in exciting style by three lengths.

The progress shown by Max Vega last year caught Beckett a little by surprise, but there is no doubt in the trainer's mind about where he hopes to be on the first Saturday in June.

He says: "He'll likely start at somewhere

RALPH BECKETT
KIMPTON, HAMPSHIRE

	Number of horses	Races run	1st	2nd	3rd	Unpl	Per cent	£1 level stake
2yo	50	147	24	18	15	90	16.3	+1.05
3yo	61	274	46	33	31	164	16.8	-19.70
4yo+	22	96	12	7	7	70	12.5	-8.00
Totals	**133**	**517**	**82**	**58**	**53**	**324**	**15.9**	**-26.65**
2018	130	522	88	89	62	283	16.9	-78.50
2017	136	464	66	59	69	269	14.2	-103.21

BY MONTH

2yo	W-R	Per cent	£1 level stake	3yo	W-R	Per cent	£1 level stake
Jan	0-0	0.0	0.00	Jan	0-8	0.0	-8.00
Feb	0-0	0.0	0.00	Feb	1-6	16.7	-1.50
Mar	0-0	0.0	0.00	Mar	0-6	0.0	-6.00
Apr	0-0	0.0	0.00	Apr	3-20	15.0	+0.83
May	1-6	16.7	+2.00	May	9-41	22.0	+1.78
June	2-8	25.0	-2.05	June	9-44	20.5	+8.01
July	1-14	7.1	-11.75	July	5-41	12.2	-17.69
Aug	4-33	12.1	-15.25	Aug	7-44	15.9	+3.75
Sep	7-31	22.6	-4.06	Sep	6-33	18.2	-13.39
Oct	7-28	25.0	+40.50	Oct	6-25	24.0	+18.50
Nov	2-20	10.0	-1.33	Nov	0-3	0.0	-3.00
Dec	0-7	0.0	-7.00	Dec	0-3	0.0	-3.00

4yo+	W-R	Per cent	£1 level stake	Totals	W-R	Per cent	£1 level stake
Jan	1-4	25.0	-0.25	Jan	1-12	8.3	-8.25
Feb	0-1	0.0	-1.00	Feb	1-7	14.3	-2.50
Mar	0-1	0.0	-1.00	Mar	0-7	0.0	-7.00

	W-R	Per cent	£1 level stake		W-R	Per cent	£1 level stake
Apr	1-8	12.5	-2.50	Apr	4-28	14.3	-1.67
May	2-14	14.3	+3.50	May	12-61	19.7	+7.28
June	1-20	5.0	-13.00	June	12-72	16.7	-7.04
July	1-11	9.1	+2.00	July	7-66	10.6	-27.44
August	3-11	27.3	+10.00	Aug	14-88	15.9	-1.50
Sep	1-9	11.1	-3.50	Sep	14-73	19.2	-20.95
Oct	2-12	16.7	+2.75	Oct	15-65	23.1	+61.75
Nov	0-5	0.0	-5.00	Nov	2-28	7.1	-8.00
Dec	0-0	0.0	0.00	Dec	0-10	0.0	-3.00

DISTANCE

2yo	W-R	Per cent	£1 level stake	3yo	W-R	Per cent	£1 level stake
5f-6f	4-35	11.4	-18.80	5f-6f	1-20	5.0	-15.67
7f-8f	19-105	18.1	+18.85	7f-8f	5-63	7.9	-14.25
9f-13f	1-7	14.3	+1.00	9f-13f	30-160	18.8	-4.24
14f+	0-0	0.0	0.00	14f+	10-31	32.3	+14.46

4yo+	W-R	Per cent	£1 level stake	Totals	W-R	Per cent	£1 level stake
5f-6f	3-10	30.0	+22.00	5f-6f	8-65	12.3	-12.47
7f-8f	3-47	6.4	-29.50	7f-8f	27-215	12.6	-24.90
9f-13f	5-33	15.2	0.00	9f-13f	36-200	18.0	-3.24
14f+	1-6	16.7	-0.50	14f+	11-37	29.7	+13.96

TYPE OF RACE

	NON-HANDICAPS				HANDICAPS		
	W-R	Per cent	£1 level stake		W-R	Per cent	£1 level stake
2yo	21-122	17.2	+24.14	2yo	0-7	0.0	-7.00
3yo	41-199	20.6	-19.95	3yo	32-247	13.0	-71.60
4yo+	11-80	13.8	-11.88	4yo+	21-197	10.7	-72.29

Statistics relate to all runners in Britain from January 1, 2019 to December 31, 2019

like Chester or Lingfield for a trial and I'd be keen to run him in the Derby, all things being equal, as I think he'll handle Epsom and he's a very straightforward individual.

"He's crept up on us really. His work before his debut was okay but not flash. Having said that, we felt he'd run well first time if not quite as well as he did [when second to subsequent Horris Hill winner Kenzai Warrior].

"We went to Pontefract next as he got a Plus 10 bonus and then went to the Zetland, rather than the original plan of the Silver Tankard, because it looked like he'd really improve for the step up in trip, which he did, and he'll definitely get a mile and a half.

"He copes so well with slow ground that you'd have to think he's helped by it when others aren't, but he'll cope with quicker ground if he's not raced on it before he's ready."

Max Vega may not be the only one from his stable lining up for the Investec Derby this summer with **Jacksonian**, second on his

Antonia De Vega: likely to be tried in headgear this season in a bid to extract the very best from her

only start behind subsequent Group 3 winner Military March, also earmarked for the Classic if things go to plan.

"The form of his maiden is very strong and his homework had indicated he'd run like that," Beckett says. "He'll likely be left in the Derby and I'll be looking to win a race with him as soon as possible. He's quite a free-running sort, which is why he started at seven furlongs, but he's going to definitely get a mile and a quarter in my view and possibly further too."

Classic potential

As well as two potential Derby contenders, Beckett also has the smart **Kinross** to unleash this season. The Kingman colt blew away the opposition on his debut at Newmarket before finding everything a bit too much in the rearranged Group 1 Vertem Futurity at Newcastle.

A small setback means there will be no time for Kinross to take in a trial this spring, but Beckett believes the Qipco 2,000 Guineas is distinctly possible if he is showing the right signs, a significant vote of confidence in a horse with undoubted potential to star this year.

He says: "He'll have a Guineas entry and I'd be hopeful of us getting him there. If he was working well enough I'd go straight there with him as he's already scooted up the Rowley Mile; he's got a lot of speed.

"I think he lacked the nous second time. It may be that he's not good enough, I don't know yet but, based on his homework and what he showed us first time, I'd be looking to throw him in at the deep end."

Max Vega, Jacksonian and Kinross are unusual flagbearers for Beckett, given much of his top-level success has come courtesy of fillies, with the likes of Look Here and Talent winning the Oaks at Epsom and Simple Verse landing the St Leger at Doncaster.

Best yet to come from trio

Last year, hopes had been high that one or more of **Antonia De Vega**, **Feliciana De Vega** and **Manuela De Vega** could add to that Classic haul. It was not quite to be, but all three remain in training in 2020 and Beckett is optimistic about their prospects granted a little ease underfoot.

Air Pilot (right): veteran is back again but will be waiting for the rain

He says: "I'd be looking to go a mile and a half with Antonia De Vega. She may start in the John Porter at Newbury, or possibly the Daisy Warwick at Goodwood a fortnight later. At some point it's likely we'll try headgear with her as well. For me, she's not reluctant but she races lazily and headgear will get her to travel through her race better.

"Feliciana De Vega really does need soft ground. It's likely she'll step up to a mile and a quarter and she'll end up in France at some point too.

"Manuela De Vega is so straightforward and takes her racing very well. The only thing I would say is that the only time she got genuinely soft ground she nearly won a Group 1 when she was beaten a neck in Germany at the end of the year. I'd be looking forward to getting her head in front as it's been frustrating that she's been second a lot, but she's a good filly."

Going key for Pilot to take off

Soft going will be essential for the evergreen **Air Pilot**, who returns to training this year at the age of 11. A regular in stakes races on the continents, Air Pilot achieved a long-held goal for Beckett when landing his first black-

type race in Britain last year in the Listed Foundation Stakes at Goodwood in September.

"The reason he's back in training again this year is that he doesn't really like being on holiday," Beckett says. "He really likes the routine of training, so we've just got to work out what to do with him. We'll wait our time and make sure he's in the right shape when the rain comes. He's not really a horse whom you make plans for."

Also back for this year are multiple winners **Hereby** and **Moon King**. The former ended last season with a Listed victory at Ascot, having won the first of her four in a row off a mark of 72, and she could start her year in the Ormonde Stakes at Chester.

"She was a rabbit at two, there was nothing of her. We barely trained her, just for a few months, but that's often ample to get enough into them," Beckett explains. "I would think she's going to start off in the Ormonde, having shown such a liking for Chester, and then go on from there. The Bronte at York is an alternative as it's important she gets her toe in. You'd hope in time she might be able to go for races like the Lillie Langtry and the Park Hill."

Roodee aim for King

Chester is also a likely starting point for Moon King, who rocketed from a rating of 60 at the start of the season to 91 by the end of it after winning five races on the spin. Beckett says: "I don't think he'll get into the Chester Cup but he should get into the Plate, so that will be our first target with him.

"Gelding helped him a lot last year and he's going to be a great, fun horse again. The owners bought him as a dual-purpose horse and he's likely to go over obstacles for someone else in the future."

The future is at the top of Beckett's thinking for **Aloe Vera**, with Kirsten Rausing's filly returning to training this year after being absent for much of 2019 due to a serious injury.

Beckett says: "She struck into herself so badly when she won the Height of Fashion

Ralph Beckett keeps a watchful eye on his string

DID YOU KNOW?

Beckett began his racing career in Australia, working for training legends Bart Cummings and Colin Hayes. On returning to the UK he was attached to two more greats in Jimmy FitzGerald and Peter Walwyn, taking over the licence when Walwyn retired in 2000

Tomfre scores at Newmarket and has his trainer thinking of another successful campaign

■ Beckett has a 36% strike-rate at Ayr during the last five years – and a level-stake profit of £17.35

Stakes at Goodwood that she had to have the rest of the year off; it was a severe injury.

"She's back cantering and moving well, but we'll be taking plenty of time to get her to the racecourse. We'll start in a Listed race and take it from there, but she'll be a slow burner as we need to get it right."

A Listed contest is the proposed starting point for **Mascat**, who followed a debut second to the promising Palace Pier with victory in a Newmarket novice.

"I think he'll probably show up in the Feilden [at Newmarket] and then we'll go on from there," Beckett says. "He's pretty useful. What level he is, I'm not sure, but I think he'll stay and we'll end up over a mile and a half eventually. I'd be fairly confident he's a stakes horse."

Similar sentiments apply to **Trefoil**, another unexposed novice winner unleashed by Beckett in the closing weeks of the Flat season.

"It was a good effort from her to win first time out," Beckett says. "I would be thinking she'll go for an Oaks trial in the spring. She's a much better individual than her sister [Thimbleweed] physically and with a better temperament too."

Bright prospects

Beckett is also looking forward to the year ahead with promising three-year-olds **Wyclif**, a "King George V-type of horse", **Tomfre** and **Heart Reef**, who all begin the season with plenty of lofty ambitions behind them after their exploits at two.

"Tomfre's in good shape and is winging away," Beckett says. "I hope he'll give his extraordinarily lucky owner-breeder a lot of fun again this year.

"Heart Reef was a bit clueless but has done very well physically through the winter. I'd be pretty hopeful about her prospects too."

Last year showed that things are rarely straightforward when it comes to horses and racing. However, with plenty of ammunition to fire, Beckett looks well placed to keep the good times rolling right through the season.

REPORTING BY PETER SCARGILL

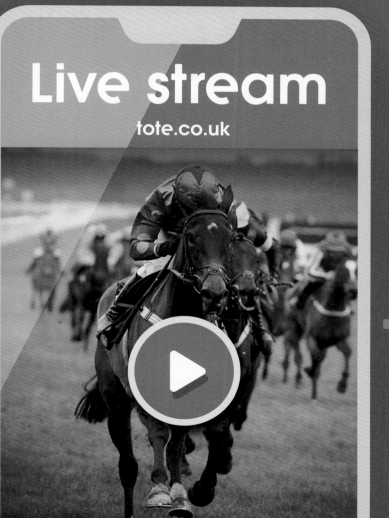

RICHARD FAHEY

Master of the numbers game

PUNTERS have been able to set their watches by Richard Fahey training the lion's share of 200 winners a season in recent years. While unable to break through that noteworthy barrier last campaign, the trainer's Musley Bank operation ran like clockwork once more to yield an impressive 178 victories.

That was a handful shy of the previous season and, although drawing a blank at the highest level, Fahey was responsible for a healthy amount of Group triumphs as we have grown so accustomed to seeing.

Emerging star Space Traveller captured the Jersey Stakes at Royal Ascot and Leopardstown's Boomerang Stakes to establish himself as arguably the yard's new leading light, while acclaimed Group 2-winning poster boys Forest Ranger and Mr Lupton also paid their way with major contributions.

Reflecting on another strong season, Fahey says: "We were happy enough. We didn't break any records but we held our own. We trained plenty of winners again and admittedly we were down slightly on the previous season, but it was still a good campaign. We'll look to keep the owners happy again."

Sands Of Mali provided Fahey's last success at the highest level when denying Harry Angel in the 2018 Qipco British Champions Sprint Stakes. However, his four-year-old season was not quite so productive. "Sands Of Mali is back and under full ownership with the Cool Silk Partnership," says Fahey. "It should be an easier year for him. He'll have no Group 1 penalty to contend with and he'll probably start at Doncaster in the Cammidge Trophy. We'll feel our way from there.

"**Mr Lupton** won a Group 2 very early on last year and it made life harder for him

■ Watch Fahey's runners in claimers and sellers. He has a five-year 26% strike-rate and profits of £13.25

carrying the penalty. He's a year older but remains no back number and we're happy with him. We'll probably go the handicap route with him and find our level there.

"We'll hopefully get **Forest Ranger** to Chester again to try to win three Huxley Stakes in a row. He's a little bit like Mr Lupton in that he suffered from carrying a Group 2 penalty all year. He's in good form and we're happy. All roads lead to Chester.

"**Space Traveller** is carrying a Group 2 penalty but improved a good chunk last season and won a couple of nice races for us. We'll try to make him into a Group 1 horse if we can. He'll probably have a prep run before tackling the Lockinge and it'd be great if he could replicate Ribchester there."

Off to pastures new

The continuous conveyor belt at the Malton yard is illustrated by the absence of Acomb Stakes winner Valdermoro and Two-Year-Old Trophy scorer Summer Sands this season. The pair have moved on to pastures new along with Flying Childers fourth Flaming Princess.

The Cheveley Park-owned **Exhort** defeated the 2018 1,000 Guineas heroine Billesdon Brook in Listed company at Pontefract last season and is destined for the breeding sheds. The useful Clipper Logistics-owned filly Red Balloons will also take up a position in the paddocks.

Gabrial, part of the furniture at Musley Bank, is another to vacate his stable box. Marwan Koukash's popular 11-year-old has been handed a well-earned retirement after a remarkable 93-race career.

Intriguing new recruit

The 112-rated stayer **Magic Circle** is arguably Fahey's most interesting acquisition for the coming season. The eight-year-old arrives from the Ian Williams yard and was last seen finishing ninth in the Ascot Gold Cup to Stradivarius. Fahey says: "Magic Circle is getting on in years and we'll probably need some relief from the handicapper, but we're looking to run him in the Chester Cup."

Discussing other key members of the team, Fahey says: "**Growl** isn't getting any younger but he had a good enough season last year. He deserved his victory in the William Hill Silver Trophy and was unlucky not to follow up in the Ayr Gold Cup. We're happy with him. He'll be going a similar route and tackling these top sprint handicaps again.

"**George Bowen** had an excellent campaign the season before last but completely lost his way last time. However, he's done that before and came back. He needs to find his form again but he's got

'Mr Lupton (left) is a year older but remains no back number and we're happy with him. We'll probably go the handicap route with him and find our level there'

himself dangerously well handicapped if we can just get him back. There's no reason why he shouldn't and we're happy with him."

"**Show Me Show Me** was third to Liberty Beach in the Molecomb and is a good, hardy horse. We wanted to geld him all of last season and thankfully he has been now. He was a bit of a playboy but he's grown over the winter and done well. We're happy enough with him but he's got to be pretty smart to compete off 101.

"**Mighty Spirit** was very consistent last season. She's a good, tough little filly and it would be nice to get her some black type. It took her ages to win as she just kept bumping into one. We're happy with her.

"**Istanbul** is quite nice. He's pretty quick and will be tackling the decent sprints.

"**Toro Strike** could end up being one for the Britannia Stakes at Royal Ascot. He's a progressive colt and could go the right way.

"**Bond's Boy** was a fine debut winner for us and then finished third to Under The Stars in a big-field contest at Newmarket. He's a big horse and looks a nice prospect. He's done well and you'd like to think he'll progress again.

"**National League** had a decent juvenile

Crownthorpe: expected to bag another decent prize this season

campaign and has been back cantering for two months. We haven't done anything quick with him but there'll be plenty of races for him as a three-year-old.

"**Eva Maria** isn't very big but she's extremely tough and genuine. I was disappointed with her last run but I'm inclined to forgive her for that. The plan is to get some black type with her if we can.

"**Crownthorpe** loves soft ground and we'll search for those conditions. We're trying to get him ready for the Lincoln but he's not sure to get in. I think he has what it takes to secure another nice prize this season."

Guineas trial for Rasmah

Renowned for his level-headed approach and keeping his cards relatively close to his chest, Fahey is particularly upbeat when talking about the filly **Al Rasmah**. The daughter of Iffraaj was an impressive debut winner at Chester before running below par in the Firth of Clyde Stakes at Ayr. However, Fahey appears undeterred and is keen to test her

DISCOVER

--

Shared Racehorse Ownership

Search for your perfect ownership experience at

inthepaddock.co.uk

RICHARD FAHEY
MUSLEY BANK, NORTH YORKSHIRE

	Number of horses	Races run	1st	2nd	3rd	Unpl	Per cent	£1 level stake
2yo	123	441	54	63	59	264	12.2	-95.18
3yo	84	511	66	57	64	322	12.9	-26.09
4yo+	69	562	58	51	62	389	10.3	-79.05
Totals	**276**	**1514**	**178**	**171**	**185**	**975**	**11.8**	**-200.32**
2018	256	1599	190	199	191	1017	11.9	-249.05
2017	298	1749	200	220	218	1109	11.4	-505.32

BY MONTH

2yo	W-R	Per cent	£1 level stake	3yo	W-R	Per cent	£1 level stake
Jan	0-0	0.0	0.00	Jan	4-22	18.2	-7.50
Feb	0-0	0.0	0.00	Feb	1-12	8.3	-10.27
Mar	1-2	50.0	+1.75	Mar	0-10	0.0	-10.00
Apr	2-16	12.5	+2.75	Apr	7-49	14.3	+12.50
May	6-43	14.0	+7.80	May	10-63	15.9	+1.85
June	9-66	13.6	-4.75	June	10-90	11.1	-12.25
July	9-78	11.5	-36.30	July	6-80	7.5	+22.00
Aug	12-77	15.6	-0.88	Aug	10-74	13.5	-18.15
Sep	10-73	13.7	-3.02	Sep	8-59	13.6	-15.77
Oct	5-55	9.1	-31.52	Oct	7-36	19.4	+4.75
Nov	0-18	0.0	-18.00	Nov	1-10	10.0	+1.00
Dec	0-13	0.0	-13.00	Dec	2-6	33.3	+5.75

4yo+	W-R	Per cent	£1 level stake	Totals	W-R	Per cent	£1 level stake
Jan	2-24	8.3	-7.50	Jan	6-46	13.0	-15.00
Feb	3-11	27.3	+3.50	Feb	4-23	17.4	-6.77
Mar	2-29	6.9	-13.00	Mar	3-41	7.3	-21.25
Apr	2-54	3.7	-23.00	Apr	11-119	9.2	-7.75
May	12-88	13.6	-12.55	May	28-194	14.4	-2.90
June	6-86	7.0	-30.75	June	25-242	10.3	-47.75
July	8-76	10.5	-7.25	July	23-234	9.8	-21.55
Aug	8-72	11.1	-6.75	Aug	30-223	13.5	-25.78
Sep	4-65	6.2	-31.00	Sep	22-197	11.2	-49.79
Oct	5-36	13.9	+11.00	Oct	17-127	13.4	-15.77
Nov	3-13	23.1	+23.50	Nov	4-41	9.8	+24.50
Dec	3-8	37.5	+14.75	Dec	5-27	18.5	+20.50

Statistics relate to all runners in Britain from January 1, 2019 to December 31, 2019

DISTANCE

2yo	W-R	Per cent	£1 level stake	3yo	W-R	Per cent	£1 level stake
5f-6f	43-311	13.8	-34.03	5f-6f	13-132	9.8	-44.90
7f-8f	11-129	8.5	-60.15	7f-8f	33-239	13.8	+47.45
9f-13f	0-1	0.0	-1.00	9f-13f	19-126	15.1	-17.90
14f+	0-0	0.0	0.00	14f+	1-14	7.1	-10.75

4yo+	W-R	Per cent	£1 level stake	Totals	W-R	Per cent	£1 level stake
5f-6f	20-181	11.0	-17.80	5f-6f	76-624	12.2	-96.73
7f-8f	24-237	10.1	-5.75	7f-8f	68-605	11.2	-18.45
9f-13f	13-137	9.5	-55.00	9f-13f	32-264	12.1	-73.90
14f+	1-7	14.3	-0.50	14f+	2-21	9.5	-11.25

TYPE OF RACE

	NON-HANDICAPS				HANDICAPS		
	W-R	Per cent	£1 level stake		W-R	Per cent	£1 level stake
2yo	46-347	13.3	-51.93	2yo	8-94	8.5	-43.25
3yo	11-100	11.0	-3.40	3yo	55-411	13.4	-22.69
4yo+	3-39	7.7	-1.50	4yo+	55-523	10.5	-77.55

DID YOU KNOW?

Fahey began training in 1993 and it was not until he bought Ribchester, at the Goffs Orby yearlings sale in October 2014, that he spent six figures at the sales. The €105,000 purchase is responsible for half of Fahey's eight Group 1 wins as a trainer and is the highest-rated horse he has trained

Ventura Lightning: has a date at Newmarket for the Free Handicap

Cosmic Law: could bag a decent handicap

mettle among the leading fillies of her generation in a Classic trial. "Al Rasmah is a filly I quite like," he says. "She's wintered very well and won nicely on her debut. I thought that was a really good performance. She disappointed us on her following start but if she's working all right nearer the time I'd be inclined to start her off in one of the 1,000 Guineas trials, whether that's the Nell Gwyn or the Newbury race [Fred Darling Stakes]. Looking at her pedigree you'd like to think she'll stay further than six furlongs."

Another talent destined for Newmarket is **Ventura Lightning**, who has been earmarked for the Free Handicap in April. A fruitful year culminated with a Listed second at York in October and the No Nay Never colt has been pleasing Fahey, who says: "Ventura Lightning has done very well over the winter. He's going to start off in the Free Handicap at Newmarket off a mark of 100. He should be suited by a step up in trip and I definitely think he can progress."

He continues: "**Gabrial The Saint** is a good, hardy sprinter and he had a good enough season last year. He doesn't want the ground to be too quick, though, and I'm sure he'll be running at Chester later in the campaign.

"**Furzig** won in February at Chelmsford and when things drop right he's pretty smart.

He's tough and hardy and has been on the go over the winter. He'll run into the turf now and I hope he can keep improving.

"**Another Touch** is another who has been kept busy over the winter and he racked up a nice sequence. I'm not sure whether he'll have a run beforehand but he'll end up at Finals Day at Lingfield.

"**Cosmic Law** ran some decent races in some top 6f handicaps. He's still a work in progress who likes slowish ground. Ground permitting, he'll be aimed at the big six- and seven-furlong handicaps again."

Rebel with a cause

When asked to nominate a horse to follow for the season Fahey leans towards the speedball **Ventura Rebel**, whose profitable two-year-old campaign featured a narrow second in the Norfolk Stakes to A'Ali at the Royal meeting. The trainer hopes his rapid colt will improve enough to mix it with the top sprinters at Group 1 level, with a return to Ascot pinpointed as the long-term target. He says: "Ventura Rebel just had a little setback but he'll be back cantering in six weeks. He'll be aimed at most of the top sprints. We're looking at Haydock's Temple Stakes as a starting point and I'm hoping he'll make up into a King's Stand horse."

REPORTING BY ROBBIE WILDERS

RICHARD HANNON

WINNERS IN LAST FIVE YEARS 153, 172, 194, 172, 195

'He might be the best we've ever had'

RICHARD HANNON hit the ground running when he saddled Night Of Thunder for that shock defeat of Kingman in the 2,000 Guineas in 2014, just months after taking over the licence from Richard senior, and he has maintained a stream of top-level winners since.

He rattled up 206 winners domestically in that first season and, although he hasn't managed a double-century since, he has twice gone close. If 2019's tally of 153 looks relatively disappointing on the surface, prize-money topping £4 million for the first time since that first year was compensation for the drop in numbers.

The superb QEII success of **King Of Change** on British Champions Day contributed more than £600,000 to that total, and the four-year-old, who is still relatively unexposed, leads about as powerful a team of older horses as the stable has ever had.

DID YOU KNOW?
Hannon is a triplet, with brother Henry and sister Elizabeth. He also has another three sisters – Claire, Fanny and Julie. Elizabeth is married to former dual champion jockey Richard Hughes

That Ascot win came just a fortnight after the stable's 1,000 Guineas winner Billesdon Brook had gained a second Newmarket Group 1 win in the Kingdom of Bahrain Sun Chariot Stakes, having steadily worked her way back to that level. She remains in training too.

Hannon could not have a higher opinion of King Of Change, whose programme picks itself to an extent. He says: "We've had very good milers like Toronado, Night Of Thunder, Olympic Glory and Barney Roy here in the last few years, and he might just be the best we've ever had.

"He's done very well physically and he'll probably go straight to the Lockinge, although he might go to Sandown first. Then it will probably be Queen Anne, Marois and back to Ascot. He's looking really well and I couldn't be happier with him."

Although the ground was very testing in the QEII, Hannon does not believe King Of

King Of Change (leading); Richard Hannon is full of enthusiasm for last season's QEII winner

■ Back Hannon's horses four and older on the all-weather. His five-year 16% strike-rate gives a profit of £61.06

Change needs it that way and points out: "He goes very well in soft ground, but he was second in the Guineas on good ground and he'll handle anything really."

Brook back for more

Billesdon Brook has benefited from a good break with owner-breeder Jeanette McCreery since her unsuccessful trip to the Breeders' Cup. Hannon says: "She was right back to her best in the Sun Chariot and I don't think

she quite stayed at Santa Anita. We'll probably start quite early with her and there are loads of possibilities. She could run in the Lockinge too."

Anna Nerium could be aimed at similar races to Billesdon Brook. Hannon says: "She has the advantage of not having a Group 1 penalty, and she goes very well in soft ground. Whenever she gets her ground she should be hard to beat. She might start at Goodwood on Guineas weekend."

Raymond Tusk took until December to win a race last year, but he is one of the highest-rated horses in the yard. Hannon says: "He ran pretty well in the Melbourne Cup, where he was going as well as any turning in, and he'll be travelling again – he'll probably go back to Australia and we'll work back from there.

"He would have gone to Saudi in February but got a stone bruise. He's very versatile trip-wise and will probably start at Newbury or Newmarket. He's a top-class horse."

Early season aims

Last year's Burradon Stakes winner **Fox Power** has the Unibet Lincoln as a likely early target, while German 2,000 Guineas winner **Fox Champion** will have a choice between the Doncaster Mile and Group races at Newmarket and Sandown. **Oh This Is Us** is also a Lincoln possible, but his main target in the first part of the season is the All-Weather Mile Championship at Lingfield on Good Friday. "He wants a mile and he loves Lingfield," said the trainer. "He's a star and he won it last year."

Fox Power: could have the Lincoln on his agenda

There are quite a few others in a broadly similar ratings bracket, including Goodwood's Golden Mile winner **Beat Le Bon** ("must have fast ground"), Ascot 1m4f winner **Floating Artist**, dual Kempton all-weather winner **Kuwait Currency**, Dubai Duty Free Cup winner **Tabarrak**, Jersey Stakes fourth **Urban Icon** and prolific all-weather winner **War Glory**.

Hannon says: "We've got a lot of nice horses like that, and Group 3-winning sprinter **Yafta**, who didn't run again after the Diamond Jubilee, is back too after a good break at Shadwell."

There is also a good word for **Brian Epstein**. "He's a nice horse. He won at Musselburgh on Derby Day and then got a form of pneumonia and had to have the rest of the year off. There's a nice race in him."

'I've taken 33s about him'

Hannon has a clutch of credible Classic aspirants among a great team of three-year-olds and he is especially excited by **Threat**, who did the stable proud last year with wins

RICHARD HANNON
EAST EVERLEIGH, WILTSHIRE

	Number of horses	Races run	1st	2nd	3rd	Unpl	Per cent	£1 level stake
2yo	131	536	58	75	69	334	10.8	-182.58
3yo	108	546	64	60	58	364	11.7	-118.27
4yo+	34	204	31	23	23	126	15.2	+4.60
Totals	**273**	**1286**	**153**	**158**	**150**	**824**	**11.9**	**-296.25**
2018	289	1401	172	191	159	877	12.3	-345.26
2017	268	1354	194	176	164	818	14.3	-78.24

BY MONTH

2yo	W-R	Per cent	£1 level stake	3yo	W-R	Per cent	£1 level stake
Jan	0-0	0.0	0.00	Jan	2-20	10.0	-3.50
Feb	0-0	0.0	0.00	Feb	0-3	0.0	-3.00
Mar	0-0	0.0	0.00	Mar	4-27	14.8	-16.92
Apr	1-16	6.3	-12.25	Apr	11-90	12.2	-11.67
May	5-31	16.1	+12.50	May	7-94	7.4	-39.00
June	8-62	12.9	-34.75	June	12-76	15.8	-13.43
July	12-97	12.4	-42.83	July	11-80	13.8	+7.33
Aug	13-109	11.9	-65.94	Aug	6-58	10.3	-16.25
Sep	11-100	11.0	+25.20	Sep	6-51	11.8	-14.08
Oct	6-69	8.7	-29.50	Oct	4-28	14.3	+5.75
Nov	1-27	3.7	-19.00	Nov	0-13	0.0	-13.00
Dec	1-25	4.0	-16.00	Dec	1-6	16.7	-0.50

4yo+	W-R	Per cent	£1 level stake	Totals	W-R	Per cent	£1 level stake
Jan	0-7	0.0	-7.00	Jan	2-27	7.4	-10.50
Febr	1-6	16.7	-3.00	Feb	1-9	11.1	-6.00
Mar	3-12	25.0	-1.00	Mar	7-39	17.9	-17.92

	W-R	Per cent	£1 level stake		W-R	Per cent	£1 level stake
Apr	3-24	12.5	+1.00	Apr	15-130	11.5	-22.92
May	4-39	10.3	-18.00	May	16-164	9.8	-44.50
June	4-32	12.5	-11.25	June	24-170	14.1	-59.43
July	2-25	8.0	-18.50	July	25-202	12.4	-54.00
Aug	6-28	21.4	+32.75	Aug	25-195	12.8	-49.44
Sep	4-16	25.0	-4.15	Sep	21-167	12.6	+6.97
Oct	3-10	30.0	+35.00	Oct	13-107	12.1	+11.25
Nov	0-4	0.0	-4.00	Nov	1-44	2.3	-17.00
Dec	1-1	100.0	+2.75	Dec	3-32	9.4	+2.25

DISTANCE

2yo	W-R	Per cent	£1 level stake	3yo	W-R	Per cent	£1 level stake
5f-6f	38-284	13.4	-72.59	5f-6f	7-108	6.5	-58.65
7f-8f	20-241	8.3	-98.99	7f-8f	43-287	15.0	-21.08
9f-13f	0-11	0.0	-11.00	9f-13f	14-145	9.7	-32.54
14f+	0-0	0.0	0.00	14f+	0-6	0.0	-6.00

4yo+	W-R	Per cent	£1 level stake	Totals	W-R	Per cent	£1 level stake
5f-6f	8-39	20.5	+11.50	5f-6f	53-431	12.3	-119.74
7f-8f	21-140	15.0	+10.60	7f-8f	84-668	12.6	-109.47
9f-13f	1-19	5.3	-15.25	9f-13f	15-175	8.6	-58.79
14f+	1-6	16.7	-2.25	14f+	1-12	8.3	-8.25

TYPE OF RACE

	NON-HANDICAPS			HANDICAPS		
	W-R	Per cent	£1 level stake		W-R	Per cent	£1 level stake
2yo	49-409	12.0	-116.83	2yo	9-127	7.1	-65.75
3yo	15-157	9.6	-71.47	3yo	49-389	12.6	-46.81
4yo+	13-55	23.6	+17.48	4yo+	18-149	12.1	-12.88

Statistics relate to all runners in Britain from January 1, 2019 to December 31, 2019

in the Gimcrack and the Champagne Stakes and is now regarded a serious Qipco 2,000 Guineas candidate.

Hannon has never hidden admiration for the Cheveley Park Stud's Footstepsinthesand colt and he said: "Threat has done extremely well. He's grown up physically, and mentally he's now the horse I always thought he would be.

"The only way I could fault him last year was that he was a little bit faint-hearted, but he seems to have grown out of that. I've had a bit of 33-1 about him in the Guineas."

There were few more impressive two-year-old winners all last year than **Mums Tipple** in the sales race at York, but he didn't reproduce the form in the Middle Park Stakes.

Hannon says: "There were excuses – he wasn't helped by the horse in the next stall getting upset – but he underperformed there and he has to prove himself still. But you don't win the way he won at York without being very good. There was nothing flukey about it – he pulverised them – and the time was good too compared to the Gimcrack.

"He's still a Guineas colt in my estimation, but we're steering him towards the Curragh rather than Newmarket, with a run in the Greenham probably first."

'Unbelievable figures'

Superlative Stakes winner **Mystery Power** is also likely to run in a trial, while a much darker prospect who could also end up in a Guineas is **Al Madhar**, who won a good maiden at Newmarket's July Meeting first time out but wasn't seen again.

Hannon says: "The figures from Al Madhar's maiden were unbelievable and I think he's very good. He wasn't moving as well after the race, so we sent him back to Shadwell and he's come back looking fantastic. He could be anything, and I'm going to train him as if he's another Guineas colt."

There's strength in depth among the three-year-old fillies too, and one senses Hannon is especially sweet on **Cloak Of Spirits**, the Invincible Spirit filly who made such a big impression at Ascot first time out.

'I think she's very talented'

The trainer says: "I think she's very good. Her middle run last year at Doncaster disappointed me but she was still green and inexperienced. I think she's very talented and she might go straight for the Guineas. She's already been to Newmarket and run very well in the Rockfel, so she doesn't need the experience, and we know she goes very well fresh."

Dark Lady beat Millisle at Salisbury last year but was only seventh behind the runner-up in the Cheveley Park Stakes. Hannon said: "We've just touched up her throat since then. She was getting there very easily and then not really going through with it, and that might have been why. She'd run a lot of good races and I think her breathing was just catching her out. She'll start in the Fred Darling or the Nell Gwyn."

Other three-year-olds currently a little below that level but are expected to do well this year include **Tahitian Prince** ("a very promising second at Kempton") and **Manigordo** ("still a maiden but with some good form and rated in the 90s").

Noon Day Gun, by Dubawi out of the stable's 1,000 Guineas winner Sky Lantern, is one of several unraced three-year-olds about whom Hannon has high hopes. **The Seventh Day**, a Siyouni colt belonging to Sheikh Mohammed Obaid, and **The Other Side**, a filly belonging to footballer Charlie Austin, also come into that category.

The stable has forever been associated with high-class two-year-olds and this year there are between 110 and 120 of them to look forward to, with homebreds from established owners bolstering the dozens the team buy on spec at the sales every autumn.

The future is looking bright.

REPORTING BY GRAHAM DENCH

CHARLIE HILLS

'There's plenty to look forward to with Battaash. He's such an exciting horse'

Brilliant Battaash leads the way again

THE year 2019 is one that Charlie Hills will never forget.

Richly talented sprinter Battaash continued to be the trailblazing stable star, his season highlighted by a memorable Group 1 success in the Nunthorpe Stakes at York, but there was excellent support from a plethora of high-class performers.

Phoenix Of Spain provided further Group 1 glory when landing the Irish 2,000 Guineas, while the emergence of useful sprinter Khaadem, successful in the Stewards'

Cup at Goodwood, gave plenty of satisfaction.

In terms of prize-money accrued in Britain, 2019 was Hills's second-best year since he took out a trainer's licence in 2011.

He netted £2,234,907 in 2015, and £1,623,004 last year, an amount which doesn't include Phoenix Of Spain's Irish triumph.

"It was a good year," says Hills, with a hint of understatement. "The horses were pretty healthy all the way through, which helps, and we finished 12th in the trainers' table.

"We've got plenty of good horses for this year, including some well-bred two-year-olds, and we're excited about the new season."

The squad will again be led by the Hamdan Al Maktoum-owned six-year-old **Battaash**, a dual Group 1 winner, who looked better than ever when storming home three and three-quarter lengths clear of Soldier's Call on the Knavesmire last August.

His season was limited to five appearances, but he won three of them and finished a noble second to Blue Point in the Group 1 King's Stand Stakes at Royal Ascot.

Such was the impression Battaash made with a scorching Temple Stakes success at Haydock last May – his first start since

Khaadem: storming home to the win the Stewards' Cup

undergoing wind surgery – that he started favourite for the King's Stand, but the irrepressible Blue Point proved a length and a quarter too strong.

"Everyone seems happy with the way he's wintered," says Hills. "I'm told he has more of a winter coat this year.

"He's won the Temple Stakes for the last two years, and it would be a big achievement if he could make it three.

"The race works well as a starting point towards Royal Ascot. There's no Blue Point this year. Without him in the race he'd have

won the King's Stand last year.

"York will also be on the agenda. There's plenty to look forward to with Battaash again. He's such an exciting horse."

Phoenix Of Spain has gone to stud, but hopes are high that rising star **Khaadem** could fill the void left by his departure.

The four-year-old son of Dark Angel was unable to cut the mustard on his Group 1 bow in Royal Ascot's Commonwealth Cup, finishing seventh to Advertise, but took full advantage of the drop in class to land a significant gamble in the Stewards' Cup.

CHARLIE HILLS
LAMBOURN, BERKSHIRE

	Number of horses	Races run	1st	2nd	3rd	Unpl	Per cent	£1 level stake
2yo	37	103	11	9	8	75	10.7	-14.21
3yo	51	244	38	28	39	139	15.6	-65.77
4yo+	26	133	19	16	12	86	14.3	-12.50
Totals	**114**	**480**	**68**	**53**	**59**	**300**	**14.2**	**-92.48**
2018	136	541	62	59	59	360	11.5	-72.59
2017	143	590	70	68	67	384	11.9	-161.41

BY MONTH

2yo	W-R	Per cent	£1 level stake	3yo	W-R	Per cent	£1 level stake
Jan	0-0	0.0	0.00	Jan	2-9	22.2	-5.46
Feb	0-0	0.0	0.00	Feb	0-1	0.0	-1.00
Mar	0-1	0.0	-1.00	Mar	4-10	40.0	+1.08
Apr	0-1	0.0	-1.00	Apr	1-33	3.0	-29.25
May	3-9	33.3	+16.00	May	6-38	15.8	-2.93
June	0-13	0.0	-13.00	June	4-36	11.1	-19.38
July	3-21	14.3	-14.96	July	8-37	21.6	-4.63
Aug	3-24	12.5	+25.00	Aug	6-32	18.8	+1.17
Sep	0-14	0.0	-14.00	Sep	3-17	17.6	+8.25
Oct	0-12	0.0	-12.00	Oct	1-21	4.8	-13.50
Nov	1-3	33.3	+2.00	Nov	2-3	66.7	-0.63
Dec	1-5	20.0	-1.25	Dec	1-7	14.3	+0.50

4yo+	W-R	Per cent	£1 level stake	Totals	W-R	Per cent	£1 level stake
Jan	1-9	11.1	-5.75	Jan	3-18	16.7	-11.21
Feb	2-5	40.0	+3.67	Feb	2-6	33.3	+2.67
Mar	1-7	14.3	-3.50	Mar	5-18	27.8	-3.42
Apr	3-19	15.3	+5.25	Apr	4-53	7.5	-25.00
May	3-18	16.7	-5.42	May	12-65	18.5	+7.65
June	2-18	11.1	+11.00	June	6-67	9.0	-21.38
July	2-16	12.5	-4.50	July	13-74	17.6	-24.09
Aug	2-18	11.1	-14.00	Aug	11-74	14.9	+12.17
Sep	3-17	17.6	+6.75	Sep	6-48	12.5	+1.00
Oct	0-3	0.0	-3.00	Oct	1-36	2.8	-28.50
Nov	0-1	0.0	-1.00	Nov	3-7	42.9	-1.63
Dec	0-2	0.0	-2.00	Dec	2-14	14.3	-1.50

DISTANCE

2yo	W-R	Per cent	£1 level stake	3yo	W-R	Per cent	£1 level stake
5f-6f	7-73	9.6	-38.21	5f-6f	10-52	19.2	+1.66
7f-8f	4-30	13.3	+24.00	7f-8f	23-144	16.0	-44.42
9f-13f	0-0	0.0	0.00	9f-13f	5-45	11.1	-20.00
14f+	0-0	0.0	0.00	14f+	0-3	0.0	-3.00

4yo+	W-R	Per cent	£1 level stake	Totals	W-R	Per cent	£1 level stake
5f-6f	10-54	18.5	-18.75	5f-6f	27-179	15.1	-55.30
7f-8f	6-31	19.4	+28.25	7f-8f	33-205	16.1	+7.83
9f-13f	2-33	6.1	-10.25	9f-13f	7-78	9.0	-30.25
14f+	1-15	6.7	-11.75	14f+	1-18	5.6	-14.75

TYPE OF RACE

	NON-HANDICAPS				HANDICAPS		
	W-R	Per cent	£1 level stake		W-R	Per cent	£1 level stake
2yo	9-85	10.6	-16.21	2yo	2-18	11.1	+2.00
3yo	18-100	18.0	-34.89	3yo	20-144	13.9	-30.88
4yo+	6-22	27.3	-4.67	4yo+	13-111	11.7	-7.83

Statistics relate to all runners in Britain from January 1, 2019 to December 31, 2019

Afaak (blue colours): Royal Hunt Cup winner

His turn of foot inside the final furlong was that of a horse potentially much better than a mark of 107 and, while he failed to reproduce that form in two subsequent Group 1s, there seems no reason why he cannot progress again this term and make a much bigger splash in the highest company.

"I'm not sure where we'll start him off," Hills reveals. "He won't be running really early on. Perhaps the Duke of York in May will be the race for him ahead of the Diamond Jubilee Stakes at Royal Ascot.

■ Follow juvenile runners from the yard over a mile and further. They show a five-year profit of £54.01

"He's done really well through the winter and improved physically. Angus Gold couldn't believe how well he looked when he last saw him. We all think he's a very exciting horse for 2020, and to win a Group 1 is the ultimate goal."

Afaak, who captured the prestigious Royal Hunt Cup on his seasonal reappearance last June, a fabulous piece of training by Hills, is back for more this year.

The six-year-old failed to add to his tally in four starts after Royal Ascot, but did run an

43

DID YOU KNOW?
When training for the London Marathon in 2008 –
to raise money for the Countryside Alliance – Hills
was informed he was bow-legged and flat-footed.
However, the two impediments apparently cancelled
each other out rather than ruled him out of the
famous stamina test

excellent race when fourth to Royal Julius in a valuable conditions event in Bahrain.

"He ran a blinder in Bahrain," Hills recalls. "In two more strides he would have got up and won. He's come back into training, and is moving great – I've never seen him work so well.

"He's got a mark of 106, so we're training him for the Lincoln. If it's too soft at Doncaster after all the rain we've had this winter we'll bypass that and wait for some better ground. There are options for him over a mile and a mile and a quarter, and he might get a bit further this year."

King's Stand aim

Useful sprinter **Equilateral** has taken his form to another level since being gelded late last year, and produced two fine performances in Dubai.

A comfortable success under James Doyle in a Listed handicap was followed by a Group 2 second, and he clearly looks an improved model.

"Equilateral has thrived out in Dubai. He's really taken to it," says Hills. "If he gets invited he could run at Meydan in a race on World Cup night. He has plenty of speed, and will be aimed at the King's Stand.

Pogo (second right): unbeaten in two starts at Newmarket

"There are some very nice races over five furlongs which would suit him, particularly the Flying Five at the Curragh – that could be ideal."

Expect to see plenty of **Pogo** on the Rowley Mile. The four-year-old son of Zebedee positively bounces off the Newmarket turf where he is unbeaten in two starts.

"Pogo loves Newmarket," Hills says. "It makes sense to go there with him. He's done particularly well through the winter, and has been showing bags of energy. He's the type who could win a couple of nice races this season."

Another likely improver is **Garrus**, who joined Hills halfway through 2019 after Jeremy Noseda's retirement.

The four-year-old was outpaced behind stablemate Battaash in the Nunthorpe, but his trainer thinks there is better to come.

"He just lacks a bit of gate speed," Hills relates. "We're trying to work on that, and will step him back up to six furlongs. We'll plan a route from there.

"He's a good-looking horse, who will make a nice stallion in due course so it's important we get a Group win out of him. He's won a Listed race and been placed in Group 3 and Group 2 company."

45

Brushwork (pink cap): three-time Newcastle winner

Stable stalwart **A Momentofmadness**, hero of the 2018 Portland Handicap, remains in training as a seven-year-old.

"He's been out in Dubai, and has enjoyed a nice winter out there," Hills says. "We'll follow a similar programme with him to last year. He's a great fun horse to have, and a very sound one too."

'He's wintered very well'

Keep a look out for the three-year-old **Persuasion**, subject of a good word from his trainer. "He's a very nice horse who won his maiden at Goodwood very comfortably," Hills recalls.

"We shouldn't have run him at York when he disappointed in the Acomb, and he didn't like the ground subsequently at Newmarket.

"He's wintered very well, and we'll start him off in the Free Handicap."

Motagally also excites his trainer. It took a while for the penny to drop, but the Sheikh Hamdan-owned four-year-old rounded off last term with deeply impressive wins at Brighton and Wolverhampton and will kick off the 2020 campaign from a mark of 90.

Hills is thinking big with the gelding and says: "He clocked a very good time last autumn, but we couldn't run him after Wolverhampton due to a small problem.

"He looks fantastic, and could keep on improving this season. I'm hoping he could develop into a Wokingham horse."

Flippa The Strippa, winner of two of her seven starts as a juvenile, including Sandown's Listed National Stakes, will be on the trail of further black type this year.

"She went back to her owner Chris Wright's stud over the winter and has been training nicely since she returned," Hills says. "We may have to travel abroad in search of black type."

Brushwork, winner of his first three starts at Newcastle, lost his unbeaten record when third to Glen Shiel on a return to the north-east venue in January.

However, there is real confidence at Wetherdown House that a mark of 88 may underestimate him. "He's done well recently," Hills says. "He went weak on us in his last race, and we're giving him time to find himself. He's a nice horse."

Others to receive a favourable mention include **Breath Of Air**, an 85-rated handicapper who has been gelded since his last start, **Tommy De Vito**, a twice-raced three-year-old who will "keep on improving and go through the ranks", and **Badri**, who is earmarked for a race at Newmarket in the spring.

There is certainly plenty more to come from Hills and his team.

REPORTING BY RICHARD BIRCH

AIDAN O'BRIEN

New riding plans but same vast array of talent

IT WAS a winter of change at Ballydoyle as the retirement as champion jockey of his son Donnacha to join the training ranks will leave Aidan O'Brien with 450-plus rides to be filled and more than a century of winners up for grabs. Currently no new appointments are in the offing and the riders in situ will get every chance to pick up the slack.

In equine terms, the question at the

forefront of the mind of every trainer with a good three-year-old colt as the start of the Flat season looms is going to be the same. How will Pinatubo train on?

Irish racegoers were privileged to see him at his very best in the National Stakes at the Curragh in September. How privileged O'Brien felt is anybody's guess as he saw two of his best colts beaten upwards of nine lengths that day, but the champion trainer is unperturbed as he plots the Classic course of **Arizona** and **Armory** among others, and once again he looks likely to be mob-handed at Newmarket in early May.

In the Irish classifications, Arizona was rated 12lb inferior to Pinatubo, but was still the top-rated Irish juvenile in a season that was highlighted by his win in the Coventry Stakes. While he failed to win again last season, he finished the campaign strongly by getting to within two lengths of Pinatubo in the Dewhurst and by finishing an unlucky-in-running fifth in the Breeders' Cup Juvenile Turf.

"He was a fine big horse last year and enjoyed a bit of nice ground," says O'Brien. "We were particularly delighted with his run in the Dewhurst on ground which could have been more suitable for him. He's done well physically and we're very happy with him and it's possible that he could start in the 2,000 Guineas."

'Plenty more to come'

Armory is in a similar category. He had won the Tyros Stakes and the Futurity Stakes before Pinatubo showed him the cleanest pair of heels imaginable in the National Stakes, but his subsequent third in the Prix Jean-Luc Lagardere was probably his best run of the season.

O'Brien says: "Like Arizona, he appreciates good ground and we think there could be plenty more to come from him. He did well over the winter, and we think he'll have no trouble starting off over a mile. He could well step up in trip after that."

A little disappointing behind Pinatubo and Arizona in the

Armory: Futurity Stakes winner probably put up his best performance as a juvenile in defeat

Dewhurst was **Wichita**, but his previous performance when a decisive winner of the Tattersalls Stakes at Newmarket was much more like it.

'Lots of quality'

This son of No Nay Never is a colt O'Brien expects better things from this season: "He shows plenty of pace but we still think there's every chance that he'll get a mile. We'll give him a chance to do that – he's a fine, big horse and has done very well over the winter. We could start him in the Guineas, we could start him off before, but we think he's a horse with lots of quality."

The strength of the middle-distance colts will become more apparent as the season develops, but it is likely that most of the Ballydoyle colts with potential to be Derby horses will get their chance to prove themselves over a mile to begin with.

Royal Dornoch (right) gets the better of Kameko to win the Royal Lodge Stakes

O'Brien's best middle-distance prospect at the moment could be **Innisfree**. He's very much bred to stay the trip and showed a very good attitude to win the Beresford Stakes on heavy ground in the autumn.

"He's not short of pace, he's a good traveller in his races," says O'Brien. "He's a lovely natured horse and he could be one of those Guineas horses who will tackle the Derby trip. We'll train him for the Classics and he could start early."

The progressive **Mogul** has some of the same hallmarks and was not disgraced when dipping his hooves into Group 1 territory late last year, finishing fourth in the Futurity at Newcastle. O'Brien says: "He was a bit of a baby last year and he took a bit of time to learn, but we were delighted with his run at Newcastle, even though we might have preferred it if the race was run on grass. It was a good experience for him though and he came out of the race well. We've been happy with him over the winter and he's one we're looking forward to."

Classic contender

Royal Dornoch is one who could make good strides this season. He took his time to win a race, but his narrow defeat of Kameko in the Royal Lodge Stakes at Newmarket could not have worked out better with the latter going on to win the Futurity at Newcastle.

"He'd been running over six furlongs before he stepped up in trip, so he has plenty of pace, and he ended up seeing out the mile very well at Newmarket. He's done very well. I imagine he'll start off in the Guineas, I don't know if he'll have a run before that."

Keep British runners in races over two miles on side. They show a five-year profit of £10.10

'She's a quality filly'

The quality of the Ballydoyle juvenile fillies from last season lacked the usual strength in depth, but the principal exception to this was **Love**. Her finest hour in a busy campaign was victory in the Moyglare Stud Stakes, but she turned up in a lot of the big fillies' races and acquitted herself with credit every time.

O'Brien says: "She's a lovely mover and wants good ground. I'd imagine she'll start off over a mile and step up to a mile and a quarter. She might even get the Oaks trip. She's a quality filly and will be trained for the Classics."

A filly possibly coming in a little under the radar is **Peaceful**. After running an eyecatching race on her debut at Leopardstown, she bolted up in an ordinary maiden at Thurles before going down narrowly at Newmarket.

"She's a lovely filly," says the trainer, adding: "She ran a lovely race at Newmarket on very bad ground. We've always liked her and she has plenty of quality. We might start off in a Guineas trial over seven furlongs, go on to one of the 1,000 Guineas and see from there."

A couple of last season's juveniles who might prove best at sprint trips include **Monarch Of Egypt**. He came up against the unbeaten Siskin twice, getting closest to him in the Phoenix Stakes, and it appears O'Brien may well give him a chance to see if he can get a mile. The trainer says: "We always thought he might stay seven furlongs but we're not sure. We'll probably start him off over seven and then decide whether we go up or come back in trip. We've always thought he's a bit better than we managed to get out of him last season."

Just behind Monarch Of Egypt on the latter occasion was stablemate and July Stakes winner **Royal Lytham**. "He's one we'll start in a trial over seven and then maybe go up to a mile," says O'Brien. "He's a good-natured horse with plenty of speed and he's tough."

The strength of the Ballydoyle team this year looks to be very much among their older horses with multiple Group 1 winners coming back for more. It may or may not include last season's dual Champion Stakes heroine **Magical**, about whom O'Brien says: "She was due to be covered by No Nay Never but she's done so well physically over the winter that I asked the owners if they wanted to keep her in training for another year. It would be great if we could get her back."

Even without Magical, O'Brien has an enviable hand to work with among his older horses, including Derby winner **Anthony Van Dyck**, Irish Derby winner **Sovereign**, and last season's joint top-rated Irish three-year-old **Japan**.

"We were delighted with Sovereign last year," O'Brien reports. "He's a fine, big horse who we've given plenty of time and we're looking forward to him. We always thought he'd stay well and he'll handle any ease in the ground if he has to. We can do a lot of things with him from a mile and a quarter upwards. We think he could stay well too. He wasn't stopping at the Curragh and could stay further than a mile and a half."

O'Brien adds: "Anthony Van Dyck is in very good form. He's very uncomplicated and hardly ran a bad race last year. Japan will compete in all of the middle-distance races. He was a little bit behind in the spring of last year but he seems more forward this year. He could do a bit of work at the Curragh on the first day of the new season and then maybe come back for a race like the Tattersalls Gold Cup with the Arc as the long-term target."

The progressive **Lancaster House** might be one to take note of this season, and O'Brien says: "We could start him in a Listed

DID YOU KNOW?
Like Jim Bolger, O'Brien is a member of the Pioneer Total Abstinence Association, a Catholic group whose primary aim is the promotion of sobriety and temperance

'We were delighted with Sovereign (left) last year. We can do a lot of things with him from a mile and a quarter upwards. We think he could stay well too. He wasn't stopping at the Curragh and could stay further than a mile and a half'

Big guns: 2019 Epsom Derby winner Anthony Van Dyck (centre) works alongside Kew Gardens (left) on the track at Dundalk

or Group 3 at a mile. A lot happened for him in a short space of time last year and he's done very well since."

Derby fourth **Broome** was not seen after a disappointing run in the Irish Derby, and he also returns for a four-year-old campaign. "He should be ready to start early from a mile and a quarter upwards," his trainer says. "He's done very well physically and we'll form a plan when we start working him."

Derby fancy **Mount Everest** didn't get to the track until the autumn and this looks like a year to make up for lost time, while Derby fifth and St Leger fourth **Sir Dragonet** also returns and should be effective at 1m4f.

O'Brien says: "Donnacha thought he didn't stay the trip in the Leger. He's forward and will start early. There's a mile and a quarter Listed race early in the season that he might start in and we'll campaign him over 1m2f to 1m4f. He has more speed than stamina."

Flying the stayers' flag

The stable is well represented in the staying division by **Kew Gardens**, who gave notice that a changing of the guard in that division may happen this year given his game defeat of Stradivarius on Champions Day at Ascot.

O'Brien says: "We've always thought the world of him. We were training him for the Ascot Gold Cup last year and he met a little setback and came good late in the year. We're delighted with him and he could possibly go to the stayers' race on Dubai World Cup night. He'll be prepared after that for the Ascot Gold Cup and all the big staying races."

Circus Maximus became one of the top three-year-old milers almost by accident last season as he started off by winning the Dee Stakes at Chester before finishing sixth in the Derby. When dropped back in trip though, victories in the St James's Palace Stakes and a controversial success in the Prix du Moulin made his season. "He was very comfortable back over a mile and is one to look forward to as he's done well," says his trainer."

Promising early types

As to the early progress of his two-year-olds, O'Brien reports: "We have a couple of early types by a couple of our new sires who we're very happy with. We have a colt by The Gurkha ex-Euphrasia who goes nicely and another by The Gurkha ex-Larceny. We also like a colt by Air Force Blue ex-Marylebone. We think the ones by The Gurkha are going to be like him. He didn't actually run at two but he showed lots in the spring before he got a bout of colic. I think the early ones especially will take after him."

REPORTING BY JUSTIN O'HANLON

HOSPITALITY EXPERIENCES

NEW OFFERS

PANORAMIC VIEWS AND GREAT FOOD

ENJOY FABULOUS HOSPITALITY EXPERIENCES IN ONE OF OUR STUNNING RESTAURANTS OR PRIVATE SUITES

FROM £79 PER PERSON

HENNESSY RESTAURANT | RACEGEORS RESTAURANT
30 PRIVATE SUITES

NEWBURY RACECOURSE

CALL OUR TEAM ON 01635 40015
NEWBURYRACECOURSE.CO.UK

JOSEPH O'BRIEN

Smart team of proven and progressive sorts

NOW heading into his fifth Flat season as a trainer, Joseph O'Brien is no longer the baby of the family in the training ranks – that role now falls to younger brother Donnacha, an important ally as a jockey since partnering Intricately to give the stable a first Group 1 victory in the 2016 Moyglare Stud Stakes.

Aidan O'Brien's elder son saddled exactly 100 winners in Ireland in the calendar year 2019, and ended the championship campaign a clear second-best behind his father in terms of earnings and races won.

The star of the show was the brilliant Ruler Of The World filly Iridessa, who signed off in superb fashion with a hard-earned triumph in the Breeders' Cup Filly & Mare Turf.

WINNERS IN LAST FOUR YEARS **100, 107, 52, 23**

DID YOU KNOW?

O'Brien began riding in 2009, shared the apprentice title the following year, won it outright in 2011 and was champion jockey in 2012 and 2013. He retired from riding with 518 winners to his name and then turned his attention to training. He started with a bang, sending out four winners on the first day in his new career – June 6, 2017

RACING POST

FRAN BERRY

THE QUIET DERBY HERO

Joseph and his amazing multi-winning dream start

Underlining a quickly established reputation as a trainer eager to make his presence on the international scene, O'Brien sent three runners to Saudi Arabia's showpiece meeting at the King Abdulaziz track in Riyadh at the end of February. And at home the stable was quickly out of the blocks at Dundalk, sending out a dozen winners before the end of February.

One of the most striking features of O'Brien's 2020 team is a high concentration of staying performers among the older horses, including several who have performed with distinction on the stable's Australian raids.

Cup hero returns home

Intriguingly, **Rekindling** has rejoined the Piltown stable having run just once for Australian trainer Liam Howley since his remarkable Melbourne Cup victory in 2017. "He had a few training setbacks, but he's moving well since he came back and is in good shape generally," says O'Brien.

"We're feeling our way with him, and it's too early to say if we can get him back to peak form, but I'm hopeful."

Former French-trained **Master Of Reality** started last season with a 33-1 success in the Group 3 Vintage Crop Stakes at Navan and ended it by running a storming race to chase home Vow And Declare in the Melbourne Cup, only to be demoted two places for causing interference. Last season's Ascot Gold Cup third is likely to have a similar programme this year.

Three Melbourne Cup also-rans are back in training, including the 2018 Irish Derby winner **Latrobe**, whose sole success last season came in a 1m4f Group 3 race at Leopardstown.

"Things didn't really fall right for him last season, but we still look on him as a Group 1 horse," says the trainer. "He'll probably start off at 1m4f but we'd be prepared to go further with him again."

Twilight Payment joined the stable from Jim Bolger as a six-year-old last year after beating Latrobe in the Curragh Cup, and

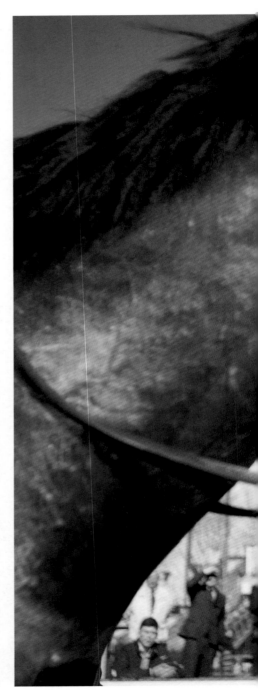

*Top team:
Joseph O'Brien
and Melbourne
Cup winner
Rekindling*

will be campaigned in the top staying races. O'Brien says: "He reached his highest rating at 113 last season and we think he has plenty of life left in him yet."

That view was endorsed by a respectable run at the big Saudi meeting, a race that produced a below-par display from stablemate **Downdraft**, a dual Listed winner in Ireland last summer and successful in a Group 3 handicap at Flemington just three days before contesting the Melbourne Cup.

An interesting addition to the stable's middle-distance squad is **Yucatan**, trained in Australia last year after winning the Group 2 Ladbrokes Herbert Power Stakes at Caulfield in 2018 for Ballydoyle.

"He was a good horse for Dad, and it's exciting to have him," says the young trainer. "We think he'll be effective in Group races at a mile and a quarter and a mile and a half."

Colours set to shine

The accent is mostly on stamina among the older horses, making **Speak In Colours** something of an exception. A three-time six-furlong winner at the Curragh and Group 1-placed over seven furlongs in the Prix de la Foret, he will be targeted at major races after starting off with a satisfactory fourth in a seven-furlong contest at the showpiece Saudi fixture.

Unraced at two, **Buckhurst** finished out of the first two only once from six starts at three and won two Group 3 races over a mile and a quarter at the Curragh before ending up with a Group 3 second over a mile and a half at Leopardstown.

Yucatan: previously a smart performer for Aidan O'Brien and has now joined Joseph for a campaign over middle distances

Side with O'Brien three-year-old runners on the all-weather. They show a profit of £14.31

63

"He progressed well last year but I always thought he'd be better at four," says O'Brien. "I'm hopeful he'll be a Group 1 horse."

Numerian was progressive last season, running well in big-value handicaps on turf after winning twice at Dundalk in the early part of the year. O'Brien explains: "He was beaten only a head in a Group 3 when he went back to Dundalk at the end of the season. That was over an extended mile and a quarter, and he might go a bit further this year."

Other four-year-olds to look out for are **No Needs Never**, back in action after running only once last season, and **Patrick Sarsfield**, unbeaten in two starts after joining the stable last year: "He's rated 86 so we'll try to win a good handicap with him at around a mile before stepping him up in class."

Classic prospect

Degraves, a colt by Camelot out of a Listed six-furlong winner by Danehill Dancer, can be rated one of the stable's best three-year-old prospects having ended the season by beating the Ballydoyle-trained Persia in the Group 3 Eyrefield Stakes at Leopardstown.

O'Brien says: "He'll probably start off in a Derby trial. I think he'll stay ten furlongs and maybe further, although he's not really bred for that. There's a lot of speed in the family, but Camelot will obviously help from a stamina angle."

The former Richard Fahey-trained **Summer Sands** was a notable acquisition last October when O'Brien paid 625,000gns for the Coach House colt after he backed up a creditable third placing in the Middle Park with victory in a valuable Listed sales race at Redcar.

"He's settled in well, and is a high-class prospect for this season," the trainer reports.

"The plan is to treat him as a sprinter, so we'll have to wait to see how things pan out."

From Intricately to Iridessa, and with several other smart performers in between, O'Brien has established a reputation for producing high-quality fillies.

The trainer is hoping for more of the same from **New York Girl** and **A New Dawn**, separated by only a neck when winner and second respectively in the Group 3 Weld Stakes over 7f at the Curragh in late September.

Discussing the pair, O'Brien says: "New York Girl was having only her second start that day and she beat a much more experienced filly. She's by New Approach, and she'll probably start off in an Oaks trial. A New Dawn has a lovely pedigree and has done well over the winter. She's been placed in three of her four stakes races and the first objective is to win one."

'She could do well this year'

O'Brien also reckons Champs Elysees filly **Brook On Fifth** has a solid future, saying: "She beat 28 rivals first time out in a maiden at the Curragh. She finished behind A New Dawn when fourth in a Group 3 over a mile on her second start and then had a little setback, but she could do well this year."

Crossfirehurricane, a colt by Kitten's Joy, has already made a significant impression in 2020. Winner of a seven-furlong Limerick maiden last June on his only juvenile start he won over the same trip on his reappearance at Dundalk in February before stepping up in class and trip to win a mile Listed race on the all-weather three weeks later.

Save for his father, no Irish trainer starts the 2020 season with such strength in depth. It looks like being another good year for O'Brien.

REPORTING BY ALAN SWEETMAN

'He progressed well last year but I always thought he'd be better at four. I'm hopeful he'll be a Group 1 horse'

HUGO PALMER

Optimist out to break the £1m barrier

DEFEAT by inches in a Group 1 race turned a fifth successive season breaking through the £1 million prize-money mark into "a disappointing one" for Newmarket trainer Hugo Palmer.

It says much for a trainer in only his tenth season that amassing £785,092 can be described in such dispiriting terms.

But Palmer, who describes himself as "an eternal optimist – you have to be to be a trainer", has clearly set himself high levels of attainment, which is not surprising after landing the Irish Oaks with Covert Love in his fifth season and the English 2,000 Guineas and St James's Palace Stakes with Galileo Gold the following year.

Powerful Breeze (centre): expected to strike at the highest level this season

So, without Palmer saying as much, his team at Kremlin Cottage Stables on the Snailwell Road will be aiming to smash through the seven-figure total again.

And the Palmer standard-bearer will be the filly **Powerful Breeze**, whose target was to have been the 1,000 Guineas at Newmarket until the yard's star filly had an early season mishap.

"Powerful Breeze has met with a setback and will not now be able to run in the 1,000 Guineas," says Palmer. "It's very disappointing for all concerned but hopefully she'll be back in the second half of the season."

Powerful Breeze had been only a couple of points behind the Guineas ante-post favourite Quadrilateral, the filly who edged out Palmer's star by a head in the Group 1 Fillies' Mile at Newmarket in October after a

sparkling last-furlong dash up the rail when Powerful Breeze had seemed to have the race in the bag 50 yards from the line.

If James Doyle had been able to edge his filly a little further right he might have legitimately denied Quadrilateral the room to make her flying finish – and change the season for Palmer's stable.

But second place was a worthy performance and her two-year-old season, which brought victory in the Group 2 May Hill Stakes at Doncaster, augurs well for this year.

"She was a star for us last year and got caught only on the line by Quadrilateral. But for those few inches we would have broken the £1m prize-money mark," says Palmer.

"We were delighted with her progress over the winter until the setback and she was

HUGO PALMER
NEWMARKET, SUFFOLK

	Number of horses	Races run	1st	2nd	3rd	Unpl	Per cent	£1 level stake
2yo	36	114	19	14	13	68	16.7	+12.66
3yo	39	177	21	29	28	99	11.9	-67.90
4yo+	24	92	13	6	12	61	14.1	-50.59
Totals	99	383	53	49	53	228	13.8	-105.83
2018	116	508	87	61	53	305	17.1	+18.56
2017	134	493	77	69	51	295	15.6	-126.71

BY MONTH

2yo	W-R	Per cent	£1 level stake	3yo	W-R	Per cent	£1 level stake
Jan	0-0	0.0	0.00	Jan	3-13	23.1	-2.50
Feb	0-0	0.0	0.00	Feb	1-7	14.3	-5.33
Mar	0-0	0.0	0.00	Mar	1-10	10.0	-4.50
Apr	0-0	0.0	0.00	Apr	1-24	4.2	-16.50
May	1-3	33.3	+2.50	May	1-20	5.0	-15.50
June	0-7	0.0	-7.00	June	4-27	14.8	-9.70
July	4-17	23.5	+6.41	July	4-24	16.7	-6.70
Aug	7-19	36.8	+36.00	Aug	1-22	4.5	-7.00
Sep	4-24	16.7	-1.25	Sep	1-9	11.1	-5.75
Oct	2-29	6.9	-18.00	Oct	2-12	16.7	-6.92
Nov	1-11	9.1	-2.00	Nov	1-6	16.7	+11.00
Dec	0-4	0.0	-4.00	Dec	1-3	33.3	+1.50

4yo+	W-R	Per cent	£1 level stake	Totals	W-R	Per cent	£1 level stake
Jan	1-8	12.5	-4.25	Jan	4-21	19.0	-6.75
Feb	0-2	0.0	-2.00	Feb	1-9	11.1	-7.33
Mar	3-8	37.5	+1.20	Mar	4-18	22.2	-3.30
Apr	4-12	33.3	+4.04	Apr	5-36	13.9	-12.46
May	0-12	0.0	-12.00	May	2-35	5.7	-25.00
June	0-16	0.0	-16.00	June	4-50	8.0	-32.70
July	0-8	0.0	-8.00	July	8-49	16.3	-8.29
Aug	1-6	16.7	-4.83	Aug	9-47	19.1	+24.17
Sep	1-8	12.5	-5.00	Sep	6-41	14.6	-12.00
Oct	2-5	40.0	+0.25	Oct	6-46	13.0	-24.67
Nov	0-4	0.0	-4.00	Nov	2-21	9.5	+7.00
Dec	1-3	33.3	0.00	Dec	2-10	20.0	+1.50

DISTANCE

2yo	W-R	Per cent	£1 level stake	3yo	W-R	Per cent	£1 level stake
5f-6f	7-45	15.6	-20.59	5f-6f	2-17	11.8	-12.83
7f-8f	11-65	16.9	+32.25	7f-8f	11-95	11.6	-19.20
9f-13f	1-4	25.0	+1.00	9f-13f	7-62	11.3	-36.12
14f+	0-0	0.0	0.00	14f+	1-3	33.3	+0.25

4yo+	W-R	Per cent	£1 level stake	Totals	W-R	Per cent	£1 level stake
5f-6f	1-21	4.8	-17.25	5f-6f	10-83	12.0	-50.67
7f-8f	1-21	4.8	-11.00	7f-8f	23-181	12.7	+2.05
9f-13f	11-45	24.4	-17.34	9f-13f	19-111	17.1	-52.46
14f+	0-5	0.0	-5.00	14f+	1-8	12.5	-4.75

TYPE OF RACE

	NON-HANDICAPS				HANDICAPS		
	W-R	Per cent	£1 level stake		W-R	Per cent	£1 level stake
2yo	15-85	17.6	+26.41	2yo	4-29	13.8	-13.75
3yo	9-63	14.3	-25.90	3yo	12-114	10.5	-42.00
4yo+	4-32	12.5	-12.08	4yo+	9-60	15.0	-38.51

Statistics relate to all runners in Britain from January 1, 2019 to December 31, 2019

looking tremendous. My priority is to make her a Group 1 horse.

"We're hoping she'll be back in the second half of the season when there are any number of options, including the Coronation Stakes, the Falmouth and the Breeders' Cup when she could stay nine or ten furlongs."

Powerful Breeze provided two of the stable's 53 winners last season, 34 down on Kremlin Cottage's record total the year before, and that was partly down to an unspecified sickness that affected Palmer's string.

"We had an illness in the yard in the spring which was very difficult to put a finger on. The horses were just not well-well," he says.

"There was a point in June when close to 50 per cent of our horses were finishing in the first four but our percentage of winners was dismal.

"It took a long time to get them right but I'm glad to say we rectified things and our year finished well, and now we have a lot to look forward to.

"We have a lot of lovely horses with lovely pedigrees and some nice two-year-olds."

'He looks tremendous'

Another horse Palmer hopes can boost the Kremlin Cottage coffers is **Collide**, who was back in Newmarket in late February after a round trip of 2,350 miles to Cagnes-sur-Mer on France's Mediterranean coast.

The Khalid Abdullah-owned five-year-old entire was Palmer's first venture to the French Riviera after a planned trip to Saudi Arabia had to be cancelled when Collide failed to get into a valuable handicap having a mark of only 98.

Hugo Palmer keeps a close eye on his string

But the change of plan paid off with victory in the Listed Grand Prix Departement for the Frankel brother to last year's St Leger winner Logician.

"He had a week out of training after his heroics on the Mediterranean and now looks tremendous," says Palmer, who is considering pencilling in the Group 3 John Porter Stakes over 1m4f at Newbury in early April for his wandering star.

"He'll be governed by the ground – he doesn't want it too quick. But his mark has only gone up to 101 – the handicapper took a dim view of the French form and put him up only 3lb, so we may look at valuable handicaps and run him over 1m6f, perhaps at the York Dante meeting in May.

"He might even become an Ebor horse, although you need to be rated around 105 to win that, so he needs to improve. But we've always thought he was a 1m6f horse and he could be a possible for the Northumberland Plate.

"His wind was an issue last year but I'm delighted to say we've put that right and he's paying us rewards."

Caravan Of Hope, a son of Nathaniel, won his last two starts of the 2019 season at Ascot and Doncaster and was never out of the frame in the other five outings.

In the same Dr Ali Ridha ownership as Powerful Breeze, Caravan Of Hope is expected to pay his way again this year.

"He won as easy as you like at Doncaster over 1m6f. He'll be a nice staying horse who needs cut in the ground," says Palmer.

"He's been gelded and has done very well over the winter and could really improve into

a top-class staying handicapper. He's a Northumberland Vase type of horse. Nathaniels improve with time, so we're hopeful his rating will go up."

'He's made giant strides'

Ironclad, a four-year-old gelding by leading sire Dubawi, is another on whom Palmer is relying for winners.

"He's one of the best-bred horses I've trained and he has the looks to match," says the trainer. "He was a late arrival into the yard last year – he picked up an injury but he recovered from it and won races at Beverley and Newmarket.

"He's made giant strides and we're really pleased with how he's done over the winter. He'll be a ten-furlong horse but he should get a mile and a half in time."

Evergreen seven-year-old **Gifted Master** has been one of the major reasons Palmer's prize-money has been ticking over, his ten victories having brought in almost £760,000 during the last five seasons, including the 2018 Stewards' Cup.

Last year was the first time he didn't win, including a disappointing run in the Wokingham when he was eased after meeting interference.

"He wasn't quite right last spring and it took a long time for him to recover. He was crying out for a break and now he's had one he's come back rejuvenated and is a happy horse," says Palmer.

"He might just have lost half a yard of pace, so I might explore the option of going up to seven furlongs with him and might consider the Victoria Cup at Ascot in May."

RACING POST

Hoping to serve it up on turf

Backers might like to take serious note of Palmer's comments about five-year-old entire **El Ghazwani**, who has racked up six wins from seven outings on Lingfield's all-weather surface and might have a perfect record but for being struck into on the losing occasion.

"He's done wonderful things at Lingfield and I can't see why he won't win on turf too. He's rated 101 on sand and 90 on turf – an 11lb pull.

"He's in the Easter Classic on Good Friday at Lingfield and will not be a forlorn hope.

■ Palmer has had 16 winners from 31 runners at Haydock in the last five years – for a profit of £83.82

DID YOU KNOW?

Doesn't that take the biscuit . . . in the 19th century, the ancestors of Hugo Palmer, eldest son of the fourth Baron Palmer, helped set up Huntley & Palmers, which by the turn of the 20th century had become the world's largest biscuit firm, employing 5,000 people at its height

Gifted Master (second right): 2018 Stewards' Cup winner is back in action after a break

On turf he'll need a flat track, not one with undulations like Newmarket. Somewhere like Ascot would suit him."

Almufti is another older horse kept in training and expected to pay his way after recovering from a wind operation to win twice on Lingfield's all-weather track.

Of Kremlin Cottage's three-year-olds, it could pay to take note of **Eastern Sheriff**, a brother to St Leger winner Harbour Law.

He raced and won once last year, an easy victory over a mile on Kempton's all-weather in November and he could be a Queen's Vase or King Edward VII type.

Palmer is clearly sweet on the son of Lawman and says: "He's definitely one I'm looking forward to."

Golden dreams of Classics

If there is to be a Classic contender in the yard apart from Powerful Breeze, the honour could sit on the shoulders of **Golden Pass**, a highly promising, well-bred daughter of Derby winner Golden Horn.

She finished a creditable third in a warm Newmarket fillies' maiden in September, the winner of which ran in the Group 1 Fillies' Mile.

"We don't know what she might turn into but I suspect she'll get an Oaks entry. I would strongly fancy her to win her maiden and then she'll go for one of the Oaks trials," says Palmer.

The trainer also singles out **Powertrain**, a winner on the July Course and at Chester, as a possible for the Britannia Stakes at Royal Ascot, and double-scorer **Acquitted**, who will be aimed at the valuable London Gold Cup handicap at Newbury in May.

"Acquitted looks nicely weighted on 89 and could be better than a handicapper," says Palmer.

Among Kremlin Cottage's other three-year-olds worth mentioning are: **Arthur's Court**, a Derby entry now ineligible after being gelded, an operation which "will be the making of him"; the "exciting" **Emissary**, a Workforce half-brother who was a comfortable winner over nine furlongs at Wolverhampton on his only start in the autumn and comes into the "could be anything category" and could yet get a Derby entry; **Zoran**, a tall, narrow horse "who has improved physically more than any other in the yard"; **Imrahor**, a well-bred son of Kingman who is expected to be a 100-plus rated horse; **Chankaya**, who could be "a very nice ten to twelve furlong horse"; and **Hot Touch**, a winner last year who has done physically well over the winter and "has the potential to be a black-type horse".

Palmer also gives a trio of two-year-olds to follow who have already taken his fancy.

An unnamed colt by Showcasing out of Dam Beautiful, a €65,000 purchase at Tattersalls Ireland sale, is an exceptionally good mover who is "showing all the right signs". Another unnamed colt, by Starspangledbanner out of Via Lattea, is raising Palmer's pulse.

"I've had only one Starspangledbanner before, Home Of The Brave, and he did phenomenally well for us," the trainer says.

Between 2014 and 2017 he won six times, including two Group 3s and a couple of Listed races.

"This horse reminds me very much of Home Of The Brave. He was bought for €68,000 at the Arqana sale in August. He's got the most beautiful attitude and I'm very happy with the way he's training.

"He's a flashy Starspangledbanner with a flaxen tail, so whoever buys him will be able to spot him easily in a race!"

Echo Beach, a two-year-old colt by Adaay out of Last Echo, was an inexpensive purchase at Tattersalls, bought by one of Palmer's syndicates to replace Hariboux, sold to America after landing three of his five races and being placed in his other two outings.

"He's a replacement for Hariboux and looks just the same sort – hardy and good in his work. He's grown and developed physically."

REPORTING BY LAWRIE KELSEY

RacingBlue

20%
introductory
discount code
RPGF20

STORM

Speed & Power for Longer

For sustained speed and power · Aids training and performance
Targets muscle acidosis to delay fatigue · Scientifically proven

Tel: 01638 814155   www.racingblue.com

Designed by Nature, Improved by Science

JAMES TATE

Going from strength to strength and thinking big

THESE are exciting times for James Tate, who is expanding his Newmarket operation after enjoying his best-ever season in 2019.

Tate, who saddled 74 winners last year, completed the purchase of the now retired Alan Bailey's Cavendish Stables, adjacent to his own Jamesfield Place yard on the Hamilton Road, at the start of the year and will house more than 100 horses between the two yards for the first time in his eight-year training career.

"I've always said I didn't want another yard that you had to get in the car and drive to," says Tate. "So when the chance to have one I can literally walk to came up, it made sense to have it. We were overflowing at Jamesfield and now our backward two-year-olds are at the new stable and they go out fourth lot in the morning."

After success at Group 2 level, three Group 3 wins and four in Listed company last season, Tate is hoping this will be the campaign he makes his breakthrough at the highest grade, and there certainly appears to be the required quality among his expanding team.

"A Group 1 is the next step but it's probably something you don't have a massive amount of control about but it would be great to get one," he says. "I think we need to concentrate on our top horses running to their top potential."

Although stable stalwart Invincible Army has left for stud, there is a lovely blend of new and familiar faces peering over his stable doors, while the trainer's hand in the three-year-old division looks exceptionally strong, with Group 3 winner **Under The Stars** *(above)*, who will start her season in a Classic trial, among the front rank.

"She's so hard to judge," says Tate of the three-time winner. "She doesn't overdo it in

WINNERS IN LAST FIVE YEARS **72, 41, 34, 54, 43**

DID YOU KNOW?
Tate is the nephew of Michael Dickinson, the three-time champion trainer who saddled the first five home in the 1983 Gold Cup and created the Tapeta racing surface

■ Take note when PJ McDonald is on board Tate runners. His 26% strike-rate gives a profit of £17.97

JAMES TATE
NEWMARKET, SUFFOLK

	Number of horses	Races run	1st	2nd	3rd	Unpl	Per cent	£1 level stake
2yo	22	64	10	9	9	36	15.6	-11.45
3yo	46	212	53	32	23	104	25.0	-4.34
4yo+	7	30	9	3	4	14	30.0	+2.91
Totals	75	306	72	44	36	154	23.5	-12.88
2018	79	263	41	43	32	147	15.6	-63.83
2017	54	241	34	39	36	132	14.1	-118.13

BY MONTH

2yo	W-R	Per cent	£1 level stake	3yo	W-R	Per cent	£1 level stake
Jan	0-0	0.0	0.00	Jan	2-19	10.5	-4.50
Feb	0-0	0.0	0.00	Feb	6-13	46.2	+5.64
Mar	0-0	0.0	0.00	Mar	4-18	22.2	-6.62
Apr	0-0	0.0	0.00	Apr	8-21	38.1	+7.25
May	1-4	25.0	+0.50	May	6-25	24.0	+0.41
June	0-6	0.0	-6.00	June	4-20	20.0	+0.11
July	3-9	33.3	+22.25	July	6-30	20.0	-5.38
Aug	2-10	20.0	-5.80	Aug	3-22	13.6	-0.50
Sep	1-10	10.0	-4.00	Sep	9-22	40.9	+8.66
Oct	2-6	33.3	-1.65	Oct	4-18	22.2	-8.04
Nov	0-8	0.0	-8.00	Nov	1-3	33.3	-0.38
Dec	1-11	9.1	-8.75	Dec	0-1	0.0	-1.00

4yo+	W-R	Per cent	£1 level stake	Totals	W-R	Per cent	£1 level stake
Jan	0-0	0.0	0.00	Jan	2-19	10.5	-4.50
Feb	0-0	0.0	0.00	Feb	6-13	46.2	+5.64
Mar	1-2	50.0	+3.00	Mar	5-20	25.0	-3.62
Apr	2-4	50.0	+1.50	Apr	10-25	40.0	+8.75
May	1-4	25.0	+0.50	May	8-33	24.2	+1.41
June	1-7	14.3	-5.09	June	5-33	15.2	-10.98
July	3-4	75.0	+9.00	July	12-43	27.9	+25.87
Aug	1-3	33.3	0.00	AuG	6-35	17.1	-6.30
Sep	0-4	0.0	-4.00	Sep	10-36	27.8	+0.66
Oct	0-2	0.0	-2.00	Oct	6-26	23.1	-11.69
Nov	0-0	0.0	0.00	Nov	1-11	9.1	-0.38
Dec	0-0	0.0	0.00	Dec	1-12	8.3	-1.00

DISTANCE

2yo	W-R	Per cent	£1 level stake	3yo	W-R	Per cent	£1 level stake
5f-6f	8-43	18.6	+5.20	5f-6f	21-63	33.3	+26.35
7f-8f	2-21	9.5	-16.65	7f-8f	23-105	21.9	-23.51
9f-13f	0-0	0.0	0.00	9f-13f	9-44	20.5	-7.18
14f+	0-0	0.0	0.00	14f+	0-0	0.0	0.00

4yo+	W-R	Per cent	£1 level stake	Totals	W-R	Per cent	£1 level stake
5f-6f	5-17	29.4	+0.91	5f-6f	34-123	27.6	+32.46
7f-8f	4-13	30.8	+2.00	7f-8f	29-139	20.9	-38.16
9f-13f	0-0	0.0	0.00	9f-13f	9-44	20.5	-7.18
14f+	0-0	0.0	0.00	14f+	0-0	0.0	0.00

TYPE OF RACE

	NON-HANDICAPS				HANDICAPS		
	W-R	Per cent	£1 level stake		W-R	Per cent	£1 level stake
2yo	10-57	17.5	-4.45	2yo	0-7	0.0	-7.00
3yo	20-79	25.3	-21.46	3yo	33-133	24.8	+17.13
4yo+	5-15	33.3	+2.66	4yo+	4-15	26.7	+0.25

Statistics relate to all runners in Britain from January 1, 2019 to December 31, 2019

the morning and on top of that she's not the biggest but she's 30 kilos heavier than last season, which is a good sign and she's absolutely full of herself.

"She didn't disappoint at all last season and her sire Night Of Thunder certainly trained on so I would be optimistic she will. She'll get entries in the Nell Gwyn and Fred Darling and then I'd have thought we'd have a crack at a Guineas and go from there.

"She's a come-from-behind horse so I think she'll get a mile but what will turn out to be her best trip I don't really know. I suspect she'll go close in one of those seven-furlong trials, which might be around her optimum trip, and she likes a bit of cut in the ground."

Magical Journey has less experience than Under The Stars after just two runs last season but could yet make up into a Classic contender herself.

"I thought she was very unlucky in the Bosra Sham Stakes on her second start and just got checked when she was challenging," Tate says. "She's got plenty of ability and the question will be 'what trip?' I could see us starting out in a novice race over seven furlongs and then deciding whether to go for a Classic trial or drop back in trip. She's exciting."

Black-type aim for Charm

Melodic Charm was not beaten far in a Group 3 on the second of her two starts last year and, although down the field in Listed company on her return at Lingfield, she is another filly who will be hunting Pattern races for the yard.

High Accolade (left): reported to have strengthened up from last year

"There's a chance she'll end up being better on the all-weather based on her pedigree and I thought it was wise getting her out early at Lingfield," says Tate. "She's a fine, big filly and we'll look for some black type."

Sky Commander and **High Accolade** could be two colts from the Classic generation to look out for, with a trip to Newcastle on Good Friday on the radar.

"We were pretty confident Sky Commander would win at Kempton on his second start and he did easily," says his trainer. "He's still a big baby and I feel he needs to grow up a little bit before we see his full potential. We'll get him out in a novice at the end of March and then I think we might have a crack at the £100,000 Burradon Stakes.

"High Accolade was tall, weak and gangly last year but always went well and he duly won his only start at two. He's strengthened up from last year and wouldn't be far off 17hh. He could be anything and we look forward to finding out.

"I think he's a miler and, a little bit like Sky Commander, I could see him having a run in a novice at the end of March and, if everything goes well, he could have a crack at something like the Burradon."

Dream Shot, a bargain yearling buy at 12,000gns, crammed nine races into his first season, including a good second in the Group 2 Flying Childers and ended the season at the Breeders' Cup.

"No one wanted him at the breeze-ups but he's turned out to be good," he says. "He's quirky and sometimes hangs but has loads of ability. Physically from two to three he's done well and we're looking forward to him. We'll try six furlongs this year and he should get it."

Searching for next star

While strongest numerically in the three-year-old division, it is four-year-old sprinter **Far Above** who Tate hopes can fill Invincible Army's shoes.

"He's the fastest horse I've ever had at home on the gallops and he's very talented," says the trainer. "He'll be dropping down to five furlongs as I thought he was far too keen when he won his Listed race over six furlongs in France.

"We'll be looking at all the top five-furlong sprints and look forward to taking on Battaash and co. He's delicate but he's good and looks like a bull. As things stand, he'd be the stable's number-one hope I'd say."

Dream Shot: speedball gets his career on the track off to a winning start with victory at Newmarket

Top Rank, unbeaten in three starts, is another four-year-old who sets Tate's pulse racing. "I think he's a Group horse," he says with conviction. "He's cantering while others are galloping to keep up with him. I should preserve his handicap mark but that's not what we're really about. If we get him in a big handicap great, but if not we'll pop him in a Pattern race and I think he's well up to it."

Best to come from Sameem

Sameem rattled off three wins last season, including a Listed contest at Hamilton, and could well benefit from a gelding operation over the winter.

"He's a tough front-runner but has his own ideas and lost it at the big meetings last year where the occasion got to him," recalls his trainer. "He's been gelded, which I hope will help him with that and we'll start with a mile-and-a-quarter handicap."

Four-year-old fillies **Shimmering Dawn** and **Wise Words** are on the trail of black type, while **Alnasherat** could be a dark horse in the camp.

Tate says: "Shimmering Dawn is a great big filly, who progressed a lot as a three-year-old and I think she should progress physically again this year. With a filly like that, rated 91, the main target is a Listed race.

"Wise Words didn't run at two and is a proper five-furlong filly. We'd be optimistic she should improve this year and it's Listed races we're after, starting at Bath in April."

He continues: "We bought Alnasherat out of Sir Michael Stoute's and he should be ready to run soon. He'd been out of training for some time when we got him and we'll see how we do with him, starting at six furlongs."

'This should be his year'

Stable stalwart **Hey Gaman** will be back to fly the stable's flag in the top seven-furlong races and Tate is confident the five-year-old can make an overdue breakthrough at Group 2 level.

"He was a Listed and Group 3 winner last season and it would be nice to win a Group 2 this year. I think he's capable if everything falls his way and this should be his year."

New Graduate, another familiar name, suffered a hind cannon bone fracture on his last run in France but has made a pleasing recovery and is on his way back.

"He's come back from the vets as sound as a pound and is cantering away," says his trainer. "I'm not sure if he's a high-class handicapper, Listed or Group 3 horse but he's somewhere around that level and is going to be a fun Saturday horse."

At the other end of the scale, Tate has plenty of unraced three-year-olds and a healthy number of juveniles, with one or two already standing out from the crowd.

Bright young hopes

"**Enchanted Night** (Night Of Thunder - Khaseeb) looks very fast," he says. "Another one to look out for is **Headliner** (The Last Lion - Countess Ferrama). She's a half-sister to Top Rank and going very nicely, while **Entrapment** (Iffraaj - Rebecca De Winter) is a sister to Mrs Danvers and looking speedy."

Of the unraced three-year-olds, he adds: "**Big Impression** is a lovely big horse and very well bred by Dubawi. He was never going to run at two because of his size but he's shaping up nicely and you'd expect him to be above average.

"**Blazing Hot** is by Hot Streak and worked well last year but we decided to put him away and he's going well again. I'd be optimistic he'd be pretty good. The same goes for **Driving Force**, who cost only 7,000gns from Book 3 but works very well and will make his debut sooner rather than later.

"**Hot To Handle** came from the breeze-ups and clocked a fast time. He picked up an injury last year and we couldn't run him. He's working now and is looking pretty fast.

"**Night Approaching** is a little bit fragile but gallops really well, while **Opening Night** is a massive Night Of Thunder filly and a three-parts sister to Gm Hopkins."

REPORTING BY LEWIS PORTEOUS

ROGER VARIAN

DID YOU KNOW?

As a teenager Varian's family moved to California for two years and he rode trackwork at Hollywood Park for Frank Garza Jr

Quality team can help maintain momentum

ROGER VARIAN last season cemented his place at the top table of Newmarket's elite, with 116 wins and 17 stakes successes both eclipsing the yard's previous best efforts.

In his third year at Carlburg Stables Varian was able to produce Group 1 wins for a pair of patiently nurtured long-term projects, with Sheikh Mohammed Obaid's Zabeel Prince winning the Prix d'Ispahan at the age of six in late May, while the same owner's five-year-old Defoe *(left)* struck in the Coronation Cup just five days later.

Defoe went on to add the Hardwicke Stakes, one of three Royal Ascot winners for Varian in what was a memorable week.

With both of his Group 1 winners back for more as well as Wokingham winner Cape Byron – he would be a stakes winner before the year was out – Varian is well stocked with older horses to ensure a continued flow of success.

No less exciting is this year's crop of three-year-olds, with the colts led by unbeaten Mill Reef Stakes winner Pierre Lapin and the teak-tough Daahyeh heading a strong challenge for Classic honours among the fillies.

Daahyeh: heading to victory in the Group 2 Rockfel Stakes

Classic hopes are high

Daahyeh is the most obvious starting point, given her string of consistent performances at two.

Nasser Bin Hamad Al Khalifa's filly burst to prominence when bounding clear of her rivals in the Albany Stakes to give both her owner and rising star of the weighing room David Egan a first Royal meeting success.

While her defeat of stablemate Stylistique in the Group 2 Rockfel Stakes would be her sole subsequent victory, that told a fraction of the story, given runner-up efforts in the Duchess of Cambridge Stakes, the Moyglare Stud Stakes and the Breeders' Cup Juvenile Fillies Turf.

Daahyeh is speedily bred, being by Bated Breath out of an Oasis Dream mare, but appeared to stay the mile around two turns of Santa Anita fine.

"She showed that she stayed a mile over in America, albeit it's more of a speed test than she will face over here," says Varian. "She has early two-year-old form, having won at Royal Ascot, but she's done well over the winter and the Guineas would be her aim. I think the mile will be her limit."

Queen can fulfil promise

In the same ownership as Daahyeh, **Queen Daenerys** broke her maiden second up in a Newmarket novice event last September.

The daughter of Frankel – a $500,000 Keeneland purchase as a yearling and a sister to stakes performers on both sides of the Atlantic – she was then stepped up dramatically in grade when returning to the Rowley Mile for the Group 1 Fillies' Mile, where she finished five and a half lengths adrift of Quadrilateral in sixth.

While Queen Daenerys holds an Irish 1,000 Guineas engagement, she looks more of a middle-distance prospect, as evidenced by her presence among the entries for the

Prix de Diane and the Irish Oaks.

Varian says: "It wouldn't be typical for one of ours to go from a novice straight into a race like the Fillies' Mile. We felt that she was likely to stay well, but she was maybe lacking a bit of experience and was never in a position to get involved.

"We think she'll certainly stay further this year and she could start out in something like the Pretty Polly here at Newmarket. She's very likely to stay a mile and a half in time and has class about her."

'He's only going to get better'

Pierre Lapin spent the winter in the upper reaches of the betting for the Commonwealth Cup, and Varian looks set to pursue the sprinting route with the speedy son of Cappella Sansevero, who was two from two last term.

The form of his comfortable success in the Mill Reef Stakes at Newbury received a boost the following month when third-placed Shadn scored in the Criterium de Maisons-Laffitte, while fifth home Malotru bolted up in a Lingfield Listed race in February.

"The Commonwealth Cup is very much his aim with races like the Pavilion Stakes – in which he would have a 4lb penalty – and the Sandy Lane as options along the way," says Varian. "We think he's very smart and will be treated like a sprinter. He is a half-brother to Harry Angel by a sire who was an early two-year-old, although that's not a concern as Pierre Lapin has done well over the winter and everything about him physically suggests he's only going to get better as a three-year-old."

Royalty heads exciting squad

Varian has in his care a raft of unexposed three-year-olds, several of whom broke their maidens in exciting fashion on the all-weather towards the end of last year.

Delta's Royalty would have been on many radars before her debut at Kempton in December, owing to her regal breeding.

The sole progeny of dual Breeders' Cup heroine Royal Delta, Delta's Royalty already carries a special place in owner-breeder Benjamin Leon's affections.

Despite racing in snatches early on and finding plenty of trouble in running, the powerful daughter of Galileo showed talent and determination to make her first start a winning one.

"We were pleased she won even though she hung across the track at Kempton," says Varian. "It will be a big ask of her to live all the way up to her pedigree but she has the natural ability that gives her a chance to do so. She was a big two-year-old and has continued to grow so, although she has won over a mile, that would be an absolute minimum now.

"She's highly likely to start over ten furlongs, either in a trial or else in a novice under a penalty. A lot went wrong on her debut so it may be we decide to learn more about her in calmer waters before a step up in class."

Sheikh Ahmed Al Maktoum's **Fooraat** is another filly bred to thrive at the highest level, being a sister to Benbatl. That makes her extra special for Varian, as she is out of her owner's 2011 Prix de l'Opera heroine Nahrain, the trainer's first Group 1 winner.

Fooraat faced another impeccably sourced debutant at Newcastle in Godolphin's Maria Rosa last October and showed a fine attitude to battle back for a neck success against a filly who can boast Kentucky Derby hero Nyquist as a sibling.

That was over seven furlongs but entries in the Prix Saint-Alary and the Prix de Diane suggest her future might lie at around a mile and a quarter.

Varian says: "I felt she could run very well and could be in the first three on her debut but for her to win and look like a good filly in doing so was very pleasing. She's strengthened up over the winter and will improve with age, so I see no reason why she

Molatham: Listed winner might take in a Guineas trial

won't stay ten furlongs. She's completely unexposed and, while she's not flashy in her work, she clearly has class and we would expect her to progress well."

Shadwell stock promises

Hamdan Al Maktoum will be hoping that at least one of a trio of inmates at Carlburg Stables can kick on from promising efforts at two.

Khaloosy picked up in electric fashion to scoot four and a half lengths clear of his toiling rivals when scoring at the second time of asking over a mile and half a furlong at Wolverhampton.

The son of Dubawi holds a Derby entry as well as Classic engagements at a mile and a mile and a quarter in France.

Varian says: "You wouldn't see too many win a novice as easily as he did, although the race slightly fell apart. He works well and he's not short of speed, so he's been given a 2,000 Guineas entry and we're hopeful he can develop

into a smart performer at up to ten furlongs."

Montather had clearly been showing plenty ahead of his first public appearance over a mile at Chelmsford and overcame an unpromising position to justify odds of 8-11 a shade cosily.

A Prix du Jockey Club entry suggests he is not short of ability while Varian knows the family well, having trained Montather's Listed placed dam Lanansaak.

"He was less flashy than Khaloosy in his novice but always looked like he was going to win," says Varian. "He could be one for a race like the Feilden and should stay a mile and a quarter. He might stretch out to a mile and a half."

'He's one to look forward to'

Another to carry the Shadwell silks is **Molatham**, who was campaigned more ambitiously than the two mentioned above in four starts.

Having had the misfortune to bump into Mums Tipple at Ascot in July – the margin of defeat was a neck whereas the winner went on to land a valuable sales race next time out by a yawning 11 lengths – Molatham made no mistake in the often informative Convivial Maiden Stakes at York's Ebor Meeting.

Better was to come when the imposing Night Of Thunder colt fought off all-comers to win the Listed Flying Scotsman Stakes at Doncaster.

Molatham's final start of the season came in the Group 3 Autumn Stakes, where being drawn in the middle of the track on the softest ground he had encountered meant he was unable to get involved in the duel between Military March and Al Suhail.

"We'll avoid soft ground with him where we can as we feel he didn't go on it at Newmarket," says the trainer. "He could go to a Guineas trial as long as he doesn't face those conditions. He was progressing well until that

ROGER VARIAN
NEWMARKET, SUFFOLK

	Number of horses	Races run	1st	2nd	3rd	Unpl	Per cent	£1 level stake
2yo	56	137	28	33	24	52	20.4	-35.96
3yo	84	344	65	54	48	175	18.9	-58.62
4yo+	30	121	23	17	16	65	19.0	-26.50
Totals	170	602	116	104	88	292	19.3	-121.08
2018	175	603	106	107	82	306	17.6	-127.45
2017	162	558	109	113	91	244	19.5	-117.57

BY MONTH

	2yo W-R	Per cent	£1 level stake	3yo W-R	Per cent	£1 level stake
Jan	0-0	0.0	0.00	1-8	12.5	+13.00
Feb	0-0	0.0	0.00	1-4	25.0	-1.25
Mar	0-0	0.0	0.00	2-7	28.6	-1.75
Apr	0-0	0.0	0.00	10-41	24.4	-3.78
May	2-4	50.0	+2.00	9-68	13.2	-9.77
June	3-9	33.3	+3.38	10-51	19.6	-16.42
July	0-12	0.0	-12.00	8-42	19.0	-20.39
Aug	3-15	20.0	-2.38	10-49	20.4	-3.85
Sep	8-35	22.9	-13.59	8-38	21.1	+3.08
Oct	7-32	21.9	+6.70	5-23	21.7	-9.49
Nov	4-21	19.0	-12.74	1-10	10.0	-5.00
Dec	1-9	11.1	-7.33	0-3	0.0	-3.00

	4yo+ W-R	Per cent	£1 level stake	Totals W-R	Per cent	£1 level stake
Jan	0-1	0.0	-1.00	1-9	11.1	+12.00
Feb	0-2	0.0	-2.00	1-6	16.7	-3.25
Mar	1-4	25.0	-2.38	3-11	27.3	-4.13
Apr	7-18	38.9	+11.11	17-59	28.8	+7.33
May	7-24	29.2	+12.10	18-96	18.8	+4.33
June	4-26	15.4	-9.75	17-86	19.8	-22.79
July	0-10	0.0	-10.00	8-64	12.5	-42.39
Aug	2-17	11.8	-11.45	15-81	18.5	-17.68
Sep	0-12	0.0	-12.00	16-85	18.8	-22.51
Oct	2-5	40.0	+0.88	14-60	23.3	-1.91
Nov	0-1	0.0	-1.00	5-32	15.6	-6.00
Dec	0-1	0.0	-1.00	1-13	7.7	-4.00

DISTANCE

	2yo W-R	Per cent	£1 level stake	3yo W-R	Per cent	£1 level stake
5f-6f	12-50	24.0	-9.26	8-44	18.2	-14.69
7f-8f	16-86	18.6	-25.71	38-185	20.5	-30.08
9f-13f	0-1	0.0	-1.00	19-109	17.4	-7.85
14f+	0-0	0.0	0.00	0-6	0.0	-6.00

	4yo+ W-R	Per cent	£1 level stake	Totals W-R	Per cent	£1 level stake
5f-6f	5-23	21.7	+1.88	25-117	21.4	-22.07
7f-8f	10-47	21.3	-14.22	64-318	20.1	-70.01
9f-13f	8-45	17.8	-8.15	27-155	17.4	-17.00
14f+	0-6	0.0	-6.00	0-12	0.0	-12.00

TYPE OF RACE

	NON-HANDICAPS W-R	Per cent	£1 level stake	HANDICAPS W-R	Per cent	£1 level stake
2yo	27-124	21.8	-34.96	1-13	7.7	-1.00
3yo	35-156	22.4	-8.56	30-188	16.0	-50.06
4yo+	8-59	13.6	-26.05	15-62	24.2	-0.45

Statistics relate to all runners in Britain from January 1, 2019 to December 31, 2019

point and we're happy to put a line through it. He's a three-year-old to look forward to."

Defoe leads older brigade

Varian and owner Sheikh Mohammed Obaid Al Maktoum must have gained satisfaction from seeing **Defoe** blossom in the highest grade last season, having first entered the winners' enclosure at Group level in August 2017 when landing the Geoffrey Freer Stakes at Newbury.

His determined rebuff of Kew Gardens in the Coronation Cup under Andrea Atzeni vindicated connections' long-held faith in the son of Dalakhani's ability at Group 1 level and he then followed that up with another gutsy effort in the Hardwicke Stakes at Royal Ascot.

The ups and downs of racing were then demonstrated when Defoe failed to fire in the King George, after which Varian elected to give him an extended break ahead of a crack at the major mile-and-a-half prizes in Dubai this spring.

The Dubai City of Gold / Sheema Classic double was one which owner and trainer pulled off successfully with Postponed in 2016, before rolling on to success in the Coronation Cup and the Juddmonte International later in the summer.

Varian says of the now six-year-old Defoe's potential European campaign: "The plan will be similar to last year, although he'll have a break after Meydan and will likely start back at Epsom. Last year's King George was too bad to be true after running extremely well to win the Coronation Cup and the

■ Watch out for two-year-old raids on Beverley. Six from 11 runners have won for a profit of £15.08

Zabeel Prince: set to return in the second half of the season

Hardwicke, which were career-bests at the age of five."

The same yellow and black-spotted silks could also be seen in the second half of the season by the likes of **Zabeel Prince** and **Barsanti**, while **UAE Prince** could bid to kick off his campaign in the same York handicap in which he was successful on his only start of 2019.

The third member of the Royal Ascot trio from last term, **Cape Byron**, has turned out to be a real specialist over the Berkshire venue's straight track, having bagged the Victoria Cup and the Group 3 Bengough Stakes in addition to his romp in the Wokingham.

Having proved himself Pattern class, this year will be geared towards a return to the Royal meeting.

"The plan is very much the Diamond Jubilee as he seems to love it at Ascot," says Varian. "There's not an obvious race in which

to prep with his Group 3 penalty and he could start off at York back up at seven furlongs. As well as he went on soft ground when winning the Bengough, he didn't really handle it on Champions Day."

Before the riches of Ascot Varian has his sights set on another lucrative payday, with **Invitational** firmly on target for the fillies' race at Lingfield on All-Weather Finals Day.

Ziad Galadari's homebred four-year-old qualified with the minimum of fuss at Wolverhampton, defying a 3lb penalty for her Listed success on turf at Fontainebleau in November.

Varian says: "All-Weather Finals Day is very much the next point of call and then races like the Chartwell Stakes at Lingfield come into play. As she's already a Listed winner the aim will be to find her a Group race."

REPORTING BY SCOTT BURTON

GALLOP

WITH CONFIDENCE

TRAIN ON THE BEST

Established for 30years

Fully Synthetic Surfaces

We Specialise In
- Gallops
- Lunge Pens
- Arenas
- Turnout Pens

Free Site Visits
& Quotations

THE
EXPERTS

O'Brien powerhouses leading the way again

THE Longines World's Best Racehorse rankings for 2019 underlined the global nature of the sport and provided food for thought about the stature of Irish Flat racing. No Irish-trained horse appeared in the top 18 worldwide, and only three Irish races made it to the list of the world's top 100 events.

However, these details are of limited relevance in the context of a racing landscape largely defined by the ability of Irish-trained horses to defend the main domestic prizes and to plunder a healthy proportion of major British races.

In 2019, Irish-trained horses successfully defended ten of the country's 13 Group 1 races, and captured an array of major races in Britain, including three Classic wins for Aidan O'Brien.

Ballydoyle's team of older horses will include the trainer's record-equalling seventh Derby winner **Anthony Van Dyck** and his 13th Irish Derby winner **Sovereign**, a pair likely to challenge for top races at up to 1m4f.

However, neither may be quite in the same league as the Derby third **Japan**, who went from strength to strength after finishing third in the Epsom Derby, winning the King Edward VII Stakes, the Grand Prix de Paris and the Juddmonte International and signing off with a fourth placing in the Arc. Japanese owner Masaaki Matsushima has acquired a half-share in the Galileo colt who will have the Arc as his long-range target.

Also returning to action at four are the horses who took the next three places behind Japan at Epsom: **Broome**, who did not appear again after a disappointing run in the Irish Derby, Chester Vase winner **Sir Dragonet**, likely to revert to shorter distances after apparently failing to stay in the St Leger, and **Circus Maximus**, who was a revelation when dropped back to a mile, landing the St James's Palace Stakes and the Prix du Moulin and proving best of the European raiders when fourth in the Breeders' Cup Mile.

There is an intriguing prospect that the brilliant **Magical**, who emerged from the giant shadow cast by Enable to add three Group 1 wins to her record in 2019, will be back in action at five.

The 2018 St Leger winner **Kew Gardens** returns as a battle-hardened five-year-old, his prospects of giving O'Brien an eighth Ascot Gold Cup buoyed by a terrific effort in lowering the colours of Stradivarius in the Long Distance Cup at Ascot in October.

Lancaster House, who won his first three races in quick succession last summer, had a valid excuse for his eclipse in a mile Group 2 contest during Irish Champions Weekend. He is viewed as a horse who could prosper over middle distances at four.

Any preview of the Classic campaign can have only one starting point, and that is the overwhelming superiority of champion juvenile Pinatubo.

Ballydoyle's best juvenile, Coventry Stakes winner **Arizona**, was deprived of second place by stablemate **Armory** when blown away by Pinatubo in the National Stakes. He showed himself in a more favourable light when beaten only two lengths in the

Dewhurst and was unlucky not to finish closer when fifth in the Breeders' Cup Juvenile Turf. He looks set to lead O'Brien's team for the 2,000 Guineas.

Armory won the Tyros and the Futurity Stakes and was a creditable third in the Prix Jean-Luc Lagardere. It is probably safe to forgive his final run when he was trounced in an unsatisfactory match for the Criterium International in testing conditions at Longchamp.

Dewhurst third **Wichita** was a stylish winner of the Group 3 Tattersalls Stakes at Newmarket, and is another 2,000 Guineas contender. He ended the season as joint-second Irish-trained colt, sharing a mark of 114 with **Siskin**, the Ger Lyons-trained winner of the Railway Stakes and Phoenix Stakes whose bid for further honours ended ignominiously when he played up at the start of the Middle Park Stakes and had to be withdrawn. A top-flight sprinting agenda is on the cards for him.

The 2019 Vertem Futurity Stakes was a novelty, transferred from Doncaster to the all-weather at Newcastle. None of the five O'Brien runners could match the Andrew Balding-trained Kameko, yet two who made the frame could spearhead the stable's Derby challenge.

Fourth-placed **Mogul**, winner of a mile Group 2 event at Leopardstown in September, should come into his own over further, while runner-up **Innisfree**, a narrow winner of the Beresford Stakes, also appeals as a probable Epsom candidate.

The Newcastle result boosted the credentials of the Ballydoyle-trained **Royal Dornoch**, who stepped up considerably on previous form when beating Kameko in the Royal Lodge.

In the juvenile fillies' department Jessica Harrington eclipsed O'Brien with a powerful squad. **Albigna** recovered from an off-day in the Moyglare Stud Stakes to land the Prix Marcel Boussac and rounded off the season by finishing second-best of the European contingent in taking fourth place in the Breeders' Cup Juvenile Fillies' Turf.

On balance, Albigna, a Niarchos-owned daughter of Zoffany, is a more enticing Classic prospect than stablemate **Millisle**, who ended up one pound higher in the European Classifications by virtue of beating the Queen Mary and Duchess of Cambridge Stakes winner Raffle Prize in the Cheveley Park. The Starspangledbanner filly may well be given the chance to prove herself at a mile, but looks speedy enough to have an early season campaign geared towards the Commonwealth Cup.

Harrington also has a bright three-year-old-prospect in **Cayenne Pepper**, winner of all three starts on home soil before finishing fourth behind the unbeaten Quadrilateral in the Fillies' Mile. The daughter of Australia staged a late rally after getting outpaced and gives the impression she will be suited by middle distances.

O'Brien will be hopeful that Moyglare Stud Stakes winner **Love**, one place in front of Cayenne Pepper at Ascot, can develop into a Classic candidate. **Peaceful**, who went close in a Listed event at Newmarket on her third and final start, is a relatively unexposed daughter of Galileo and could prosper at three, while **So Wonderful** is a 108-rated filly who will begin the season as one of the best maidens in training.

The retirement of Donnacha O'Brien will impact on the Irish racing landscape in 2020. Aidan and Joseph O'Brien have lost a top-class rider, while they and every other trainer will have to cope with the emergence of another significant force on an already competitive playing field.

Joseph O'Brien has already staked a strong claim as Ireland's number-two Flat trainer, making a significant impact on the global scene thanks to Rekindling's triumph in the 2017 Melbourne Cup and a landmark victory for Iridessa at last year's Breeders' Cup.

Iridessa has been retired, but **Rekindling** has returned to Ireland after experiencing training setbacks in Australia. If he recovers his form he will take his place in a strong squad of stayers, including last year's demoted Melbourne Cup runner-up **Master Of Reality**, **Downdraft**, a Flemington Group 3 handicap winner three days before the big race, and **Twilight Payment**, who joined the team from Jim Bolger for the latter stages of a campaign during which he beat O'Brien's 2018 Irish Derby winner Latrobe in the Group 2 Curragh Cup.

O'Brien believes he can rebuild **Latrobe**'s Group 1 profile. He also has top-level ambitions for last season's Royal Whip winner **Buckhurst**, and is looking forward to training former Ballydoyle inmate **Yucatan**, repatriated along with Rekindling after an Australian stint.

Speedier types on the team include last season's Prix de la Foret third **Speak In Colours**, high-class handicapper **Numerian**, and the lightly raced **Patrick Sarsfield**, unbeaten in two starts since joining and potentially well handicapped on a mark of 86 before being given a shot at Listed or Group races.

In the Classic crop a trio of fillies have considerable potential. **New York Girl** and the more experienced **A New Dawn** fought out the finish of the Group 3 Weld Park Stakes in late September, and **Brook On Fifth**, who made a good first impression in a Curragh maiden, is reckoned capable of building on a subsequent Group 3 fourth behind Cayenne Pepper. Among the colts, **Crossfirehurricane** underlined his potential as a Group horse in the making with a Dundalk Listed win which stretched his unbeaten record to three.

Dermot Weld's team is headed by two exciting four-year-old fillies in the staying division – last season's Irish St Leger heroine **Search For A Song**, and **Kastasa**, nominated by the trainer as a possible Gold Cup contender for the Aga Khan after bringing her score to five wins from seven starts with a scintillating Group 3 win over two miles at the Curragh in September.

Weld's best hope for high honours among the three-year-old colts is **Shekhem**, a son of Zoffany, beaten only a neck by Innisfree in the Beresford Stakes. He is owned by the Aga Khan, whose Michael Halford-trained Kingman colt **Sinawann** looked a smart prospect in taking the runner-up spot behind Mogul in a mile Group 2 contest at Leopardstown.

Jim Bolger had a relatively quiet year on the juvenile front in 2019 but **Ten Year Ticket** appeals as a colt who could prosper at three on the strength of a 33-1 victory on his belated debut in a backend maiden.

Cayenne Pepper (right): three-time winner looks a bright prospect

A Classic team for the portfolio

1,000 GUINEAS

A HALLMARK of Frankel's career at stud has been his ability to sire horses who stayed a lot further than the trips over which he ran.

This was particularly evident last season where his first two domestic Classic winners came in the Oaks and St Leger. He can, however, still get good milers – Falmouth Stakes winner Veracious a notable example – and in **Quadrilateral** he has a genuine shot at getting a 1,000 Guineas winner.

She goes into the spring as ante-post favourite having won all three starts last season in contrasting fashion – a nine-length win at Newbury in September sandwiched between two other wins by a neck and a head.

Her last victory came in the Fillies' Mile where she came with a powerful late surge to beat Powerful Breeze and, while there's a strong chance she will get further this season, the strength she showed inside the final furlong in October will serve her well when she lines up for the Guineas.

She is 6-1 favourite so is each-way value and it will be hard to get her out of the three.

Quadrilateral: appealing at 6-1 for the 1,000 Guineas

2,000 GUINEAS

The colts' Classic is currently dominated by the unbeaten Pinatubo. He took a rather unconventional route to the top, going from the all-weather to the Woodcote and then the Chesham – but there can be no doubting he is from the very top drawer.

Those wanting to oppose him can cling to the fact that other, later developers last season may have caught up with him over the winter, but that is more likely to reveal itself the further into the season we get.

If there is a horse to challenge Pinatubo it could be **Kameko**. He improved with racing last season, saving his best for last with a three-and-a-half-length beating of Innisfree in the Vertem Futurity.

As there is a doubt about him getting a Derby trip, it seems logical to at least give him a chance in the Guineas.

OAKS

Quadrilateral will be all the rage if she wins the Guineas and would have a great chance. However, in the spirit of adventure, it's worth considering **Domino Darling** too and she can be backed at 20-1.

The William Haggas-trained filly is well bred and will have no issue with the trip. She won on her only start at Doncaster in October on heavy ground which was thought not to suit her. It would be no surprise to see her in an Oaks trial in the spring – possibly the Pretty Polly which Haggas won last season with Maqsad.

DERBY

The Derby picture, as with the fillies, is dominated by what many assume will be the 2,000 Guineas winner – Pinatubo. He is favourite, but there are a few interesting ones at bigger prices, including **Sinawann**.

This Kingman colt showed a good level of form as a two-year-old, winning a maiden at the Curragh before finishing second behind Mogul in a Group 2 at Leopardstown. He stayed on well that day and will only improve over middle distances.

ST LEGER

Keep an eye on Aidan O'Brien's **Iberia**. He's not at this stage one of Ballydoyle's best, but he did run some useful races in defeat last season and looks like he will stay well and the type who might be aimed at the Queen's Vase at the halfway point of the season.

The trainers who can help us lock in a profit

IT IS time for speedballs, regally bred milers, middle-distance Classic contenders and resilient stayers to hit the track after a cold and wet six months that had Flat fans desperately wishing winter didn't exist. Buckle up because the 2020 Flat season is about to get under way – and it looks like being one to remember.

The likes of Stradivarius and Logician are set to dominate the staying division and get the hearts of favourite-backers pumping on the biggest stages, while Pinatubo is perhaps the most discussed thoroughbred in training after a hugely impressive juvenile campaign.

The likes of John Gosden, Aidan O'Brien, William Haggas and Mark Johnston will undoubtedly dominate the total prize-money and winners tables again this season thanks to their highly impressive, meticulous training routines, powerful owners and spot-on race planning, but punters are warned that although their horses attract plenty of attention and win a significant number of races, rarely do any of the quartet end the season with a level-stake profit.

Relying on their big performers at the showcase meetings can often provide profitable dividends, but it is a losing battle backing their runners day in, day out and therefore you cannot completely focus on them throughout the campaign.

There are plenty of up-and-coming trainers surging through the ranks though, not least **Archie Watson**. Many of his horses can prove to be punters' pals this year, with his runners often underbet in the markets against rivals with more established connections.

Although he is not an up-and-coming trainer by any means, given he succeeded his father and started training in 2003, **Andrew Balding** is a name to note.

The Kingsclere trainer, who has fantastic facilities at his mercy at Park House Stables, set himself a hard target to match in his first year of training 17 years ago by landing the Group 1 Epsom Oaks with Casual Look, but he has generally improved his total year-on-year and has been supported by the extremely powerful King Power Racing among other owners in recent seasons.

The beginning of multiple new strong partnerships, as well as the fact he has had the assistance of top jockeys Oisin Murphy and Silvestre De Sousa, has led to Balding hitting personal best totals of 123 and 126 winners in the last couple of years. And aside from the likes of Gosden and O'Brien, it is hard to find a trainer with a better young crop of horses.

Bangkok, Dashing Willoughby, Good Birthday, King's Lynn and Be More are just five with exciting futures, and that is without mentioning the likes of Vertem Futurity winner Kameko and Balding's lightly raced, backend three-year-olds, who will have improved for an extra year under their belt.

It is fair to assume Balding could be in for another exceptional campaign and he may have the firepower to propel him into the top echelon for the first time in his career.

Steady progression up the total prize-money table provided him with a top-five position last year and although he has a huge margin to make up with the likes of Gosden (£8 million compared to Balding's £3.6m), all he needs is that one dominant Group 1 performer and he will be well on his way.

The same applies to **Charlie Appleby**, who if anything has become shrewder with his placement and targeting of races for his horses in Britain.

A former travelling head lad and assistant trainer for Sheikh Mohammed, Appleby started his training career in 2013 and has recorded over 600 winners, with the vast majority of his successes coming in the royal blue silks.

Appleby is now known worldwide having secured victories in Britain, Ireland, France, Italy, Dubai, America and Australia among plenty of other countries, and it is this phenomenal usage of the racing programme that has provided him with the esteemed status as number one trainer for Godolphin.

What makes Appleby stand out, aside from his brilliance at getting horses to peak at the right time, is that he has a different strategy to the vast majority of British trainers.

Appleby had a mere 275 runners in Britain last year – by far the fewest of any trainer in the top 30 bar Aidan O'Brien, who had 220 despite mainly coming over for the big days.

Furthermore, Appleby finished 11th in the total prize-money table and 19th in total winners last year, but the average amount of

Bright hope:
Vertem
Futurity
winner
Kameko

runners of the trainers who finished above him in each category were 864 and 804, so over 500 more than Godolphin's head honcho.

Thanks to a winter spent in Meydan, most of Appleby's best horses return to Britain fit as fleas, so he should start the campaign in fine form, and he could well hit 100 winners for the season for the first time since 2017 thanks to the likes of Pinatubo, Cross Counter and Space Blues among others. Look for Appleby to take full advantage of Newmarket's fixtures.

Newmarket often plays host to a vast selection of the best two-year-olds over the duration of a season and one of last year's standouts, Brentford Hope, will be the main flagbearer for trainer **Richard Hughes** this campaign.

The son of Camelot fairly romped home by five lengths in a backend maiden at the track, after which Hughes described his pace as 'unbelievable', and his entry in the Irish Derby speaks for itself.

However, Brentford Hope isn't the only top prospect for the Lambourn trainer this year and although his seasonal totals have rather stalled over the last three years (63, 62, 55), Hughes looks well on his way to recording a career-best tally.

The north doesn't host anywhere near as many meetings as we see down south, but it would be folly to ignore those based near Yorkshire, and two trainers who look well worth keeping an eye on this campaign are **Grant Tuer** and **Phillip Makin**.

Tuer, who used to predominantly train jumpers, recorded his first Flat winner with his only runner in 2006, and following an eight-year hiatus between 2008 and 2016, returned with a small string.

His first couple of seasons since the prolonged break produced modest totals of

just four and eight winners, but Tuer showcased his abilities last year by notching 21 scorers and it wouldn't be surprising if he hit the 30-mark this campaign.

Former rider Makin took up training only last year and made an instant impact, albeit he was rather unlucky with numerous placed efforts that could have taken his strike-rate to different heights.

A solid 11 winners were joined by 20 seconds, 18 thirds and 15 fourths from just 159 runners – a 40 per cent strike-rate inside the first four – and the majority came with unexposed, young horses. With a year under the trainer's belt and a new bunch of juveniles set to make a noise on the track, Makin might quickly become a force at the northern venues.

Similar thoughts apply to **Andrew Hughes**, a County Kilkenny-based trainer who is 0-20 with runners in his native Ireland but 6-50 in Britain, producing a £1 level-stake profit of £37. Hughes won't have the same depth as Makin and his impact will be far smaller, but he seems to target Hamilton and you could do far worse than back all of his horses at that venue this year.

Ireland has been stuck in groundhog day for the last few years, with the likes of Aidan and Joseph O'Brien, Ger Lyons, Dermot Weld and Jessica Harrington dominating, but aside from the obvious introduction of Donnacha O'Brien to the training ranks, the guy you want to keep onside is **Paddy Twomey**.

Twomey has proved prolific with his small, but select squad in recent seasons, recording strike-rates of 25 and 29 per cent for the last two years, and punters will reap the rewards if sticking with him once again. Look for Raven's Cry and Sunday Sweet to prove his best yardsticks.

'With a year under the trainer's belt and a new bunch of juveniles set to make a noise on the track, Makin might quickly become a force at the northern venues'

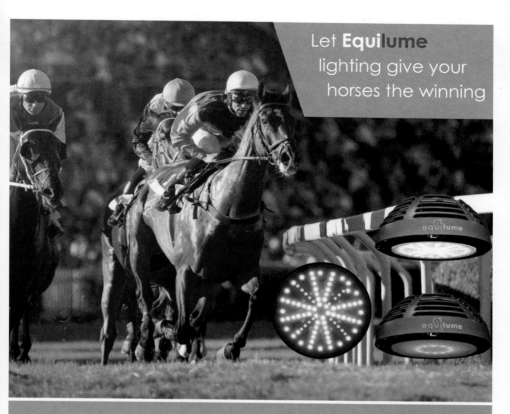

DARK HORSES DAVE ORTON

A dozen whose best days are yet to come

BOSS POWER

Boss Power was sent off at 7-1 for his debut at Yarmouth over 7f last summer, and did a lot wrong when finishing last of the four runners. Trained by a master in Sir Michael Stoute, however, it is safe to assume the choicely bred colt will have wintered well, and he certainly has races in him as a three-year-old. His pedigree suggests going up to 1m2f ought to be ideal.

BRENTFORD HOPE

Brentford Hope looked a smart prospect in winning a 1m2f Newmarket maiden by five lengths on his sole juvenile outing. The ground was soft and there may not have been much depth to the race, but there is no doubt he has a lot of talent. There is a conditions race over the same trip at Newbury in April that has been contested by some decent types over the years so that could be a good spot for his reintroduction.

DARAIN

Darain has some top-notch siblings, none more so than his brother Too Darn Hot, albeit followed closely by his sisters So Mi Dar and Lah Ti Dar. John Gosden, who trained those three, didn't manage to get this 3,500,000gns colt to the track at two, but has stated that the son of Dubawi was a lot like his dam, needing a bit of time to develop. His racecourse debut will be one of the most anticipated during 2020.

DOMINO DARLING

By the owner's 2015 Derby winner Golden Horn, this filly could be one for the Oaks. She narrowly won a mile Doncaster maiden on her only start at two, in October, with 14 rivals in behind. The ground was testing but she should be effective on better going and she will presumably resume in either a novice or a Classic trial. Her trainer William Haggas won the 2011 Oaks with Dancing Rain.

ENEMY

Enemy is a half-brother to consistent Group 1 winner Magic Wand, plus the 2013 Irish Oaks winner Chicquita. He won his only juvenile start, getting up just narrowly over seven furlongs at Ascot. He had a good deal in hand, though, and sets him up for an exciting season at three. He'll surely be tried in Group company.

ENNISTYMON

This choicely bred filly was a major eyecatcher on her debut over 7f at the Curragh last summer, looking as though she had plenty to give but repeatedly denied a clear run. With a smart pedigree that contains a mix of speed and stamina, she could be worth following.

HEART REEF

A €220,000 yearling, and the first foal of a half-sister to King George/Arc winner Danedream, Heart Reef (right) made the perfect start when winning on her debut at Haydock despite showing signs of greenness. She was given a break before taking her chance at Listed level, but she performed well below expectations when just fifth in heavy ground. Her pedigree screams middle distances, so this season she can be placed to fulfil her undoubted potential.

HEAVEN OF HEAVENS

Although unplaced in both juvenile starts, Heaven Of Heavens is one to note, being a sister to her all-conquering connections' Group 1 winners Rhododendron and Magical. She ought to do much better this term.

HIGHEST GROUND

This beautifully bred colt looks to have gone somewhat under the radar with the Derby in mind. He was an impressive debut winner over 7f at Leicester last September, powering home despite a sluggish start. The sound surface that day was ideal and he is highly regarded by Sir Michael Stoute. The dam has already produced a winner over as far as 1m7f, and going over the Derby trip should be right up his street.

POET'S LADY

Poet's Lady showed more than enough in two runs during 2019 to suggest she can make the grade. Sent off a 25-1 chance for her debut over 6f at Thirsk in August, she kept on stoutly from midfield to post a most encouraging performance. Three weeks later she went to Haydock, where again she showed a great deal of promise at the same distance. Both those efforts were on soft ground, which she seemed to handle, but it is likely a faster surface might suit even better.

SKY LAKE

Despite being sent off at 20-1 and finishing eighth of 11 runners on her debut in a 7f fillies' novice at Chelmsford last September, Sky Lake did show ability and she proved it in no uncertain terms when overcoming a slow start to bolt up by over four lengths in a mile novice contest at Newcastle the following month. Related to German Group/Listed winners on the dam's side of her pedigree, it would be wrong to suggest that she is merely an all-weather performer and she can develop into a useful handicapper.

TENBURY WELLS

At $1,600,000 as a yearling, Tenbury Wells wasn't cheap and plenty was expected on his debut in late December last year, when he was sent off the 11-10 market leader over an extended mile at Wolverhampton. However, nothing went right that day. The hope is that he learnt plenty for that outing and is straighter when next seen, as his price tag and pedigree suggest he could be smart.

BREEDING LINES MARTIN STEVENS

Pedigrees that suggest victory on the big stage

CAPE PALACE
3yo b c Golden Horn-Mia Diletta (Selkirk)

John Gosden's charge was backed as if defeat was out of the question on debut at Newcastle in August and he duly hosed up by eight lengths. He was sent off odds-on again for the Haynes, Hanson & Clark but finished third after running too freely. It might be worth forgiving Hamdan bin Mohammed Al Maktoum's colt, though, as he should improve bundles for turning three: he is by the later-maturing Derby and Arc hero Golden Horn and is a half-brother to Italian 2,000 Guineas winner Poeta Diletto.

CHIASM
2yo b f Galileo-Kind (Danehill)

All eyes will be on this juvenile filly if she makes her debut at two for John Gosden in 2020 as she is a sister to Frankel and fellow multiple Group 1 winner Noble Mission, and is the first foal out of Kind in five years. A note of caution, though: not all of the dam's produce have been superstars – Proconsul was unplaced on both starts for Andre Fabre and Morpheus reached a peak RPR of 95.

EVEN SO
3yo b f Camelot-Breeze Hill (Danehill)

Ger Lyons could have an Oaks filly on his hands with Even So, a wide-margin winner of a Gowran Park maiden that had been taken by last season's narrowly beaten Epsom runner-up Pink Dogwood in 2018. The Coolmore-owned filly is by Pink Dogwood's sire Camelot out of Breeze Hill, a middle distance-winning Danehill half-sister to Derby hero Dr Devious and to the dam of Oaks winner Dancing Rain.

Premier Power: should be making his mark in Group company

FREE SOLO
3yo ch c Showcasing-Amuser (Galileo)

Not seen since coasting to a five-length success in a mile maiden in July, the Niarchos family's homebred is a serious three-year-old prospect if he has maintained that level of form. He is by Showcasing, better known for siring ace sprinters such as Advertise and Quiet Reflection, but has seemingly inherited more stamina from his dam Amuser, an unraced daughter of Galileo and brilliant miler Six Perfections.

IDES OF AUGUST
2yo b c Dubawi-Alina (Galileo)

This Godolphin-owned colt, the most expensive yearling sold in Europe last year at 3,600,000gns has been entrusted to Charlie Appleby. His sire Dubawi tends to get going with two-year-olds from summer onwards, while one half-sibling, Barney Roy, won on his sole start at two in the September before shining at three and older, so he may be at his peak this year in the autumn.

KHAYZARAAN
3yo b f Kingman-Riqa (Dubawi)

Freddy Head saddled this Kingman filly to win two of her three starts in France, both over a mile, by an aggregate 13 and a half lengths last year. There are mixed messages for her optimum trip as her half-sister Tantheem was a three-time Group 3-winning sprinter, while her dam, Listed-placed over a mile, is a half-sister to last year's Prix du Jockey Club third Motamarris. One thing is for sure: class flows through this family.

PALACE PIER
3yo b c Kingman-Beach Frolic (Nayef)

John Gosden sent out this colt to win both starts over seven furlongs at Sandown last year by more than eight lengths combined, despite showing greenness both times. He is another feather in the cap of exciting young sire Kingman and is a three-parts brother to ten-furlong scorer Tatweej out of an unraced Nayef half-sister to Dante winner Bonfire, so a step up in trip should suit in time.

PREMIER POWER
3yo ch c Siyouni-Pelerin (Shamardal)

This colt cruised to a five-length victory over subsequent Newmarket novice stakes winner Tom Collins on his second start in a six-furlong contest at Kempton last October. He should make up into a Group-class three-year-old and stay further, being by Siyouni – source of French Classic scorers Ervedya, Laurens and Sottsass – out of Pelerin, a daughter of Shamardal who won Listed heats over seven furlongs to a mile.

RHYTHM MASTER
2yo b c Dark Angel-Pastoral Girl (Pastoral Pursuits)

This colt could be a sprinting two-year-old to follow as his sire Dark Angel excels with such horses and he is the first foal out of Pastoral Girl, a daughter of the speedy Pastoral Pursuits who was a fair ninth in the Queen Mary Stakes and runner-up in the Princess Margaret Stakes as a juvenile.

WALDKONIG
3yo b c Kingman-Waldlerche (Monsun)

Those who have backed him ante-post for the Classics can be reassured he has the pedigree to back up his debut promise, as a half-brother to Arc hero Waldgeist and Prix de Malleret winner Waldlied. He hails from a solid middle-distance family, often late maturers, so connections are unlikely to be in a rush with him.

Ten horses to focus on throughout the season

BOCCACCIO

Boccaccio may have the best part of 3st to improve to challenge his more illustrious stablemate Pinatubo for Classic honours, but it wouldn't be a great surprise if he turned out to be a high-quality miler in his own right this season. He was ready relatively early in the season and had some fair horses behind him when making his winning debut at Yarmouth in May – the Group-placed Ropey Guest, now rated 101, was fourth. However, things obviously did not go to plan for him as he didn't run again until the end of November, although he was a non-runner due to the unsuitably soft ground in the Horris Hill at Newmarket a few weeks earlier. Instead, he went to Kempton for a 14-runner novice and strolled to a three-and-a-quarter-length victory, picking up really nicely when asked. He is going to need to improve a great deal on the bare form of that, but he looks straightforward and he's by Dubawi out of a mare by 2,000 Guineas winner Footstepsinthesand, so he's bred for the job.

CAPE PALACE

On the basis that you should forgive a horse one bad run, the John Gosden-trained Cape Palace has to be included. He was backed as though defeat was out of the question on his

Powerful Breeze (7): looks a likely candidate for high honours

debut in August, and so it proved when he sauntered to an eight-length success. Not surprisingly he was all the rage next time out in the often informative Haynes, Hanson and Clark Conditions Stakes at Newbury, but he could manage only third at odds of 1-2. It's quite possible that run came too soon after his debut three weeks earlier, and it's worth recalling how the horse he treated with such contempt on his debut, King Carney, won his next two starts and is now rated 102.

DAL HORRISGLE

The William Haggas-trained Dal Horrisgle was progressive early last season and I'm sure we didn't see the best of him. Having broken his duck in a two-year-old novice in November 2018, he won his first two starts at three, another novice at Nottingham in June and a handicap at Haydock a month later. Upped in class for the Group 3 Gordon Stakes at Glorious Goodwood, he didn't really get the run of the race but stayed on nicely when switched out to be beaten just under four lengths in fifth behind Nayef Road. He wasn't seen after finishing a well-beaten last of five to Sir Ron Priestley back at the same track when upped to 1m6f next time, but if he comes back this summer he's one to look out for as his half-brother Dal Harraild progressed with age.

DOMINO DARLING

The market normally speaks when it comes to Haggas juveniles running first time out. Before last season the trainer had sent out only seven winners from 246 runners when they were priced at 10-1 or more, a strike-rate of less than three per cent. However, when he does have an unexpected first-time scorer they tend to be fairly useful as six of

the seven went on to achieve RPRs of at least 96 and four were well over 100. Haggas had three first-time-out juveniles win at big prices last season, all fillies, and the one I like the most is Domino Darling. She showed a good attitude to get up and win by a head on heavy ground at Doncaster in October. Stamina certainly looked to be her forte, which is no surprise given this daughter of Golden Horn is closely related to Queen's Vase winner Namibian.

EMISSARY

This three-year-old made only one appearance on the all-weather at the end of the season, but comes with a super pedigree that makes him interesting. He's a Kingman half-brother to Derby and Arc winner Workforce, and he has clearly inherited some of his sibling's ability given the way he scored on his debut at Wolverhampton in October. He was a good six lengths behind runner-up Glenties – who had been allowed to dictate a steady pace alongside one other and pulled nine lengths clear of the rest – when originally asked to make ground, so the fact he did it so readily has to bode well.

FELICIANA DE VEGA

Much was expected of Feliciana De Vega as a three-year-old following easy victories on both starts as a juvenile at the end of 2018. However, she didn't have a clear run as she didn't run again until August and was below par then at Haydock and in a Listed race at Saint-Cloud in October. However, she sprang back into life in the Group 3 Darley Stakes at Newmarket just over a week later, winning in commanding fashion. That success confirmed Feliciana De Vega to be a proper Group filly and there's every chance she will have considerably more to give.

KAMEKO

Kameko was green when scoring at Sandown on his debut in July and still looked to have plenty to learn when a nose second at 14-1 to Positive in the Solario the following month. However, he continued to progress in his next two starts, running a neck second to Royal Dornoch in the Group 2 Royal Lodge and then winning the Vertem Futurity. The latter contest had been transferred from a waterlogged Doncaster to Newcastle's Tapeta surface, on which Kameko's sire Kitten's Joy has a decent strike-rate. However, it would be unwise to suggest his impressive three-and-a-quarter-length success was down to the surface as he had improved with every run and was doing so again. Kitten's Joy was in any case a turf horse in America and is the sire of Roaring Lion who ran only four times as a juvenile, ending with a close defeat in the Futurity. He blossomed as a three-year-old and there's a fair chance Kameko will too.

LOUGANINI

Here's one to keep an eye out for when the mud is flying. Louganini was taken out of a heavy-ground novice contest with a self certificate in October, but made his debut just a few days later on soft ground at Newmarket and he looked like he relished the conditions. That was a race full of debutants, including an odds-on shot of Aidan O'Brien's, but none of them handled the surface as well as Louganini, who strode nearly three lengths clear at odds of 10-1. Louganini is by Zoffany, who gets plenty who act in the mud, while his dam is Princess Loulou, who ran six of her best seven races on soft or heavy ground, including a second place in the Group 1 Prix Romanet. Her first foal has plenty to do to match her talent, but Jason Watson said he was still very raw for his debut and clearly thinks a lot of him.

POWERFUL BREEZE

Powerful Breeze achieved an awful lot in a short space of time last season and would have been ideal for the 1,000 Guineas before meeting with a setback that rules her out until the second half of the season. She didn't make her debut until the second-last week of August, when she was an unconsidered 20-1 shot in a Newmarket novice, but travelled over all her rivals and won going away by nearly three lengths. That was a fine start, but it still looked a big ask for her to be running in the Group 2 May Hill at Doncaster just under three weeks later. However, she again showed just how well she can travel even in much better company and, once switched to the outside around three furlongs out, she breezed into the lead and had more than enough to spare when seeing off Boomer and strong-finishing Alpen Rose. It was Group 1 company next in the Fillies' Mile at Newmarket and, while she was beaten a head by Quadrilateral, I got the impression she was much the best filly in the race. It's all a learning process with these young horses, and if she is able to take up from where she left off at two there are plenty of big days ahead for her.

WALDKONIG

John Gosden has introduced his share of top horses on the all-weather surfaces, and Waldkonig is bred to be very decent, being a half-brother to Arc winner Waldgeist. The son of Kingman ran only once as a two-year-old and didn't make his appearance until December, but he gave notice then that he has the potential to develop into a serious racehorse by making a sparkling winning debut at Wolverhampton. Very green in the 11-runner field, the 6-4 market leader looked all at sea when it came to handling the bends, but turning for home he quickened up in terrific style to pull nine lengths clear at the line, having been eased down. His sire was a miler, but there's obviously plenty of stamina on the dam's side of the pedigree, and it won't be a surprise if his next outing comes in a Derby trial.

GLOBAL CHALLENGE NICHOLAS GODFREY

Ten horses trained outside Europe whose presence could be felt in Britain this season

DARK POWER
Allan Smith (Bahrain)

A four-time winner in Britain when trained in Lambourn by Clive Cox, this son of Dark Angel has gone from strength to strength since joining Bahrain's habitual champion trainer Allan Smith, breaking track records over five and six furlongs at the kingdom's Sakhir racecourse. However, the veteran trainer always felt he would get seven and he duly kept on powerfully off a fast pace to claim a shock 66-1 triumph under Frankie Dettori in a $1 million event over 1,351 metres (about 6¾f) on the Saudi Cup undercard, where he beat an international field full of proper Group-class animals. Smith is keen to send the gelding to race in Britain in the summer, though first he will need to persuade Sheikh Isa, who owns Dark Power under his Al Adiyat Racing banner. "We could look at a variety of races," says Smith. "He's fast enough for five but on the other hand, he's not your typical type of sprinter, he extends his stride, he's a big-moving horse. He's a bit of a Cadillac."

DEIRDRE
Mitsuru Hashida (Japan)

There may be better Japanese-trained horses than Deirdre *(above)* but you would be hard pressed to find many more popular after last season's exploits, when she added lustre to her nation's overseas record by winning the Group 1 Nassau Stakes at Glorious Goodwood, thereby becoming the first Japanese-trained horse to win in Britain since Agnes World landed the July Cup in 2000. Big, strong and tough, Deirdre became a flagbearer for Japan's international ambitions in an adventurous campaign, winning admirers around the racing world with valiant efforts in Dubai (where she made the frame in the Dubai Turf for the second year in a row), Hong Kong (twice) and Ireland. She will be stationed at Newmarket again for her six-year-old season with the Arc as her primary target, her world tour having continued in February when she suffered an odds-on defeat when narrowly beaten by outsider Port Lions in a $1m event over an extended mile and a quarter on the Saudi Cup undercard in Riyadh. Whatever happens now, she has done her connections proud.

Four Wheel Drive: celebrations after the Breeders' Cup Juvenile Turf

EXCEEDANCE
Michael, Wayne and John Hawkes (Australia)

Nick Smith, Royal Ascot's director of racing and communications, is especially hopeful of luring this three-year-old, whom he has labelled "a proper class act", adding: "He would be one who would certainly be a candidate. I know Neil Werrett [head of Black Caviar's syndicate] very, very well and he is linked in with the Vinery team [owners] and they are making all the right noises." Exceedance exploded from mid-division on the far side at a soft-ground Flemington for a half-length victory in the Coolmore Stud Stakes, Melbourne's premier sprint for his age group at the spring carnival in November. Runner-up that day (pair clear) was Godolphin's Bivouac, another son of Exceed

And Excel with whom he has traded blows in Australia but whose connections are not keen on a tilt at Royal Ascot. Exceedance's Grade 1-winning stablemate Brutal is a possible for the Queen Anne, however.

FOUR WHEEL DRIVE
Wesley Ward (USA)

Wesley Ward's heroics have become the stuff of Royal Ascot folklore and the meeting's favourite adopted American son can be relied upon to field his usual team of formidable juveniles. However, Ward's successes have not been restricted to the two-year-old division, and he will be hoping for big things from the unbeaten Four Wheel

Drive, who made all from a wide gate in a totally dominant victory in the Breeders' Cup Juvenile Turf Sprint at Santa Anita. The son of American Pharoah is likely to be considered for both the Commonwealth Cup and the King's Stand Stakes; despite his abundant speed, he won over six furlongs as a two-year-old at Belmont Park before his Breeders' Cup success. That said, his abundant speed would surely be a potent weapon in the King's Stand, a race Ward won four years ago with a spectacular display from the three-year-old Lady Aurelia.

GYTRASH
Gordon Richards (Australia)

While it is beginning to be a long time between drinks for Aussie sprinters at Royal Ascot, every one, including Black Caviar, who has won at the Royal meeting won the Lightning Stakes before boarding the plane. That said, Ascot recruiter Nick Smith admitted this South Australian sprinter hadn't been on his radar before his shock victory in the Flemington dash in February, but the gelding's enthusiastic connections were left mulling over a trip to Britain after that 20-1 success for veteran 68-year-old trainer Gordon Richards, who had never before saddled a Group 1 winner in a career spanning five decades. Looking at Royal Ascot, Richards says: "To be totally honest, it's not something I had previously considered but there are a lot of positives. He is such a relaxed customer and travels around without turning a hair. He is also obviously very effective up the straight."

HAWWAAM
Mike de Kock (South Africa)

Due to be sent into three months' quarantine in Mauritius in February, the plan is for this South African star to spend the majority of the season in England as part of Sheikh Hamdan's operation – although whether he will continue in the care of Mike de Kock

had yet to be finalised at the time of writing. Either way, Hawwaam is a really talented individual effective at a mile to a mile and a quarter with six Graded successes to his name. They include three at the top level in a sensational three-year-old campaign during which he rattled off a hat-trick between March and June 2019, winning the S A Classic and the Premier's Champions Challenge at Turffontein (trounced older horses) before adding the Daily News 2000 at Greyville. Although he was a beaten favourite in both the Queen's Plate and Sun Met before getting ready to wave farewell to his homeland, it will be interesting to see how he fares in England, though it will be a surprise if he is in action before the second half of the season.

KIMARI
Wesley Ward (USA)

With slightly better luck, Kimari could feasibly have ended her two-year-old campaign unbeaten in five with victories at both Royal Ascot and the Breeders' Cup on her CV. Instead, she won three out of five – among them a stunning last-to-first effort at Keeneland where she overwhelmed subsequent Breeders' Cup runner-up Chimney Rock. Elsewhere, she was overhauled late on by an above-average Queen Mary winner in Raffle Prize *(right)*, having so nearly made all on ground softer than ideal, and then came fourth in the Breeders' Cup Juvenile Turf Sprint after flying late from an utterly impossible position at the rear at Santa Anita. "She's proved she likes the Ascot track – hopefully she can go back, probably for the Commonwealth Cup against the boys," says Ward.

NATURE STRIP
Chris Waller (Australia)

Having saddled Brazen Beau to finish second to Undrafted in the Diamond Jubilee Stakes in 2015, Winx's trainer Chris Waller may have spurned the opportunity to bring the legendary mare to Britain. However, he is setting his eyes on Royal Ascot in 2020 with blazingly fast sprinter Nature Strip. Originally trained by now disgraced Darren Weir, this five-year-old has improved since joining Waller midway through his four-year-old campaign to win three Group 1s, most notably with a devastating front-running display in the A$2m Darley Sprint Classic over six furlongs at Flemington in November, where he broke alertly and proceeded to blitz a field full of top Aussie sprinters by more than three lengths. Royal Ascot was immediately mentioned as a likely target and, while a subsequent odds-on fourth in the Lightning Stakes was below par, Nature Strip was back to form with a Group 2 victory over 6f at Randwick in early March. He has plenty of form over six furlongs at home, but the straight track at Ascot is a different proposition, making the King's Stand Stakes the more probable destination.

SHARING
Graham Motion (USA)

British-born trainer Graham Motion, who has made more than one sortie to Royal Ascot, mentioned the Coronation Stakes as a possible target for Sharing almost as soon as she crossed the wire to complete a hat-trick with a solid performance in the Breeders' Cup Juvenile Fillies at Santa Anita. The form looks strong: the daughter of top sprinter Speightstown beat British visitor Daahyeh fair and square by a length and a quarter,

with Prix Marcel Boussac winner Albigna further away in fourth. "One of my ambitions is to come home to England to win a race," explains Maryland-based Motion, who won the Kentucky Derby and Dubai World Cup with subsequent Queen Anne disappointment Animal Kingdom. "To win a race in Europe would be a goal of mine whether it's Ascot or somewhere else but now that we've been to Ascot a couple of times, we have that familiarity whereas it's always going to be a bit adventurous to try somewhere like Newmarket."

SUNLIGHT
Tony & Calvin McEvoy (Australia)

Australia's Royal Ascot pathfinder Choisir and Godolphin's Blue Point set the example for the McEvoy father-and-son training partnership when it comes to triple Group 1-winning sprinter Sunlight, whom they intend to run in both the King's Stand and Diamond Jubilee Stakes. The filly is on the mend after surgery in December for a splint-bone injury, a setback that meant revising plans for her autumn campaign at home and made a trip to Britain a more tempting opportunity. Her three-year-old form in Melbourne in the 2018-19 season was red-hot as she won the Coolmore Stud Stakes and Newmarket Handicap at Flemington before another Group 1 success at Moonee Valley in the William Reid Stakes; all three were six-furlong events, and she won another Group 2 at the trip in the spring before injury struck. She's expected to have a couple of races in Adelaide in April before jetting to England.

New season – shining stars set to make it big

WHAT a difference a year makes. Twelve months ago it was hard to know where to start with the French-trained three-year-olds such was the paucity of evidence from the backend of 2018.

Will the 2020 crystal ball be any clearer? Well the hopeful answer is yes given Andre Fabre has three Group 1-winning sophomores at his disposal.

Earthlight was the subject of a campaign that recalled the exploits of the Fabre-trained Zafonic as well as Arazi (Francois Boutin) and Blushing Groom (Francois Mathet) before him, all two-year-olds who had multiple questions asked of them at the highest levels in their debut seasons in a way that rarely seems to be the case these days with top-class horses trained in France.

Earthlight was a cosy enough winner when introduced over five and a half furlongs at Maisons-Laffitte last June, a performance that convinced Fabre the son of Shamardal needed more experience.

Over the course of the next two months he rattled off another three wins, taking an extra step at conditions level before adding the Group 3 Prix de Cabourg and then the juvenile highlight of the Deauville summer, running down Raffle Prize to secure a second Darley Prix Morny for Fabre, 27 years on from Zafonic.

The soon-to-be 30-time French champion trainer then turned Earthlight's sights to a trip to Newmarket for the Dewhurst and a first crack at seven furlongs.

But in a theme that could repeat itself throughout the first part of the 2020 season, the continued emergence of another Godolphin star, the Charlie Appleby-trained Pinatubo, led to a change of plan and a crack at the Middle Park Stakes.

Morny third-placer Golden Horde got an awful lot closer this time, going down by

only a neck but there was much to like about the way Earthlight ate up the ground coming out of the Dip and he now has that all-important experience of the Rowley Mile which has been a prerequisite of so many successful French raids on the Guineas.

Fabre is in no doubt Earthlight will stay beyond a mile, and so the Prix du Jockey Club may be on the medium-term target list after a crack at one of Europe's top mile prizes.

Whether Sheikh Mohammed is inclined to pitch Earthlight against Pinatubo at such an early stage of the year remains to be seen, especially given the lofty rating awarded to Appleby's inmate by European handicappers.

In normal circumstances Fabre might have no objection to staying at home for the Poule d'Essai with Earthlight but, such are the riches at both his and Godolphin's disposal, he and they also have the Prix Jean-Luc

Lagardere winner in **Victor Ludorum**. He is yet another son of Shamardal and a horse whose raw ability was obvious at two but whose limits may be less easily estimated at this point.

It seems an odd statement about a Group 1 winner but, even after three starts last term, Victor Ludorum is still filed firmly in the category of "could be anything".

Having earned his Arc day spurs on testing ground over a mile, he has even fewer stamina concerns than Earthlight and, if things progress well during the spring, it would not be the biggest surprise to see connections supplement an Investec Derby entry in April to the Poule d'Essai, Jockey Club and Grand Prix de Paris options he was handed in February.

The form of his Lagardere win was no more than confirmed when, three weeks later, Alson and Armory finished in the same

Big guns: Earthlight (left) and Victor Ludorum (winning the Lagardere)

order in a two-runner edition of the Criterium International over seven furlongs.

But it is the visual impression of his three wins rather than any raw weights and measures that prompts the thought there is still more to come from Victor Ludorum, who remained a work in progress even in winning at Longchamp.

Alson completes Fabre's trio of Group 1 winners having been moved to Chantilly by his German owner-breeders after completing a fine two-year-old campaign with Jean-Pierre Carvalho, one that earned him a spot on the final shortlist of three for 2019 Horse of the Year across the Rhine.

Carvalho felt a mile was the absolute limit for Alson last season and was more than happy to bring him back in trip after the Lagardere so it will be interesting to see how he is campaigned by Fabre.

On the fillies' side, **Tropbeau** flew the flag for the stable last season, finishing a fine campaign when third to Millisle in the Cheveley Park Stakes.

That performance paved the way for a return trip to Newmarket for the Qipco 1,000 Guineas should Fabre and Lady Bamford elect to go that route. It would be no surprise to see her start off over seven furlongs in the Prix Imprudence, now relocated to Deauville after the closure of Maisons-Laffitte.

But it cannot be taken for granted Tropbeau will stay a strongly run mile, with her sire Showcasing and her maternal grand dam Frizzante having enjoyed their finest hours over six furlongs in the Gimcrack and July Cup respectively.

Perhaps of more interest at Classic distances could be **Savarin**, who failed to handle a mile on very deep ground in the Prix Marcel Boussac but had previously looked every bit as good as her stellar parentage.

A daughter of the late Deep Impact and Classic heroine Sarafina, Savarin is co-owned by Teruya Yoshida, who arguably covets a

Tropbeau finishes third in the Group 1 Cheveley Park Stakes at Newmarket

win in the Prix de Diane almost as highly as the Arc.

Should she make it to the start of either the Diane or, before that, the Poule d'Essai des Pouliches, expect to see Yutaka Take make the trip from Japan to take the ride at the behest of the filly's other owner Masaaki Matsushima.

While Fabre has a seemingly unshakable grip on the French three-year-old scene, hopes will be as high as ever at this early stage in plenty of stables.

The smaller stables

The Boussac is often a race in which it pays to keep track of those who filled the places, and **Marieta** produced a fine effort in chasing home the Niarchos Family's Albigna, leaving her vastly underrated trainer Mauricio Delcher Sanchez to spend the winter plotting her future.

Delcher Sanchez's initial reaction was that the daughter of Siyouni was outstayed on the soft ground but that is not to say she won't get the mile trip this year, although that looks her absolute limit and she has not been given an entry in either the Saint-Alary or the Diane.

Third-placed **Flighty Lady** is bred to relish further in time and was closing Marieta down fast, giving young Chantilly-based Irishman Gavin Hernon a day to remember.

Flighty Lady has since joined Jean-Claude Rouget, having been bought privately to race in the Sottsass colours of Peter Brant.

One who might easily have made an impact in the Boussac but for a minor setback is Hamdan Al Maktoum's **Khayzaraan** – trained like her talented sister Tantheem by Freddy Head – whose two wide-margin victories at Deauville and Chantilly marked her down as a filly with Group 1 potential.

Kenway was well backed against Victor Ludorum and Armory in the Lagardere and, although he failed to shine on that occasion, Frederic Rossi will have further Group-race aspirations for the son of Galiway.

Marseille-based Rossi now operates a Chantilly satellite yard and enjoyed a fine 2019 season, finishing sixth in the trainers' championship.

Perhaps the most plausible case from the beaten horses behind Victor Ludorum can be made for **Ecrivain**, who was two short necks away from being second at Longchamp and will be given a Classic preparation by Carlos Laffon-Parias.

The Criterium de Saint-Cloud continues to be scheduled hard up against the Vertem Futurity Trophy but that didn't prevent Aidan O'Brien, Andrew Balding and Brian Meehan sending promising horses to challenge for Group 1 honours.

In that context **Mkfancy** produced a decent performance to score for Theo Bachelot and Pia Brandt, who has identified the UAE Derby on World Cup night as a potential starting point.

Should he take to the dirt then the Kentucky Derby comes into play but Brandt has also given the son of Makfi the more conventional Jockey Club option at Chantilly.

Fond farewell

Before leaving the three-year-olds it is worth marking the fact that 2020 is scheduled to be Alain de Royer-Dupre's final season as a licence holder.

The principal trainer for the Aga Khan since 1983, Royer-Dupre has been without peer over that period in achieving Classic success with slower-developing horses, several of whom didn't see a racecourse until the spring of their three-year-old season.

Among the Aga Khan's Classic entries for this year, Royer-Dupre has six unraced colts engaged in the Prix du Jockey Club, while five of the same combination's eight Diane possibles have yet to make their debut.

Of the three to have run, **Vanada** might be a name to keep an eye on, having come out on top in a Saint-Cloud newcomers' race which has recently been won by fillies of the calibre of Obligate and The Juliet Rose.

The older generation

The churn of older horses is a mixture of waving goodbye to some champions and counting down the days to the reappearance of others.

The good news is very good: Sottsass and Persian King return to the fray with the two Classic-winning colts having plenty of scope to reach even greater heights.

Sottsass was rated the best three-year-old in the world by international handicappers, 1lb ahead of Japan and the first French-trained colt to claim that title since Makfi in 2010 (Treve took the crown in 2013 while Almanzor was the best in Europe for 2016, although adrift of Arrogate on the global stage).

His third place behind Waldgeist and Enable in the Arc was a fine effort in extremely testing conditions and a return bid at Longchamp will be the main priority, with the Prix Ganay and the Prince of Wales's Stakes a potential route through the early months of the season.

Persian King was brilliant on his return to action in the Fontainebleau last April and then overcame softer-than-ideal ground in the Poulains to claim his Classic the following month.

Fabre felt initially that the son of Kingman didn't stay the extended mile and a quarter of the Jockey Club when readily brushed aside by Sottsass but has since come to the conclusion Persian King was not quite right on the day.

Among the benefits of resting him for the rest of the year was allowing time to do some more growing and, all being well, we can expect to see an even finer physique at four.

Francis Graffard enjoyed a June to remember in 2019 and, while his Diane heroine Channel has been retired to the paddocks, Coronation Stakes winner **Watch Me** will be back to do battle once more.

So too will **The Revenant**, who progressed with every run last year and finally found just one horse too good when finishing runner-up to King Of Change in the QEII Stakes on Champions Day.

An early sighter at Saint-Cloud is on the cards, with Graffard – who this year has been added to the roster of owners for the Aga Khan and for Khalid Abdullah – citing the Lockinge as a realistic target for the lightly raced son of Dubawi.

Laffon-Parias will look for further international opportunities with Canadian International third **Ziyad**, while he remains convinced **Shaman** is a Group 1 performer; the Head-trained **Soudania** looked a filly with a bright future when running away with the Prix du Prince d'Orange; and arguably Fabre's most interesting four-year-old could be **Slalom**, whose reluctance out of the gate has hopefully been solved by a gelding operation.

Godolphin's **Impulsif** was not the only horse whose wheels spun in the mud at Longchamp over Arc weekend and a return to a sound surface could see him regain the steeply progressive curve he was on last summer.

All ground seems to come alike to **Skalleti**, and the patience shown by trainer Jerome Reynier in avoiding Group 1 company up until now could very conceivably earn its recompense in 2020.

That's all folks

Finally, a check list of those who will not be returning this year: among a host of horses sold to continue their careers abroad can be counted Delaware, Flop Shot and Villa Marina – all now in the US – while Olmedo has gone to Australia; as for the fillies now out of training and sent to the breeding sheds, wave farewell to Fount, Morgan Le Faye, With You, Polydream and Siyarafina to name but five.

Injured Jockeys Fund

As a not-for-profit, self funding organisation

we are reliant on the support and generosity of our supporters.

To find out how you can become involved and support the Injured Jockeys Fund or make a donation, please visit us at:

www.ijf.org.uk

or call: **01638 662246**

Compassion • Care • Support

Sir Anthony McCoy OBE
President - Injured Jockeys Fund

Injured Jockeys Fund (Registered Charity No. 1107395)

THIS SEASON'S KEY HORSES

By Dylan Hill

A'Ali (Ire)

3 b c Society Rock - Motion Lass (Motivator)

Simon Crisford   Shaikh Duaij Al Khalifa

PLACINGS: 211510-   RPR **112+**

Starts	1st	2nd	3rd	4th	Win & Pl
6	3	1	-	-	£173,336
	9/19	Donc	5f Cls1 Gp2 2yo gd-fm		£39,697
	7/19	Deau	5½f Gp2 2yo gd-sft		£66,757
	6/19	Asct	5f Cls1 Gp2 2yo soft		£56,710

Leading two-year-old sprinter last season, winning three Group 2 races from 5f-5½f; coped with soft ground when winning the Norfolk Stakes but proved even better on a quicker surface when taking the Flying Childers at Doncaster; set to stick to sprinting.

Accidental Agent

6 b g Delegator - Roodle (Xaar)

Eve Johnson Houghton   Mrs RF Johnson Houghton

PLACINGS: 148/36105/3R4823033-   RPR **115**

Starts	1st	2nd	3rd	4th	Win & Pl
25	5	3	5	2	£683,672
	6/18	Asct	1m Cls1 Gp1 2yo gd-fm		£367,197
104	10/17	Asct	7f Cls2 98-109 Hcap gd-sft		£112,050
85	9/17	Kemp	7f Cls4 77-87 Hcap std-slw		£5,822
	10/16	NmkR	6f Cls2 Auct 2yo gd-fm		£81,165
	7/16	Chep	7f Cls4 Mdn Auct 2yo good		£5,175

Surprise winner of the 2018 Queen Anne Stakes and showed patches of smart form last season, notably when third in the Lockinge; disappointing overall, though, and even refused to race when back at Royal Ascot; has since been gelded.

Addeybb (Ire)

6 ch g Pivotal - Bush Cat (Kingmambo)

William Haggas   Sheikh Ahmed Al Maktoum

PLACINGS: 41131/11803/41212-   RPR **122**

Starts	1st	2nd	3rd	4th	Win & Pl
15	7	2	2	2	£578,542
	8/19	Hayd	1m2½f Cls1 Gp3 heavy		£35,727
	6/19	Asct	1m2f Cls1 List soft		£56,710
	4/18	Sand	1m Cls1 Gp2 gd-sft		£56,710
99	3/18	Donc	1m Cls2 97-107 Hcap soft		£62,250
93	9/17	NmkR	1m1f Cls2 65-93 Hcap gd-sft		£18,675
88	7/17	Asct	1m Cls3 74-88 3yo Hcap good		£9,704
	6/17	Hayd	1m Cls4 Mdn 3yo gd-sft		£4,690

Mudlark who benefited from ideal conditions last season, winning Group 3 and Listed races before a close second to Magical in the Champion Stakes; has been kept away from anything quicker than soft ground since flopping in the 2018 Lockinge.

Al Hilalee

4 b c Dubawi - Ambivalent (Authorized)

Charlie Appleby   Godolphin

PLACINGS: 11/031-   RPR **106**

Starts	1st	2nd	3rd	4th	Win & Pl
5	3	-	1	-	£132,805
	6/19	Chan	1m4f Gp2 2yo gd-sft		£66,757
	8/18	Deau	1m List 2yo gd-sft		£53,982
	7/18	NmkJ	7f Cls3 Mdn 2yo gd-fm		£7,763

Unbeaten in two runs as a juvenile in 2018 and

sent off just 8-1 for last season's 2,000 Guineas only to trail home in rear; disappointed again next time but got back on track after a short break when making all on first run over 1m4f in a Group 2 at Chantilly; top middle-distance prospect.

Al Madhar (Fr)

3 b c Siyouni - Phiz (Galileo)

Richard Hannon   Hamdan Al Maktoum

PLACINGS: 1-   RPR **88+**

Starts	1st	2nd	3rd	4th	Win & Pl
1	1	-	-	-	£7,762
	7/19	NmkJ	7f Cls3 Mdn 2yo gd-fm		£7,763

Did really well to win a hot Newmarket maiden on only run last July, knuckling down well to beat subsequent smart performer Al Suhail a shade cosily; not seen after that but has the potential to make up into a useful miler.

Al Suhail

3 b c Dubawi - Shirocco Star (Shirocco)

Charlie Appleby   Godolphin

PLACINGS: 2132-   RPR **114**

Starts	1st	2nd	3rd	4th	Win & Pl
4	1	2	1	-	£25,441
	8/19	Yarm	7f Cls4 2yo gd-fm		£4,852

Showed high-class form in defeat when beaten in two of the strongest Group 3 races run last season, finishing a length third in a red-hot Solario Stakes and pipped by a smart prospect in Military March in the Autumn Stakes; just outstayed that day and could still win good mile races.

Albigna (Ire)

3 ch f Zoffany - Freedonia (Selkirk)

Jessica Harrington (Ir)   Niarchos Family

PLACINGS: 11614-   RPR **112+**

Starts	1st	2nd	3rd	4th	Win & Pl
5	3	-	-	1	£329,081
	10/19	Lonc	1m Gp1 2yo v soft		£205,910
	6/19	Curr	6f Gp2 2yo good		£69,099
	5/19	Curr	6f Mdn 2yo gd-fm		£11,099

Looked all about stamina towards the end of last season, making it all the more remarkable that she had earlier won a 6f Group 2; relished the step up to a mile when winning last season's Prix Marcel Boussac at Longchamp and got going just too late when fourth at the Breeders' Cup.

Alligator Alley

3 b c Kingman - Overturned (Cape Cross)

Joseph O'Brien (Ir)   Smith, Magniers, Shanahan & Carthy

PLACINGS: 4312168-   RPR **104+**

Starts	1st	2nd	3rd	4th	Win & Pl
7	2	1	1	1	£76,154
	8/19	York	5f Cls1 List 2yo gd-fm		£39,697
	7/19	Navn	5f Mdn 2yo gd-fm		£8,785

Developed into a smart sprinter last season,

overcoming traffic problems to win a Listed race at York having been slightly unlucky when second in the Molecomb Stakes; reportedly upset in the stalls when a disappointing favourite in the Flying Childers.

Alpha Delphini

9 b g Captain Gerrard - Easy To Imagine (Cozzene)

Bryan Smart   The Alpha Delphini Partnership

PLACINGS: /836928711/232210/2-   RPR **114**

Starts		1st	2nd	3rd	4th	Win & Pl
28		8	7	3	-	£388,166
	8/18	York	5f Cls1 Gp1 gd-fm			£198,485
	10/17	Muss	5f Cls3 soft			£12,938
	9/17	Bevl	5f Cls3 soft			£12,450
	8/16	Bevl	5f Cls1 List good			£28,355
88	7/16	Asct	5f Cls2 85-109 Hcap gd-fm			£28,013
83	7/16	York	5f Cls3 81-94 Hcap good			£11,644
79	4/16	Muss	5f Cls4 67-80 Hcap gd-fm			£5,175
	8/15	Bevl	5f Cls4 Mdn good			£5,175

Veteran sprinter who showed remarkable improvement as a seven-year-old in 2018, winning the Nunthorpe in a thriller against Mabs Cross; backed that up with a fine second in last year's Temple Stakes (second best ever run on RPRs) but missed the rest of the year through injury.

Alpine Star (Ire)

3 ch f Sea The Moon - Alpha Lupi (Rahy)

Jessica Harrington (Ir)   Niarchos Family

PLACINGS: 311-   RPR **108**

Starts		1st	2nd	3rd	4th	Win & Pl
3		2	-	1	-	£73,209
	8/19	Curr	7f Gp2 2yo yield			£61,126
	8/19	Gway	7f Mdn Auct 2yo good			£10,649

Won two out of three last season, notably getting up close home to edge out Petite Mustique in the Debutante Stakes (form worked out well); 7f already looked the bare minimum for her that day and should flourish when stepped up to middle distances.

Alrajaa

4 b g Dubawi - Ethaara (Green Desert)

John Gosden   Hamdan Al Maktoum

PLACINGS: 452/21111-   RPR **113+aw**

Starts		1st	2nd	3rd	4th	Win & Pl
8		4	2	-	1	£39,746
100	11/19	Ling	1m Cls2 85-102 Hcap stand			£11,972
93	10/19	Kemp	1m Cls2 83-100 3yo Hcap std-slw			£15,563
82	10/19	Chmd	1m Cls4 76-87 Hcap stand			£5,531
	9/19	Chep	7f Cls5 App good			£3,429

Massive improver during a late summer/autumn campaign last year, winning his last four races, all by more than two lengths; hacked up off 100 at Kempton last November and looks ready for Pattern level on that evidence.

Alright Sunshine (Ire)

5 b g Casamento - Miss Gibraltar (Rock Of Gibraltar)

Keith Dalgleish   Paul & Clare Rooney

PLACINGS: 1321121-   RPR **107+**

Starts		1st	2nd	3rd	4th	Win & Pl
7		4	2	1	-	£52,994
97	9/19	Ayr	2m1½f Cls3 72-97 Hcap good			£10,350
88	8/19	Muss	1m6f Cls3 74-91 Hcap soft			£12,450
84	7/19	Ripn	1m4f Cls4 78-85 Hcap good			£5,369
	5/19	Muss	1m4½f Cls5 Auct gd-fm			£3,881

Prolific in both codes, winning three bumpers before starting on the Flat last season and winning four times; particularly progressive since sent handicapping, winning three out of four with a neck defeat in the valuable Old Borough Cup at Haydock; still unexposed.

Alson (Ger)

3 b c Areion - Assisi (Galileo)

Andre Fabre (Fr)   Gestut Schlenderhan

PLACINGS: 41121-   RPR **113+**

Starts		1st	2nd	3rd	4th	Win & Pl
5		3	1	-	1	£257,666
	10/19	Lonc	7f Gp1 2yo heavy			£128,694
	8/19	Badn	7f Gp3 2yo good			£28,829
	8/19	Claf	7f 2yo good			£15,315

High-class juvenile for Jean-Pierre Carvalho last season, though Group 1 win was effectively a walkover with sole rival Armory well below par; had previously finished second behind unbeaten Victor Ludorum in the Prix Jean-Luc Lagardere; now with Andre Fabre.

Anthony Van Dyck (Ire)

4 b c Galileo - Believe'N'Succeed (Exceed And Excel)

Aidan O'Brien (Ir)   Sue Magnier, Michael Tabor & Derrick Smith

PLACINGS: 7111239/1120330-   RPR **119**

Starts		1st	2nd	3rd	4th	Win & Pl
14		5	2	3	-	£1,817,166
	6/19	Epsm	1m4f Cls1 Gp1 3yo gd-fm			£921,538
	5/19	Ling	1m3½f Cls1 List 3yo soft			£34,026
	8/18	Curr	7f Gp2 2yo yield			£67,876
	7/18	Leop	7f Gp3 2yo gd-fm			£31,327
	7/18	Klny	1m Mdn 2yo good			£8,177

Won a thrilling five-way finish in last season's Derby; yet to prove anything other than a very moderate Derby winner after five subsequent defeats, though had ground/trip against him more than once and showed promise in placed efforts in the Irish Derby and Breeders' Cup Turf.

124

Arizona (Ire)

3 b c No Nay Never - Lady Ederle (English Channel)

Aidan O'Brien (Ir)   Sue Magnier, Michael Tabor & Derrick Smith

PLACINGS: 2114325-   RPR **117**

Starts	1st	2nd	3rd	4th	Win & Pl
7	2	2	1	1	£288,248

6/19	Asct	6f Cls1 Gp2 2yo good	£85,065
5/19	Curr	6f Mdn 2yo gd-fm	£11,099

Didn't quite build on narrow Coventry Stakes win last season, coming up short in four Group I races; still did well to keep Pinatubo honest when second in the Dewhurst and flashed home late when a closing fifth from the rear in the Breeders' Cup Juvenile Turf.

Armory (Ire)

3 b c Galileo - After (Danehill Dancer)

Aidan O'Brien (Ir)   Sue Magnier, Michael Tabor & Derrick Smith

PLACINGS: 3111232-   RPR **111**

Starts	1st	2nd	3rd	4th	Win & Pl
7	3	2	2	-	£273,281

8/19	Curr	7f Gp2 2yo yield	£69,099
7/19	Leop	7f Gp3 2yo good	£31,892
6/19	Curr	7f Mdn 2yo gd-yld	£9,712

Seemingly top of the pecking order at Ballydoyle for much of last season, winning three times at odds-on including the Futurity Stakes, but came up short subsequently; fair efforts when placed behind Pinatubo and Victor Ludorum before below-par second in two-runner Group I last time.

Alright Sunshine: four-time winner open to further improvement

Arthur's Kingdom (Ire)

3 b c Camelot - Madeira Mist (Grand Lodge)

Aidan O'Brien (Ir)   Michael Tabor, Derrick Smith & Sue Magnier

PLACINGS: 2212-   RPR **104**

Starts	1st	2nd	3rd	4th	Win & Pl
4	1	3	-	-	£65,863

10/19	Gowr	1m Mdn 2yo heavy	£8,785

Missed much of last season after being beaten at 2-9 in a Killarney maiden on good ground but returned in good form on heavy ground in the autumn, winning well at Gowran Park and finishing second in a Group I at Saint-Cloud; seems sure to stay 1m4f and beyond.

Bangkok (Ire)

4 b c Australia - Tanaghum (Darshaan)

Andrew Balding   King Power Racing Co Ltd

PLACINGS: 244/1102522-1   RPR **118**aw

Starts	1st	2nd	3rd	4th	Win & Pl
11	3	4	-	2	£167,986

2/20	Ling	1m2f Cls1 List stand	£25,520
4/19	Sand	1m2f Cls1 Gp3 3yo gd-fm	£39,697
3/19	Donc	1m2f Cls5 Mdn 3yo good	£3,752

Boiled over when 9-1 for last year's Derby after two impressive wins early in the season; got back on track with good runs to finish second in the King Edward VII and Strensall before winning on the all-weather, though only third in the Winter Derby.

Barney Roy

6 b g Excelebration - Alina (Galileo)

Charlie Appleby   Godolphin

PLACINGS: 1/121239/218-1   RPR **117**

Starts	1st	2nd	3rd	4th	Win & Pl
11	5	3	1	-	£731,895

1/20	Meyd	1m1f Gp2 good	£112,782
5/19	Lonc	1m List gd-sft	£23,423
6/17	Asct	1m Cls1 Gp1 3yo gd-fm	£226,840
4/17	Newb	7f Cls1 Gp3 3yo gd-fm	£34,026
9/16	Hayd	1m Cls4 Mdn 2yo good	£4,270

Top-class from 1m-1m2f in 2017 (won the St James's Palace Stakes and beaten a nose in the Eclipse) but subsequently failed at stud; slightly mixed bag since returning last season but has shown enough to suggest he can be a force at Group 1 level again.

Battaash (Ire)

6 b g Dark Angel - Anna Law (Lawman)

Charlie Hills   Hamdan Al Maktoum

PLACINGS: 3/11141/12144/12110-   RPR **129**

Starts	1st	2nd	3rd	4th	Win & Pl
20	10	2	3	3	£1,394,751

8/19	York	5f Cls1 Gp1 gd-fm	£226,840
8/19	Gdwd	5f Cls1 Gp2 gd-fm	£176,935
5/19	Hayd	5f Cls1 Gp2 gd-fm	£56,710
8/18	Gdwd	5f Cls1 Gp2 gd-fm	£176,935
5/18	Hayd	5f Cls1 Gp2 good	£56,710
10/17	Chan	5f Gp1 soft	£170,932
8/17	Gdwd	5f Cls1 Gp2 soft	£176,992
7/17	Sand	5f Cls1 Gp3 gd-fm	£36,862
6/17	Sand	5f Cls1 List 3yo gd-fm	£20,983
5/16	Bath	5f Cls4 2yo good	£4,690

Lightning-fast sprinter who has produced several devastating performances in recent seasons, notably in becoming a three-time winner of the King George Stakes; yet to win at Royal Ascot (twice second in the King's Stand) but did break his Nunthorpe hoodoo last year.

Beat Le Bon (Fr)

4 b c Wootton Bassett - Frida La Blonde (Elusive City)

Richard Hannon   Sullivan B'Stock/ Merriebelle Irish Farm

PLACINGS: 2322/18411156-   RPR **113+**

Starts	1st	2nd	3rd	4th	Win & Pl
12	4	3	1	1	£278,834

104	8/19	Gdwd	1m Cls2 94-108 Hcap gd-fm	£93,375
101	7/19	Hayd	7f Cls2 84-101 Hcap gd-fm	£16,173
94	5/19	Gdwd	1m Cls2 82-103 3yo Hcap gd-fm	£62,250
	3/19	Ling	6f Cls5 stand	£3,752

Took a long time to fulfil his potential (regarded as a Guineas hope by his trainer as a two-year-old) but form took off with a hat-trick last summer, including victory in the Golden Mile at Goodwood; too keen off a slower gallop in the Celebration Mile before a fair sixth in Australia on final run.

Ben Vrackie

5 b g Frankel - Kinnaird (Dr Devious)

John Gosden   Princess Haya Of Jordan

PLACINGS: 7212033/2074-   RPR **113+**

Starts	1st	2nd	3rd	4th	Win & Pl
11	1	3	2	1	£65,116

7/18	Ling	1m4f Cls5 std-slw	£3,752

Long held in high regard (had been quickly stepped up to Group level as a three-year-old after winning a novice by 11 lengths) and justified the faith with a short-head second in the Duke of Edinburgh last season; form tailed off subsequently but has since been gelded.

Benbatl

6 b h Dubawi - Nahrain (Selkirk)

Saeed bin Suroor   Godolphin

PLACINGS: 5156/112101512/10-11   RPR **124**

Starts	1st	2nd	3rd	4th	Win & Pl
20	10	3	1	-	£4,325,443

2/20	Meyd	1m1½f Gp2 fast	£203,008
1/20	Meyd	1m1f Gp2 good	£112,782
9/19	NmkR	1m Cls1 Gp2 good	£56,710
10/18	Caul	1m2f Gp1 good	£348,410
7/18	Muni	1m2f Gp1 good	£88,494
3/18	Meyd	1m1f Gp1 good	£2,666,667
2/18	Meyd	1m1f Gp1 good	£88,889
1/18	Meyd	1m1f Gp3 good	£77,778
6/17	Asct	1m2f Cls1 Gp3 3yo gd-fm	£51,039
4/17	Donc	7f Cls5 Mdn 3yo good	£3,235

Group 1 winner in Dubai, Australia and Germany who has yet to break through at that level in Britain, being a beaten favourite in the 2018 Queen Anne and last season's QEII; heavy ground a valid excuse that day, though, and had been a brilliant five-length winner of the Joel Stakes.

Bielsa (Ire)

5 b g Invincible Spirit - Bourbon Ball (Peintre Celebre)

Kevin Ryan   Highbank Stud

PLACINGS: 1/1101-   RPR **109**

Starts	1st	2nd	3rd	4th	Win & Pl
5	4	-	-	-	£33,668

93	10/19	Donc	6f Cls2 84-97 Hcap heavy	£12,450
87	8/19	Thsk	6f Cls3 81-94 Hcap good	£12,938
	5/19	Donc	6f Cls5 gd-fm	£3,752
	10/18	Rdcr	6f Cls5 soft	£4,528

Exciting sprinter who has won four of his five races; lost his unbeaten record when favourite for the Portland at Doncaster but returned there in October to produce a stunning two-and-a-quarter-length win off 93; should have much bigger handicaps and perhaps Group races on his agenda.

Billesdon Brook

5 ch m Champs Elysees - Coplow (Manduro)

Richard Hannon   Pall Mall Partners & Mrs R J McCreery

PLACINGS: 13115/41445/3912118-   RPR **116**

Starts		1st	2nd	3rd	4th	Win & Pl
20		7	3	3	3	£711,987
	10/19	NmkR	1m Cls1 Gp1 gd-sft			£151,345
	8/19	Gdwd	7f Cls1 Gp3 good			£45,368
	6/19	Chmd	7f Cls1 List stand			£42,533
	5/18	NmkR	1m Cls1 Gp1 3yo gd-fm			£310,487
	8/17	Gdwd	7f Cls1 Gp3 2yo good			£22,684
87	8/17	Gdwd	7f Cls2 70-87 2yo Hcap soft			£16,173
	7/17	Kemp	7f Cls5 2yo std-slw			£3,235

Shock 66-1 winner of the 1,000 Guineas in 2018 and managed a second Group 1 win on the Rowley Mile when landing last season's Sun Chariot Stakes; had largely struggled at the top level in between but also won Group 3 and Listed races last term.

Bless Him (Ire)

6 b g Sea The Stars - Happy Land (Refuse To Bend)

David Simcock   Tony Perkins & Partners

PLACINGS: 213515/6937/742011-   RPR **110+**

Starts		1st	2nd	3rd	4th	Win & Pl
16		4	2	2	1	£121,373
97	9/19	Asct	1m Cls2 97-101 Hcap gd-fm			£18,675
92	8/19	Yarm	1m Cls3 80-94 Hcap firm			£9,767
90	6/17	Asct	1m Cls2 90-105 3yo Hcap gd-fm			£74,700
	4/17	Chmd	1m Cls5 Mdn 3-4yo stand			£5,175

Bounced back to form with a couple of handicap wins at the end of last season after a couple of years in the doldrums following his win in the 2017 Britannia; easy Ascot win over subsequent

Cambridgeshire/Listed winner Lord North couldn't have worked out any better.

Boomer

3 b f Kingman - Wall Of Sound (Singspiel)

Tom Dascombe   Chasemore Farm

PLACINGS: 41125-   RPR **108**

Starts		1st	2nd	3rd	4th	Win & Pl
5		2	1	-	1	£63,615
	8/19	Gdwd	7f Cls1 Gp3 2yo good			£28,355
	7/19	Newb	7f Cls4 Mdn 2yo gd-fm			£4,464

Not far off the best juvenile fillies last season, cosily winning a strong Group 3 and chasing home Powerful Breeze in the May Hill; didn't seem to quite get the trip on softer ground in the Fillies' Mile but should stay at least that far as a three-year-old (dam won over 1m2f).

Born With Pride (Ire)

3 b f Born To Sea - Jumooh (Monsun)

William Haggas   Sunderland Holding Inc

PLACINGS: 1-   RPR **101+**

Starts		1st	2nd	3rd	4th	Win & Pl
1		1	-	-	-	£17,013
	11/19	NmkR	1m Cls1 List 2yo heavy			£17,013

Did remarkably well to win a strong Listed race at Newmarket on only run last season; big, scopey filly with realistic Oaks pretensions and seems sure to get at least that far (half-sister to 2m Group 1 winner Shraaoh and 1m6f Listed winner Raheen House).

Billesdon Brook: Classic winner ended last season on a high and might have more to give

Brando

8 ch g Pivotal - Argent Du Bois (Silver Hawk)

Kevin Ryan — Mrs Angie Bailey

PLACINGS: 976/1242824/3717244-   RPR **119**

Starts		1st	2nd	3rd	4th	Win & Pl
37		9	9	4	5	£1,012,424
	6/19	Haml	6f Cls2 soft			£16,808
	4/18	NmkR	6f Cls1 Gp3 good			£34,026
	8/17	Deau	6¹/₂f Gp1 good			£185,583
	4/17	NmkR	6f Cls1 Gp3 gd-fm			£34,026
110	9/16	Ayr	6f Cls2 98-110 Hcap gd-sft			£124,500
	7/16	Sand	5f Cls1 Gp3 soft			£36,862
88	4/16	NmkR	5f Cls3 81-89 Hcap gd-sft			£9,057
84	9/15	Hayd	6f Cls3 80-89 Hcap soft			£8,086
	8/15	Haml	6f Cls5 Mdn good			£3,235

Won the Group 1 Prix Maurice de Gheest in 2017 and has run well in many other top sprints in recent seasons, including when second in the July Cup and Sprint Cup in 2018; generally below that level last year but still fourth in the Sprint Cup and Champions Sprint.

Brentford Hope

3 b c Camelot - Miss Raven (Raven's Pass)

Richard Hughes — Bernardine & Sean Mulryan

PLACINGS: 1-   RPR **93 +**

Starts		1st	2nd	3rd	4th	Win & Pl
1		1	-	-	-	£6,469
	10/19	NmkR	1m2f Cls3 Mdn 2yo soft			£6,469

Hugely impressive winner of his sole run last season at Newmarket, taking apart what looked a good maiden as he led on the bit and was shaken up to win by five lengths; had been green beforehand and seems sure to improve; could be a Derby horse.

Broome (Ire)

4 b c Australia - Sweepstake (Acclamation)

Aidan O'Brien (Ir) — Michael Tabor, Derrick Smith & Sue Magnier

PLACINGS: 51622/1146-   RPR **117 +**

Starts		1st	2nd	3rd	4th	Win & Pl
9		3	2	-	1	£303,174
	5/19	Leop	1m2f Gp3 3yo gd-yld			£53,153
	4/19	Leop	1m2f Gp3 3yo soft			£31,892
	8/18	Gway	1m¹/₂f Mdn 2yo yld-sft			£9,812

Big improver when stepped up to middle distances last season, emerging as a leading Derby contender with wins in the Ballysax Stakes and Derrinstown Derby Trial before a close fourth at Epsom; disappointed in the Irish Derby and missed the rest of the season.

Buckhurst (Ire)

4 b c Australia - Artful (Green Desert)

Joseph O'Brien (Ir) — Lloyd J Williams

PLACINGS: 152112-   RPR **115**

Starts		1st	2nd	3rd	4th	Win & Pl
6		3	2	-	-	£109,016
	8/19	Curr	1m2f Gp3 yld-sft			£31,892
	6/19	Curr	1m2f Gp3 good			£39,865
	4/19	Leop	1m Mdn 3yo soft			£7,214

Progressive middle-distance performer last season, winning two 1m2f Group 3 races; stayed on well when stepped up to 1m4f on final run at Leopardstown, finishing second behind Norway, and could even get further (was entered in the Melbourne Cup).

Buffer Zone

5 br g Bated Breath - Buffering (Beat Hollow)

Ger Lyons (Ir)   Sean Jones, David Spratt & Mrs Lynne Lyons

PLACINGS: 451/1347/12510-					RPR **110**
Starts	1st	2nd	3rd	4th	Win & Pl
12	4	1	1	2	£139,322
99	9/19	Curr	6f 83-105 Hcap good		£79,730
86	6/19	Curr	6f 70-90 Hcap good		£26,577
	6/18	Wind	6f Cls5 good		£3,752
	10/17	Kemp	6f Cls5 2yo std-slw		£3,235

Massive improver following a gelding operation and switch to Ireland last season, winning two handicaps at the Curragh including on Irish Champions Weekend; probably found race coming too soon when well beaten in the Ayr Gold Cup having been smashed into favouritism.

Cape Byron

6 ch g Shamardal - Reem Three (Mark Of Esteem)

Roger Varian   Sheikh Mohammed Obaid Al Maktoum

PLACINGS: 1/13/9404227/110310-					RPR **118**
Starts	1st	2nd	3rd	4th	Win & Pl
17	5	3	2	2	£304,287
	10/19	Asct	6f Cls2 Gp3 soft		£39,697
107	6/19	Asct	6f Cls2 95-108 Hcap gd-fm		£108,938
103	5/19	Asct	7f Cls2 86-110 Hcap gd-sft		£65,363
	9/17	Asct	1m Cls3 soft		£9,704
	10/16	NmkR	7f Cls4 Mdn 2yo gd-sft		£4,528

Brilliantly reinvented as a sprinter last season; had been a nearly horse in handicaps until winning last season's Victoria Cup and then improved to win twice more over 6f at Ascot in the Wokingham and the Bengough Stakes; below par in both runs at Group 1 level.

Cape Palace

3 b c Golden Horn - Mia Diletta (Selkirk)

John Gosden   Sheikh Hamdan Bin Mohammed Al Maktoum

PLACINGS: 13-					RPR **94+**aw
Starts	1st	2nd	3rd	4th	Win & Pl
2	1	-	1	-	£10,547
	8/19	Newc	7f Cls4 2yo std-slw		£9,057

Made an explosive start to his career when an eight-length winner at Newcastle last August; sent off just 1-2 to follow up when raised in class at Newbury next time but reportedly raced too keenly when only third; seems sure to prove better than that.

Broome: dual Group 3 winner is set to return to action after missing the second half of last season

Cayenne Pepper (Ire)

3 ch f Australia - Muwakaba (Elusive Quality)

Jessica Harrington (Ir)   Jon S Kelly

PLACINGS: 1114-   RPR **109+**

Starts	1st	2nd	3rd	4th	Win & Pl
4	3	-	-	1	£91,171
8/19	Curr	1m Gp3 2yo gd-yld			£42,523
7/19	Tipp	7¹/₂f 2yo gd-fm			£8,519
6/19	Leop	7f Mdn 2yo good			£9,712

Very highly regarded even among Jessica Harrington's golden crop of juvenile fillies last season and duly won first three starts; better than she showed when fourth in the Fillies' Mile at Newmarket, finishing strongly when hitting the rising ground having struggled with the course.

Century Dream (Ire)

6 b h Cape Cross - Salacia (Echo Of Light)

Simon Crisford   Abdulla Belhabb

PLACINGS: 1611/011443d3/247725-   RPR **108**

Starts	1st	2nd	3rd	4th	Win & Pl
23	7	2	3	5	£397,621
6/18	Epsm	1m¹/₂f Cls1 Gp3 good			£51,039
5/18	Asct	1m Cls1 List soft			£20,983
101	10/17	Newb	1m2f Cls2 83-102 Hcap soft		£12,938
98	9/17	Hayd	1m Cls2 84-94 Hcap good		£12,450
93	7/17	Ayr	1m Cls2 82-94 Hcap good		£15,563
87	6/17	Donc	1m Cls3 80-94 3yo Hcap soft		£7,763
10/16	Nott	1m¹/₂f Cls5 Mdn 2yo gd-sft			£3,235

Developed into a high-class miler in 2018 when beaten less than a length in the Queen Anne and the QEII; reportedly took a long time to come to hand last year after a trip to Dubai and struggled when returning in the autumn; capable of much better.

Circus Maximus (Ire)

4 b c Galileo - Duntle (Danehill Dancer)

Aidan O'Brien (Ir)   Flaxman Stables, Sue Magnier, M Tabor, D Smith

PLACINGS: 5134/1612714-   RPR **119**

Starts	1st	2nd	3rd	4th	Win & Pl
11	4	1	1	2	£934,402
9/19	Lonc	1m Gp1 gd-sft			£231,649
6/19	Asct	1m Cls1 Gp1 3yo good			£305,525
5/19	Ches	1m2¹/₂f Cls1 List 3yo gd-sft			£42,533
9/18	Gowr	1m Mdn 2yo heavy			£8,995

Initially seen as a middle-distance horse last season (won the Dee Stakes first time out) but proved best over a mile after failing to stay in the Derby; won the St James's Palace Stakes and Prix du Moulin either side of a half-length second to Too Darn Hot in the Sussex Stakes.

Cloak Of Spirits (Ire)

3 ch f Invincible Spirit - Pivotique (Pivotal)

Richard Hannon   Sheikh Mohammed Obaid Al Maktoum

PLACINGS: 163-   RPR **108**

Starts	1st	2nd	3rd	4th	Win & Pl
3	1	-	1	-	£18,432
7/19	Asct	7f Cls4 2yo gd-fm			£6,728

Sent off just 6-4 for last season's May Hill Stakes

130

at Doncaster after a hugely impressive debut win but finished a disappointing sixth in what proved a strong race; got back on track again when a half-length third behind Daahyeh in the Rockfel Stakes.

Communique (Ire)

5 ch h Casamento - Midnight Line (Kris S)

Mark Johnston   Sheikh Hamdan Bin Mohammed Al Maktoum

PLACINGS: 5114481125/71481298-   RPR **117**

Starts	1st	2nd	3rd	4th	Win & Pl
24	7	5	4	3	£372,728
7/19	NmkJ	1m4f Cls1 Gp2 gd-fm			£56,710
5/19	NmkR	1m4f Cls1 Gp2 good			£56,710
9/18	NmkR	1m4f Cls1 List gd-fm			£22,684
103	9/18	Newb	1m4f Cls2 96-103 Hcap gd-sft		£16,173
97	8/18	Gdwd	1m2f Cls2 85-105 3yo Hcap good		£46,688
92	7/18	NmkJ	1m2f Cls2 86-104 3yo Hcap gd-fm		£49,800
84	5/18	Newb	1m2f Cls2 82-101 3yo Hcap gd-fm		£43,575

Won the Jockey Club Stakes and Princess of Wales's Stakes last season, extending a fine record at Newmarket's two courses (three most valuable wins plus a Listed victory there); second in the Grosser Preis von Berlin before form tailed off in subsequent German runs.

Cross Counter

5 b g Teofilo - Waitress (Kingmambo)

Charlie Appleby   Godolphin

PLACINGS: 1/1241121/14348-   RPR **119**

Starts	1st	2nd	3rd	4th	Win & Pl
13	6	2	1	3	£3,521,843
3/19	Meyd	2m Gp2 good			£708,661
0	11/18	Flem	2m Gd1 Hcap gd-sft			£2,456,647
8/18	Gdwd	1m4f Cls1 Gp3 3yo gd-fm			£85,065
101	7/18	Asct	1m4f Cls2 82-101 3yo Hcap gd-fm		£31,125
1/18	Wolv	1m1¹/₂f Cls5 3yo stand			£3,752
12/17	Wolv	1m¹/₂f Cls5 2yo stand			£3,881

Enjoyed his finest hour when winning the 2018 Melbourne Cup and has since backed that up with several fine performances in top staying races; just came up short behind Stradivarius and Dee Ex Bee in the Gold Cup and Goodwood Cup last season.

Crossed Baton

5 b g Dansili - Sacred Shield (Beat Hollow)

John Gosden   K Abdullah

PLACINGS: 61/117226/921-   RPR **109**

Starts	1st	2nd	3rd	4th	Win & Pl
11	4	3	-	-	£105,850
11/19	Ling	1m2f Cls1 List stand			£20,983
4/18	Epsm	1m2f Cls1 List 3yo good			£28,355
3/18	Kemp	1m2f Cls5 3yo stand			£5,175
9/17	Sand	1m Cls5 2yo good			£3,881

Quirky but talented horse who got back on track after a gelding operation and in first-time cheekpieces (has also tried blinkers) when winning a Listed race at Lingfield in November; was very highly regarded as a three-year-old and clearly retains plenty of ability, and could yet fulfil expectations.

RoR
Retraining of Racehorses

Racing to a new career at ror.org.uk

RoR Source a Horse
Retraining of Racehorses

sourceahorse.ror.org.uk

A new website for selling or loaning a horse directly out of a trainer's yard and for all former racehorses.

Owner/Trainer Helpline

A dedicated helpline to assist in the placement of horses coming out of training.

Rehoming Direct

RoR has compiled a checklist to safeguard your horse's future when moved directly into the sport horse market.

Retrainers

RoR has a list of retrainers recommended by trainers who can start the retraining process and assess each horse.

Visit ror.org.uk for rehoming options and advice

Equine Charities

Retrain former racehorses for a donation, as well as care for vulnerable horses with the help of RoR funding.

RoR is British horseracing's official charity for the welfare of horses retired from racing.

T: 01488 648998

Daahyeh

3 ch f Bated Breath - Affluent (Oasis Dream)

Roger Varian   H H Sh Nasser Bin Hamad Al Khalifa

PLACINGS: 112212-					RPR **110+**
Starts	1st	2nd	3rd	4th	Win & Pl
6	3	2	-	-	£332,450

9/19	NmkR	7f Cls1 Gp2 2yo good		£56,710
6/19	Asct	6f Cls1 Gp3 2yo gd-sft		£51,039
5/19	NmkR	6f Cls4 2yo good		£5,175

Consistent in top two-year-old races last season; won the Albany and Rockfel Stakes as well as finishing second twice at Group 1 level behind Love in the Moyglare and US filly Sharing in the Breeders' Cup Juvenile Fillies Turf; could be a big player in the 1,000 Guineas.

Dakota Gold (left) waits to be loaded into the stalls before winning at York last season

Dakota Gold

6 b g Equiano - Joyeaux (Mark Of Esteem)

Michael Dods   Doug Graham & Ian Davison

PLACINGS: 30062346100/5111121-					RPR **115**
Starts	1st	2nd	3rd	4th	Win & Pl
29	9	5	4	1	£281,202

	10/19	Asct	5f Cls1 List soft	£25,520
	9/19	York	6f Cls1 List good	£28,355
104	8/19	York	5¹/₂f Cls2 90-104 Hcap good	£43,575
99	8/19	Ripn	6f Cls2 90-102 Hcap soft	£46,688
96	7/19	York	6f Cls2 82-100 Hcap soft	£31,125
90	9/18	Hayd	5f Cls2 80-103 Hcap gd-sft	£31,125
87	7/17	York	5¹/₂f Cls4 73-87 3yo Hcap gd-sft	£7,763
79	4/17	Thsk	5f Cls3 73-88 3yo Hcap gd-fm	£7,763
	8/16	Haml	6f Cls4 Mdn 2yo gd-fm	£4,205

Hugely progressive sprinter last season; won five of his last six races, culminating in a second Listed win at Ascot under a 3lb penalty; looks well up to Group level, perhaps on softer ground than when just touched off on good to firm in a Group 3 at Newbury.

Dame Malliot

4 b f Champs Elysees - Stars In Your Eyes (Galileo)

Ed Vaughan   A E Oppenheimer

PLACINGS: **1/2116-**					RPR **111 +**
Starts	1st	2nd	3rd	4th	Win & Pl
5	3	1	-	-	£98,465
8/19	Deau	1m4¹/₂f Gp2 heavy			£66,757
7/19	Nmkl	1m4f Cls1 List good			£22,684
12/18	Wolv	1m1¹/₂f Cls4 Auct 2yo stand			£4,787

Massively impressive when winning a Listed race at Newmarket by five lengths last season and just got the job done on heavy ground when stepped up to Group 2 level at Deauville; possibly feeling the effects of that hard race when flopping in the Park Hill.

Dark Lady

3 b f Dark Angel - Ladyship (Oasis Dream)

Richard Hannon   Cheveley Park Stud

PLACINGS: **2143217-**					RPR **105**
Starts	1st	2nd	3rd	4th	Win & Pl
7	2	2	1	1	£49,278
9/19	Sals	6f Cls1 Gp3 2yo good			£25,520
7/19	Ling	6f Cls5 2yo stand			£3,429

Consistent performer in good two-year-old races last season and landed a Group 3 success at Salisbury, though perhaps flattered to beat Millisle (only seventh behind that filly in the Cheveley Park); had looked equally effective at 7f when a neck second to Boomer at Goodwood.

Dashing Willoughby

4 b g Nathaniel - Miss Dashwood (Dylan Thomas)

Andrew Balding   Mick & Janice Mariscotti

PLACINGS: 128/2314579-   RPR **113**

Starts	1st	2nd	3rd	4th	Win & Pl
10	2	2	1	1	£169,957
6/19 Asct	1m6f Cls1 Gp2 2yo soft				£127,598
8/18 Wolv	1m¹/₂f Cls4 Mdn 2yo stand				£6,728

Game winner of last season's Queen's Vase, proving a strong stayer over 1m6f on soft ground; probably ran even better when fifth in the Goodwood Cup (only faded late on) but form regressed subsequently, including when seventh in the St Leger; has since been gelded.

Davydenko

4 ch c Intello - Safina (Pivotal)

Sir Michael Stoute   Cheveley Park Stud

PLACINGS: 7/11011-   RPR **108+**

Starts	1st	2nd	3rd	4th	Win & Pl
6	4				£37,427
98	9/19 Donc	1m2f Cls2 90-98 Hcap gd-fm			£15,563
90	8/19 NmkJ	1m Cls2 90-101 3yo Hcap gd-fm			£12,938
	6/19 Thsk	1m Cls5 gd-fm			£5,175
	5/19 Wind	1m Cls5 3-4yo good			£3,752

Progressive colt whose only defeat in five runs last season came when down the field in the Britannia at Royal Ascot; bounced back to win good handicaps at Newmarket and Doncaster on quicker ground, including when stepped up to 1m2f; could be a Group horse.

Defoe (Ire)

6 gr g Dalakhani - Dulkashe (Pivotal)

Roger Varian   Sheikh Mohammed Obaid Al Maktoum

PLACINGS: /11110/113202/42119-   RPR **122**

Starts	1st	2nd	3rd	4th	Win & Pl
19	9	4	1	1	£739,613
	6/19 Asct	1m4f Cls1 Gp2 good			£127,598
	5/19 Epsm	1m4f Cls1 Gp1 good			£252,360
	5/18 NmkR	1m4f Cls1 Gp2 good			£59,546
	4/18 Newb	1m4f Cls1 Gp3 gd-sft			£34,026
	8/17 Newb	1m5¹/₂f Cls1 Gp3 good			£34,026
	7/17 Haml	1m3f Cls1 List 3yo good			£23,818
98	7/17 York	1m2¹/₂f Cls2 77-98 3yo Hcap good			£31,125
88	5/17 Newb	1m2f Cls2 77-95 3yo Hcap soft			£43,575
	9/16 Ffos	1m Cls5 Mdn 2yo soft			£3,235

Made the step up into a Group 1 horse last season after a gelding operation, winning the Coronation Cup and following up in the Hardwicke Stakes; missed the second half of the season after flopping in the King George but due to return in Dubai on World Cup night.

Degraves (Ire)

3 b c Camelot - Daganya (Danehill Dancer)

Joseph O'Brien (Ir)   Williams, Gudinski & Ateam Syndicate

PLACINGS: 4311-   RPR **104+**

Starts	1st	2nd	3rd	4th	Win & Pl
4	2	-	1	1	£41,956
10/19 Leop	1m1f Gp3 2yo sft-hvy				£33,486
10/19 Navn	1m Mdn 2yo soft				£6,389

Progressed nicely last season, comfortably winning a maiden at Navan on his third run and easily bridging the gap to Group 3 level in the Eyrefield Stakes; probably better than that bare form (idled in front) and could continue to thrive over middle distances.

Delphinia (Ire)

4 b f Galileo - Again (Danehill Dancer)

Aidan O'Brien (Ir)   Sue Magnier, Michael Tabor & Derrick Smith

PLACINGS: 071/63532221-   RPR **114**

Starts	1st	2nd	3rd	4th	Win & Pl
11	2	3	2	-	£262,008
10/19 Ling	1m5f Cls1 List std-slw				£22,684
10/18 Gway	1m¹/₂f Mdn 2yo soft				£10,358

Progressive middle-distance filly last season; ran her best race when a short-head second to Star Catcher on Champions Day at Ascot having also shown her stamina over further when second in the Park Hill Stakes and Prix de Royallieu; could finally win a top race.

Desert Encounter (Ire)

8 b g Halling - La Chicana (Invincible Spirit)

David Simcock   Abdulla Al Mansoori

PLACINGS: /93726131/38831111-5   RPR **119**

Starts	1st	2nd	3rd	4th	Win & Pl
32	12	4	7	1	£1,015,242
	10/19 Wood	1m4f Gd1 good			£275,862
	9/19 Newb	1m3f Cls1 Gp3 gd-fm			£34,026
	8/19 Wind	1m2f Cls1 Gp3 gd-fm			£34,026
	8/19 Gdwd	1m4f Cls1 Gp3 gd-fm			£56,710
	10/18 Wood	1m4f Gd1 good			£282,353
	8/18 Wind	1m3¹/₂f Cls1 List good			£20,983
	9/17 Newb	1m3f Cls1 Gp3 good			£34,026
	5/17 Asct	1m4f Cls1 List gd-fm			£25,520
91	6/16 Wind	1m3¹/₂f Cls2 85-96 Hcap soft			£12,938
89	5/16 NmkR	1m6f Cls2 86-97 Hcap gd-fm			£18,675
82	4/16 Donc	1m4f Cls4 72-82 App Hcap soft			£5,175
	10/15 Muss	1m4f Cls6 Auct Mdn 3-4yo good			£2,264

Better than ever at the age of seven last season, winning his last four races including a second successive Canadian International at Woodbine; generally kept to a lower level at home and earned a hat-trick of Group 3 wins before his travels; best on quick ground.

Domino Darling

3 b f Golden Horn - Disco Volante (Sadler's Wells)

William Haggas   A E Oppenheimer

PLACINGS: 1-					RPR **85+**
Starts	1st	2nd	3rd	4th	Win & Pl
1	1	-	-	-	£3,428
	10/19	Donc	1m Cls5 Mdn 2yo heavy		£3,429

Beautifully bred filly by her owner's Derby winner Golden Horn who became the seventh winner for her dam (1m4f-2m Group 3 scorer Namibian the most notable) when making a successful start at Doncaster last October; could be a smart middle-distance filly.

Dream Of Dreams (Ire)

6 ch g Dream Ahead - Vasilia (Dansili)

Sir Michael Stoute   Saeed Suhail

PLACINGS: 151/75532220/112080-					RPR **121**
Starts	1st	2nd	3rd	4th	Win & Pl
25	5	8	2	-	£302,947
	5/19	Wind	6f Cls1 List good		£20,983
	4/19	Chmd	6f Cls2 stand		£16,173
	11/17	Donc	6f Cls1 List soft		£22,684
	9/17	Ling	7f Cls3 gd-sft		£9,767
	5/16	Hayd	6f Cls4 2yo gd-sft		£4,270

Improved into a top-class sprinter early last season, following up wins at Chelmsford and Windsor with a fast-finishing second behind Blue Point in the Diamond Jubilee Stakes at Royal Ascot; badly lost his way subsequently but has now been gelded.

Dubai Warrior

4 b c Dansili - Mahbooba (Galileo)

John Gosden   Sheikh Mohammed Bin Khalifa Al Maktoum

PLACINGS: 1/12711-					RPR **113**aw
Starts	1st	2nd	3rd	4th	Win & Pl
6	4	1	-	-	£48,690
	12/19	Ling	1m2f Cls1 List stand		£20,983
103	11/19	Chmd	1m2f Cls2 88-105 Hcap stand		£12,602
	8/19	Kemp	1m Cls4 std-slw		£6,469
	11/18	Chmd	1m Cls5 2yo stand		£4,787

Star of the all-weather season who completed a 1m2f hat-trick when running away with the Winter Derby in February; something to prove on turf after disappointing on his only run away from synthetics at Longchamp last autumn.

Duke Of Hazzard (Fr)

4 b c Lope De Vega - With Your Spirit (Invincible Spirit)

Paul Cole   Mrs Fitri Hay

PLACINGS: 42321261/3575111-					RPR **115**
Starts	1st	2nd	3rd	4th	Win & Pl
15	5	3	2	1	£272,017
	8/19	Gdwd	1m Cls1 Gp2 good		£75,850
	8/19	Gdwd	1m Cls1 Gp3 3yo gd-fm		£56,710
	7/19	NmkJ	1m Cls1 List 3yo gd-fm		£28,355
	10/18	Deau	1m List 2yo good		£26,549
	8/18	Gdwd	7f Cls2 Mdn 2yo gd-fm		£18,903

Much improved after blinkers were fitted midway through last season, winning all three subsequent starts including the Celebration Mile at Goodwood; likely to get a crack at Group 1 level when encountering preferred fast ground.

Davydenko: the Doncaster winner could make a successful move to Group company

RACING POST

Eagles By Day (Ire)
4 b/br c Sea The Stars - Missunited (Golan)

Michael Bell | Clipper Logistics

PLACINGS: 2/21638- **RPR 111**

Starts	1st	2nd	3rd	4th	Win & Pl
6	1	2	1	-	£34,789

4/19 Sals 1m4f Cls4 Mdn 3yo gd-fm.....£6,728

Patchy form last season but showed his potential on a couple of occasions, running away with a good maiden by seven lengths and finishing third in the King Edward VII Stakes at Royal Ascot; missed the end of the season after a well-beaten favourite in the Bahrain Trophy.

Earthlight (Ire)
3 ch c Shamardal - Winters Moon (New Approach)

Andre Fabre (Fr) | Godolphin

PLACINGS: 11111- **RPR 119**

Starts	1st	2nd	3rd	4th	Win & Pl
5	5	-	-	-	£399,637

9/19 NmkR 6f Cls1 Gp1 2yo good.....£155,953
8/19 Deau 6f Gp1 2yo heavy.....£180,171
7/19 Deau 6f Gp3 2yo gd-sft.....£36,036
7/19 Deau 6f 2yo good.....£15,315
6/19 MsnL 5½f 2yo gd-sft.....£12,162

Won five out of five last season, including Group 1 victories in the Prix Morny and the Middle Park; yet to run beyond 6f but set to be aimed at the 2,000 Guineas according to his trainer, who warns he would need a prep run beforehand (hard to get fit).

Ebury
4 ch c Iffraaj - Alabelle (Galileo)

Martyn Meade | Manton Park Racing

PLACINGS: 12012- **RPR 100+**

Starts	1st	2nd	3rd	4th	Win & Pl
5	2	2	-	-	£17,396

9/19 Asct 1m Cls3 gd-fm.....£9,704
3/19 Kemp 1m Cls5 3yo std-slw.....£3,881

Slow to build on impressive debut win last spring (beaten at 1-4 and well beaten in a Listed race) but bounced back in the autumn; won a classified stakes at Ascot and finished a length second in a good Newmarket handicap; likely sort for top mile handicaps.

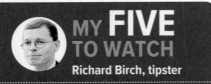

MY FIVE TO WATCH
Richard Birch, tipster

●Art Of Diplomacy ●Dreamweaver
●Give It Some Teddy ●Highest Ground
●Mr Coco Bean

El Astronaute (Ire)
7 ch g Approve - Drumcliffe Dancer (Footstepsinthesand)

John Quinn | Ross Harmon Racing

PLACINGS: 4424121/26691125853- **RPR 111**

Starts	1st	2nd	3rd	4th	Win & Pl
50	12	11	5	6	£411,141

106 6/19 Curr 5f 83-106 Hcap gd-yld.....£66,441
6/19 Cork 5f List gd-yld.....£26,577
10/18 MsnL 5½f List soft.....£23,009
101 8/18 York 5½f Cls2 88-105 Hcap gd-fm.....£43,575
98 5/18 York 5f Cls2 84-101 Hcap gd-fm.....£18,675
91 8/17 Gdwd 5f Cls2 85-104 Hcap good.....£19,407
90 5/17 Ches 5f Cls2 84-95 Hcap good.....£18,675
88 4/17 NmkR 5f Cls3 83-95 Hcap gd-fm.....£9,057
84 8/16 Epsm 5f Cls2 84-98 Hcap good.....£12,450
85 9/15 Ches 5½f Cls2 78-99 2yo Hcap gd-sft.....£16,173
77 8/15 Leic 5f Cls4 68-84 2yo Hcap good.....£3,946
7/15 Thsk 5f Cls5 Mdn 2yo gd-fm.....£3,235

Evergreen sprinter who has won 12 times during a stellar career, including two big handicaps at York in 2018; gained both wins in Ireland last season, including a second Listed victory at Cork; better than ever when third in the Prix de l'Abbaye on his final run.

Elarqam
5 b h Frankel - Attraction (Efisio)

Mark Johnston | Hamdan Al Maktoum

PLACINGS: 11/4634/4131137- **RPR 122+**

Starts	1st	2nd	3rd	4th	Win & Pl
13	5		3	3	£331,746

7/19 York 1m2½f Cls1 Gp2 soft.....£68,052
7/19 Sand 1m2f Cls1 List gd-fm.....£22,684
5/19 Gdwd 1m2f Cls1 List gd-fm.....£28,355
9/17 NmkR 7f Cls1 Gp3 2yo gd-sft.....£28,355
9/17 York 7f Cls3 2yo gd-sft.....£7,763

Bounced back from a bitterly disappointing three-year-old campaign when winning three times last season, most notably in the York Stakes; also ran well when beaten just over a length in third in the Juddmonte International, though now 0-4 at Group 1 level.

Enable
6 b m Nathaniel - Concentric (Sadler's Wells)

John Gosden | K Abdullah

PLACINGS: 1/3111111/111/1112- **RPR 128+**

Starts	1st	2nd	3rd	4th	Win & Pl
15	13	1	1	-	£10,411,972

8/19 York 1m4f Cls1 Gp1 good.....£241,018
7/19 Asct 1m4f Cls1 Gp1 gd-sft.....£708,875
7/19 Sand 1m2f Cls1 Gp1 gd-fm.....£425,325
11/18 Chur 1m4f Gd1 good.....£1,629,630
10/18 Lonc 1m4f Gp1 good.....£2,528,319
9/18 Kemp 1m4f Cls1 Gp3 std-slw.....£39,697
10/17 Chan 1m4f Gp1 soft.....£2,441,880
8/17 York 1m4f Cls1 Gp1 gd-sft.....£198,485
7/17 Asct 1m4f Cls1 Gp1 gd-sft.....£652,165
7/17 Curr 1m4f Gp1 3yo gd-fm.....£194,872
6/17 Epsm 1m4f Cls1 Gp1 3yo good.....£283,550
5/17 Ches 1m3½f Cls1 List 3yo good.....£34,026
11/16 Newc 1m Cls5 Mdn 2yo stand.....£2,911

Outstanding mare who had won 12 races in a row, including ten at Group 1 level, until agonisingly beaten in last season's Prix de l'Arc de Triomphe; had impressively dropped back to 1m2f in the Eclipse before going on to win a second King George; third Arc win again the big aim.

Enbihaar (Ire)

5 b m Redoute's Choice - Chanterelle (Trempolino)

John Gosden   Hamdan Al Maktoum

PLACINGS: 314/121113-   **RPR 118**

Starts	1st	2nd	3rd	4th	Win & Pl
9	5	1	2	1	£376,176
	9/19	Donc	1m6½f Cls1 Gp2 gd-fm		£56,710
	8/19	Gdwd	1m6f Cls1 Gp2 gd-fm		£176,935
	7/19	Hayd	1m4f Cls1 Gp2 gd-fm		£52,740
	5/19	Gdwd	1m4f Cls1 List good		£28,355
	9/18	Kemp	1m3f Cls4 std-slw		£6,469

Leading older middle-distance filly or mare last season, winning three Group 2 races and thriving over 1m6f with a five-length romp at Glorious Goodwood; fair third when stepped up to Group 1 level in the Prix de Royallieu and should do better back on quicker ground.

Enemy

3 b c Muhaarar - Prudenzia (Dansili)

John Gosden   Qatar Racing Ltd & Lady O'Reilly

PLACINGS: 1-   **RPR 86**

Starts	1st	2nd	3rd	4th	Win & Pl
1	1	-	-	-	£10,350
	9/19	Asct	7f Cls3 Mdn 2yo gd-fm		£10,350

Won sole start in what looked a strong 7f maiden at Ascot last season despite trainer feeling he

would be babyish beforehand; likely to stay further and widely quoted for the Derby (half-brother to Irish Oaks winner Chicquita), though not certain to get the trip judging by his sire.

Equilateral

5 b g Equiano - Tarentaise (Oasis Dream)

Charlie Hills   K Abdullah

PLACINGS: 16/108144/3427616-12   **RPR 112**

Starts	1st	2nd	3rd	4th	Win & Pl
17	5	2	3		£182,882
105	1/20	Meyd	5f List 95-105 Hcap good		£78,947
	9/19	Donc	5f Cls1 List gd-fm		£22,684
	9/18	Leic	5f Cls3 gd-fm		£9,452
	5/18	Donc	6f Cls5 gd-fm		£3,752
	8/17	Bath	5f Cls5 Mdn 2yo gd-sft		£2,911

Talented sprinter who hasn't always fulfilled that potential, struggling to build on a close second in the Palace House Stakes at Newmarket last season; still won a Listed race at Doncaster and showed smart form in Dubai this spring after a gelding operation.

Escobar (Ire)

6 b g Famous Name - Saying Grace (Brief Truce)

David O'Meara   Withernsea Thoroughbred Limited

PLACINGS: 02870302/0902135431-   **RPR 115**

Starts	1st	2nd	3rd	4th	Win & Pl
30	5	4	4	1	£328,595
105	10/19	Asct	1m Cls2 96-110 Hcap heavy		£155,625
99	7/19	York	1m Cls2 90-99 Hcap gd-fm		£15,563
95	6/18	Hayd	1m Cls3 81-97 Hcap gd-fm		£10,997
	8/16	Newb	7f Cls1 List 2yo gd-fm		£14,461
	7/16	Newb	7f Cls4 Mdn 2yo gd-fm		£6,469

Remarkably consistent in top handicaps last season and deservedly gained a big win in the Balmoral Handicap on Champions Day having been second 12 months earlier; particularly effective on that heavy ground but also won at York in July on good to firm.

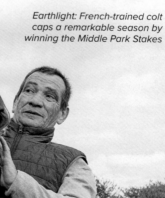

Earthlight: French-trained colt caps a remarkable season by winning the Middle Park Stakes

Etoile (USA)

3 b f War Front - Gagnoa (Sadler's Wells)

Aidan O'Brien (Ir)   Sue Magnier, Michael Tabor & Derrick Smith

PLACINGS: 180-   RPR **100+**

Starts	1st	2nd	3rd	4th	Win & Pl
3	1	-	-	-	£42,522
5/19	Naas	6f Gp3 2yo gd-fm			£42,523

Very ambitiously campaigned last season and delivered in a Group 3 first time out at Naas in May; out for four months after that race and came up short in two Group 1 races when back, finishing eighth in the Cheveley Park and tenth at the Breeders' Cup.

Falcon Eight (Ire)

5 b h Galileo - Polished Gem (Danehill)

Dermot Weld (Ir)   Moyglare Stud Farm

PLACINGS: 113/2145-   RPR **114**

Starts	1st	2nd	3rd	4th	Win & Pl
7	3	1	1	1	£71,619
7/19	Sand	2m Cls1 List gd-fm			£22,684
8/18	Kiny	1m3f good			£8,450
7/18	Curr	1m4f Mdn gd-fm			£7,359

Beautifully bred stayer who continued to progress early last season, beating Mekong by a head in a Listed race at Sandown after a near miss in the same grade behind Twilight Payment; twice found out at a higher level subsequently but lightly raced enough to improve again.

Fancy Blue (Ire)

3 b f Deep Impact - Chenchikova (Sadler's Wells)

Donnacha O'Brien (Ir)   Michael Tabor, Derrick Smith & Sue Magnier

PLACINGS: 11-   RPR **100**

Starts	1st	2nd	3rd	4th	Win & Pl
2	2	-	-	-	£35,361
10/19	Curr	1m List 2yo soft			£26,577
9/19	Naas	7f Mdn 2yo good			£8,785

Won both starts last season and did particularly well to win what looked a decent Listed race at the Curragh, storming through from last to first off a steady gallop; still looked green when asked to pick up and should have plenty more to offer.

Fanny Logan: won four on the spin last season after having headgear fitted

Fanny Logan (Ire)

4 b f Sea The Stars - Linda Radlett (Manduro)

John Gosden   Sheikha Al Jalila Racing

PLACINGS: 2/13911114-   RPR **112**

Starts	1st	2nd	3rd	4th	Win & Pl
9	5	1	1	1	£211,932
10/19	NmkR	1m2f Cls1 Gp3 gd-sft			£34,026
9/19	Yarm	1m2f Cls1 List gd-fm			£28,110
8/19	Sals	1m2f Cls1 List soft			£28,355
7/19	York	1m2½f Cls1 List good			£28,355
4/19	Weth	1m2f Cls5 good			£4,852

Transformed by having a hood applied midway through last season, going on to win her next four races (a Group 3 and three Listed events) at around 1m2f; fourth in the Breeders' Cup Filly & Mare Turf behind Iridessa when stepped up to Group 1 level.

RACING POST

Far Above (Ire)

4 b c Farhh - Dorraar (Shamardal)

James Tate   Sheikh Rashid Dalmook Al Maktoum

PLACINGS: 1411-   RPR **100**

Starts	1st	2nd	3rd	4th	Win & Pl
4	3	-	-	1	£37,139

7/19	Deau	6f List 3yo good	£24,775
6/19	Wind	6f Cls5 soft	£3,752
4/19	NmkR	7f Cls4 Mdn 3yo gd-fm	£6,469

Long held in very high regard and lived up to gallops whispers with a winning debut at Newmarket's Craven meeting when sent off just 11-8; put his sole defeat behind him with two more wins, including a Listed race at Deauville; looks an exciting prospect.

Faylaq

4 b c Dubawi - Danedream (Lomitas)

William Haggas   Hamdan Al Maktoum

PLACINGS: 65/411214-   RPR **103**

Starts	1st	2nd	3rd	4th	Win & Pl
8	3	1	-	2	£32,979

95	9/19	Kemp	1m3f Cls3 80-95 3yo Hcap std-slw	£9,338
79	6/19	NmkJ	1m4f Cls5 66-79 Hcap good	£4,528
73	6/19	Ripn	1m4f Cls4 59-82 3yo Hcap gd-sft	£5,693

Won three times last season, most notably at Kempton under top weight; reportedly struggled to cope with soft ground when only fourth in a Group 3 at Ascot, though had also been kept away from quick ground after being beaten on good to firm at the same track.

Feliciana De Vega

4 b f Lope De Vega - Along Came Casey (Oratorio)

Ralph Beckett   Waverley Racing

PLACINGS: 11/351-   RPR **111**

Starts	1st	2nd	3rd	4th	Win & Pl
5	3	-	1	-	£73,284

10/19	NmkR	1m1f Cls1 Gp3 soft	£34,026
12/18	Deau	7½f List 2yo stand	£26,549
11/18	NmkR	7f Cls4 2yo soft	£5,175

Missed the first half of last season but proved herself a very smart filly later in the campaign, easily landing the Darley Stakes at Newmarket having endured a nightmare passage in a Listed race in France; big filly who looks the type to get better with age.

Final Song (Ire)

3 b f Dark Angel - Rahiyah (Rahy)

Saeed bin Suroor   Godolphin

PLACINGS: 1336-132   RPR **103**

Starts	1st	2nd	3rd	4th	Win & Pl
7	2	1	3	-	£106,929

1/20	Meyd	7f 3yo fast	£45,113
5/19	Asct	5f Cls4 Mdn 2yo soft	£6,728

Not far off the very best two-year-olds early last season, finishing third behind Raffle Prize in the Queen Mary and Duchess of Cambridge Stakes; off for three months after that run and well below best when a beaten favourite in the Oh So Sharp on her return.

Far Above (left) heads to the track before making a winning debut

ST LEGER FESTIVAL

Experience Yorkshire's Classic

9-12 SEPTEMBER

DONCASTER-RACECOURSE.CO.UK

First In Line

4 ch c New Approach - Hidden Hope (Daylami)

John Gosden   A E Oppenheimer

PLACINGS: 2112021-				RPR **110**

Starts	1st	2nd	3rd	4th	Win & Pl
7	3	3	-	-	£85,321
105	11/19	Chmd	1m6f Cls2 84-105 3yo Hcap stand	£31,125
	8/19	Donc	1m2f Cls5 gd-sft	£3,429
	6/19	Ling	1m2f Cls5 stand	£3,752

Dual winner over 1m2f early last season but did even better when stepped up to 1m6f, finishing second behind Hamish in the Melrose and defying a big weight in a good handicap at Chelmsford; might have found 1m4f sharp enough when second to Trueshan at Newmarket.

Fleeting (Ire)

4 b f Zoffany - Azafata (Motivator)

Aidan O'Brien (Ir)   Sue Magnier, Michael Tabor & Derrick Smith

PLACINGS: 1731/03224524-				RPR **115+**

Starts	1st	2nd	3rd	4th	Win & Pl
12	2	3	2	2	£396,727
	9/18	Donc	1m Cls1 Gp2 2yo good	£39,697
	6/18	Limk	7f Mdn 2yo gd-fm	£8,177

Desperately unlucky not to win a race last season; shaped like the best filly in the race when third in the Oaks and twice chased home Star Catcher, including in the Irish Oaks, before another near miss in the Prix de l'Opera; should continue to be a force in top middle-distance fillies' races.

Forest Of Dean

4 b g Iffraaj - Forest Crown (Royal Applause)

John Gosden   Princess Haya Of Jordan

PLACINGS: 842/1214110-				RPR **116+**

Starts	1st	2nd	3rd	4th	Win & Pl
10	4	2		2	£105,639
100	8/19	York	1m2½f Cls2 79-100 Hcap gd-fm	£43,575
93	8/19	Gdwd	1m2f Cls2 89-110 3yo Hcap good	£46,688
85	4/19	Donc	1m2f Cls4 68-85 3yo Hcap good	£5,531
	2/19	Newc	1m2f Cls5 3yo std-slw	£3,235

Progressed well last season, winning three of first five handicaps including a competitive 0-105 contest at York's Ebor meeting; sent off just 13-8 for another valuable handicap at Newbury next time but raced freely and beat just two home; has since been gelded.

Forever In Dreams (Ire)

4 gr f Dream Ahead - Dora De Green (Green Tune)

Aidan Fogarty (Ir)   Phoenix Ladies Syndicate

PLACINGS: 117/512073-				RPR **113**

Starts	1st	2nd	3rd	4th	Win & Pl
9	3	1	1	-	£217,448
	5/19	Hayd	6f Cls1 List gd-fm	£26,654
	5/18	StCl	6f 2yo gd-sft	£11,504
	5/18	Bord	5f 2yo soft	£7,965

High-class sprinter who produced two massive runs at Ascot last season, finishing second in the Commonwealth Cup and third in the Champions Sprint; twice well beaten in between but had shown she can act away from Ascot when winning a Listed race at Haydock.

Fox Chairman (Ire)

4 b c Kingman - Starfish (Galileo)

Andrew Balding   King Power Racing Co Ltd

PLACINGS: 1321-				RPR **113**

Starts	1st	2nd	3rd	4th	Win & Pl
4	2	1	1	-	£53,933
	7/19	Newb	1m2f Cls1 List soft	£20,983
	4/19	Newb	1m Cls4 Mdn 3yo gd-sft	£5,531

Lightly raced colt who has achieved a high level of form in just four races, winning a Listed race at Newbury on his final run last season; had finished third in the Dee Stakes on just his second run before improving when second in the Hampton Court behind Sangarius.

Fox Tal

4 b c Sea The Stars - Maskunah (Sadler's Wells)

Andrew Balding   King Power Racing Co Ltd

PLACINGS: 3143/14-				RPR **117**

Starts	1st	2nd	3rd	4th	Win & Pl
6	2	-	2	2	£118,704
	9/19	Donc	1m2f Cls2 gd-fm	£12,450
	7/18	Ffos	7½f Cls4 2yo gd-fm	£5,434

Missed most of last season but quickly proved himself a high-class middle-distance colt in just two runs in the autumn, winning easily in a conditions race at Doncaster before finishing fourth in the Champion Stakes; lightly raced and open to further improvement.

Ghaiyyath (Ire)

5 b h Dubawi - Nightime (Galileo)

Charlie Appleby   Godolphin

PLACINGS: 311/1/1310-1				RPR **128**

Starts	1st	2nd	3rd	4th	Win & Pl
9	6	-	2	-	£399,051
	2/20	Meyd	1m2f Gp3 good	£90,226
	9/19	Badn	1m4f Gp1 good	£135,135
	4/19	Lonc	1m2f Gp2 good	£66,757
	9/18	Lonc	1m2f Gp3 3yo gd-sft	£35,398
	10/17	NmkR	1m Cls1 Gp3 2yo good	£34,026
	9/17	NmkR	1m Cls4 Mdn 2yo gd-sft	£5,175

Talented but inconsistent during injury-plagued career; stunning 14-length winner of the Grosser

Preis von Baden in Germany last season to earn a crack at the Arc but flopped in a French Group 1 for the second time (had finished only third when 1-2 for the Prix Ganay).

Glass Slippers

4 b f Dream Ahead - Night Gypsy (Mind Games)

Kevin Ryan   Bearstone Stud Limited

PLACINGS: 36116/0524111-					RPR **117**
Starts	1st	2nd	3rd	4th	Win & Pl
12	5	1	1	1	£274,669
	10/19	Lonc	5f Gp1 v soft		£180,171
	9/19	Lonc	5f Gp3 good		£36,036
	8/19	Deau	6f List 3yo good		£24,775
	9/18	Ches	6f Cls2 2yo good		£12,450
	8/18	Bevl	5f Cls5 2yo gd-fm		£4,140

Took a long time to come right last season but flourished in the second half of the year in France, most notably when running away with the Prix de l'Abbaye by three lengths; acts on any ground and could win plenty more races over 5f and 6f.

Glorious Journey

5 b g Dubawi - Fallen For You (Dansili)

Charlie Appleby   Sheikha Al Jalila Racing

PLACINGS: 11/439419/822819-1					RPR **116**
Starts	1st	2nd	3rd	4th	Win & Pl
15	5	2	1	2	£283,656
	1/20	Meyd	7f Gp2 good		£112,782
	8/19	Newb	7f Cls1 Gp2 soft		£56,710
	8/18	Deau	1m Gp3 3yo gd-sft		£35,398
	9/17	StCl	7f Gp3 2yo good		£34,188
	6/17	NmkJ	6f Cls4 2yo good		£4,528

Dropped in trip last season and proved himself among the leading 7f performers in Britain; beaten a neck by Limato in the Criterion Stakes and went one better when winning the Hungerford Stakes at Newbury; continued in good form in Dubai this spring.

Golden Horde (Ire)

3 ch c Lethal Force - Entreat (Pivotal)

Clive Cox   AlMohamediya Racing

PLACINGS: 415132-					RPR **116**
Starts	1st	2nd	3rd	4th	Win & Pl
6	2	1	1	1	£218,291
	8/19	Gdwd	6f Cls1 Gp2 2yo good		£113,420
	6/19	Wind	6f Cls4 2yo gd-fm		£5,175

Progressive juvenile last season; gained biggest win in the Richmond Stakes at Glorious Goodwood but ran even better when second in the Middle Park, pushing Earthlight much closer

than when third in the Prix Morny (seemingly unsuited by heavy ground).

Good Effort (Ire)

5 b h Shamardal - Magical Crown (Distorted Humor)

Ismail Mohammed   Abdulla Al Mansoori

PLACINGS: 31623/07090180521-11					RPR **112**aw
Starts	1st	2nd	3rd	4th	Win & Pl
20	5	2	2	1	£84,211
	2/20	Ling	6f Cls1 List stand		£25,520
	1/20	Newc	5f Cls2 std-slw		£18,903
	12/19	Deau	6½f stand		£9,459
92	8/19	NmkJ	6f Cls3 79-94 Hcap good		£9,057
79	8/18	Newb	7f Cls4 75-85 3yo Hcap gd-fm		£5,531

Massive improver on the all-weather this winter, completing a hat-trick when stepped up to Listed grade at Lingfield in February; inconsistent last year but best of his form (Newmarket win in August and Listed second in 2018) suggests he can also handle turf well.

Hamish

4 b g Motivator - Tweed (Sakhee)

William Haggas   B Haggas

PLACINGS: 213112-					RPR **114**+
Starts	1st	2nd	3rd	4th	Win & Pl
6	3	2	1	-	£154,976
98	10/19	York	1m6f Cls2 77-98 3yo Hcap soft		£62,250
92	8/19	York	1m6f Cls2 80-96 3yo Hcap gd-fm		£77,813
	6/19	Wind	1m2f Cls5 gd-sft		£3,752

Smart young stayer who improved massively when stepped up to 1m6f last season, winning the Melrose at York and following up in another good three-year-old handicap over the same course and distance; just outbattled when second to Trueshan on heavy ground on final run.

Happy Power (Ire)

4 gr c Dark Angel - Tamarisk (Selkirk)

Andrew Balding   King Power Racing Co Ltd

PLACINGS: 4131/13174356-					RPR **116**
Starts	1st	2nd	3rd	4th	Win & Pl
12	4	-	3	2	£147,014
	6/19	York	1m Cls1 List soft		£28,355
93	4/19	Newb	7f Cls2 80-96 3yo Hcap soft		£12,450
83	10/18	Donc	7f Cls3 74-95 2yo Hcap gd-sft		£7,116
	8/18	Haml	6f Cls4 Mdn 2yo good		£5,434

Smart miler who won a good handicap at Newbury and a Listed race at York early last season; subsequently acquitted himself well in top mile races, notably when a length third in the Celebration Mile and beaten less than two lengths in the Sussex Stakes.

Headman

4 b c Kingman - Deliberate (King's Best)
Roger Charlton   K Abdullah

PLACINGS: 12/61115-   **RPR 117**

Starts	1st	2nd	3rd	4th	Win & Pl
7	4	2	-	-	£344,945
	8/19	Deau	1m2f Gp2 3yo v soft		£205,405
	6/19	StCl	1m2f Gp2 3yo gd-sft		£66,757
95	5/19	Newb	1m2f Cls2 76-95 3yo Hcap good		£43,575
	11/18	Newc	1m Cls4 2yo stand		£5,531

Took a while to live up to big reputation (had been touted as a Guineas horse as a juvenile) but soon looked a potential Group 1 horse last season; won a couple of Group 2 races over 1m2f in France and ran well when fifth in the Irish Champion Stakes after botching the start.

Hello Youmzain (Fr)

4 b c Kodiac - Spasha (Shamardal)
Kevin Ryan   Haras D'Etreham & Cambridge Stud

PLACINGS: 121/41318-   **RPR 121**

Starts	1st	2nd	3rd	4th	Win & Pl
8	4	1	1	1	£380,691
	9/19	Hayd	6f Cls1 Gp1 soft		£170,130
	5/19	Hayd	6f Cls1 Gp2 3yo gd-fm		£51,039
	10/18	MsnL	6f Gp2 2yo soft		£95,841
	8/18	Carl	6f Cls5 Mdn 2yo gd-sft		£4,205

Proved himself a top-class sprinter with two terrific wins at Haydock last season, winning the Sprint Cup after claiming the scalp of Calyx earlier in the year; below that level in two runs at Ascot but blew the start when a creditable third in the Commonwealth Cup.

Hello Youmzain: top sprinter scores at Haydock last season and looks sure to be a force in similar company this year

Hereby (Ire)

4 b f Pivotal - Look Here (Hernando)
Ralph Beckett   J H Richmond-Watson

PLACINGS: 6131111-   **RPR 102+**

Starts	1st	2nd	3rd	4th	Win & Pl
7	5		1	-	£73,071
	10/19	Asct	1m6f Cls1 List 3yo soft		£45,368
79	9/19	Ches	1m4½f Cls3 76-89 Hcap good		£7,470
75	8/19	Pont	1m4f Cls3 73-91 Hcap good		£7,470
72	8/19	Ches	1m4½f Cls4 65-87 Hcap gd-sft		£6,081
	6/19	Gdwd	1m3f Cls5 Mdn soft		£5,240

Went from strength to strength last season, winning her last four races; last handicap win came off just 79 but defied a big step up in class when winning a Listed race at Ascot, relishing step up to 1m6f; filled out as last season went on and still unexposed as a stayer.

Hey Gaman

5 b h New Approach - Arsaadi (Dubawi)
James Tate   Rabbah Bloodstock Ltd

PLACINGS: 0112/327530/1122567-   **RPR 116**

Starts	1st	2nd	3rd	4th	Win & Pl
20	5	5	2	-	£378,505
	5/19	Lonc	7f Gp3 good		£36,036
	4/19	Leic	7f Cls1 List gd-fm		£34,026
	8/17	Newb	7f Cls1 List 2yo soft		£14,461
	7/17	NmkJ	6f Cls3 2yo gd-sft		£9,057
	7/17	Yarm	6f Cls4 2yo gd-fm		£4,658

Very smart 7f specialist who won Group 3 and Listed races last season before finishing second in the Lennox and Minstrel Stakes; lost his way subsequently, repeating a pattern of peaking in the first half of the season (best run as a three-year-old when second in the French Guineas).

Highest Ground (Ire)

3 b c Frankel - Celestial Lagoon (Sunday Silence)

Sir Michael Stoute   Niarchos Family

PLACINGS: 1-					RPR **86+**
Starts	1st	2nd	3rd	4th	Win & Pl
1	1	-	-	-	£6,469
9/19	Leic	7f Cls3 2yo gd-fm			£6,469

Hugely eyecatching winner of sole start over 7f at Leicester last season, blowing the start and looking green but powering through for a decisive success; seems sure to benefit from at least 1m2f as a three-year-old and could prove a smart colt.

Holdthasigreen (Fr)

8 ch g Hold That Tiger - Greentathir (Muhtathir)

Bruno Audouin (Fr)   Jean Gilbert & Claude Le Lay

PLACINGS: 3231/1711221/215513-					RPR **115**
Starts	1st	2nd	3rd	4th	Win & Pl
33	14	5	5	2	£831,600
10/19	Lonc	2m4f Gp1 v soft			£154,432
4/19	Lonc	1m7¹/₂f Gp3 gd-sft			£36,036
10/18	Chan	1m7f Gp1 gd-sft			£176,982
8/18	Deau	1m7f Gp2 good			£65,575
7/18	MsnL	1m7¹/₂f List good			£23,009
3/18	Chan	1m7f List heavy			£23,009
12/17	Toul	1m4f List v soft			£25,641
6/17	Pari	1m4f List good			£25,641
3/17	MsnL	1m7¹/₂f List good			£22,222
10/16	Nant	1m4f List v soft			£22,059
7/16	Vich	1m4f List good			£19,118
6/16	Nant	1m4f good			£9,559
5/16	Deau	1m4f 4yo Hcap stand			£9,559
2/16	Porn	1m4f 4yo stand			£5,515

High-class stayer who has won Group 1 races in each of the last two seasons in France, most recently the Prix du Cadran last year having finished second in it in 2018; has proved his stamina over the Gold Cup trip and connections have long held Royal Ascot ambitions.

Innisfree (Ire)

3 b/br c Galileo - Palace (Fastnet Rock)

Aidan O'Brien (Ire)   D Smith, Sue Magnier, M Tabor & Mrs AM O'Brien

PLACINGS: 2112-					RPR **110**aw
Starts	1st	2nd	3rd	4th	Win & Pl
4	2	2	-	-	£113,625
9/19	Curr	1m Gp2 2yo heavy			£58,468
7/19	Gway	7f Mdn 2yo good			£9,318

Won a notably weak Beresford Stakes last season (two major withdrawals meant nothing in the field had run in more than a maiden) before stepping up on that by finishing second behind

easy winner Kameko in the Vertem Futurity Trophy; likely improver over middle distances.

Japan

4 b c Galileo - Shastye (Danehill)

Aidan O'Brien (Ire)   Derrick Smith & Sue Magnier & Michael Tabor

PLACINGS: 711/431114-					RPR **125**
Starts	1st	2nd	3rd	4th	Win & Pl
9	5	-	1	2	£1,546,880
8/19	York	1m2¹/₂f Cls1 Gp1 good			£602,544
7/19	Lonc	1m4f Gp1 3yo gd-sft			£308,865
6/19	Asct	1m4f Cls1 Gp2 3yo gd-sft			£127,598
9/18	Naas	1m Gp2 2yo good			£57,434
9/18	List	7f Mdn 2yo heavy			£9,540

Proved the best horse to come out of last year's Derby despite finishing only third at Epsom after a rushed preparation; went on to win Group 1 races at 1m2f and 1m4f, notably pipping Crystal Ocean in the Juddmonte International, before a good fourth in the Arc.

Jash (Ire)

4 b c Kodiac - Miss Azeza (Dutch Art)

Simon Crisford   Hamdan Al Maktoum

PLACINGS: 112/16-					RPR **107**
Starts	1st	2nd	3rd	4th	Win & Pl
5	3	1	-	-	£98,521
5/19	NmkR	7f Cls1 List 3yo good			£22,684
9/18	Sals	6f Cls4 2yo gd-fm			£4,787
8/18	NmkJ	6f Cls4 2yo gd-fm			£5,175

High-class juvenile (close second behind Ten Sovereigns in the 2018 Middle Park) who ran just twice last season having had issues after Royal Ascot; well beaten in the Commonwealth Cup there but had won a 7f Listed race on his return; likely to be aimed at top sprints.

Juan Elcano

3 ch c Frankel - Whatami (Daylami)

Kevin Ryan   Sheikh Mohammed Obaid Al Maktoum

PLACINGS: 123-					RPR **109**
Starts	1st	2nd	3rd	4th	Win & Pl
3	1	1	1	-	£32,321
6/19	Hayd	7f Cls4 2yo heavy			£7,051

Highly tried in just three runs last season and proved himself a smart colt when beaten just a length in the Superlative Stakes and Champagne Stakes, both on quick ground; won his maiden on heavy but was withdrawn because of soft ground later in the season.

Jubiloso
4 b f Shamardal - Joyeuse (Oasis Dream)

Sir Michael Stoute | K Abdullah

PLACINGS: 11337- | RPR **111**

Starts	1st	2nd	3rd	4th	Win & Pl
5	2	-	2	-	£77,222
	5/19	Newb	7f Cls4 3yo good		£6,728
	4/19	Chmd	6f Cls3 Mdn stand		£8,086

Quickly developed into a high-class filly last season, hacking up by seven lengths in a novice at Newbury before a fine third in the Coronation Stakes at Royal Ascot; unlucky third at Goodwood next time but well below par when odds-on for a Group 3 at Sandown.

Kameko (USA)
3 b/br c Kitten's Joy - Sweeter Still (Rock Of Gibraltar)

Andrew Balding | Qatar Racing Limited

PLACINGS: 1221- | RPR **117+**aw

Starts	1st	2nd	3rd	4th	Win & Pl
4	2	2	-	-	£157,837
	11/19	Newc	1m Cls1 Gp1 2yo stand		£113,420
	7/19	Sand	7f Cls4 Mdn 2yo good		£6,792

Looked a work in progress for much of last season, running green in a couple of narrow defeats, but delivered on his potential in style in the rescheduled Vertem Futurity Trophy, hacking up by three and a quarter lengths; likely 2,000 Guineas contender before stepping up in trip.

Kastasa (Ire)
4 b f Rock Of Gibraltar - Kasanka (Galileo)

Dermot Weld (Ir) | Aga Khan

PLACINGS: 4/131111- | RPR **113+**

Starts	1st	2nd	3rd	4th	Win & Pl
7	5		1	1	£155,713
92	9/19	Curr	2m Gp3 yield		£31,892
84	9/19	Leop	1m5f 73-103 Hcap good		£79,730
79	8/19	Curr	1m4f 65-93 Hcap gd-yld		£15,946
	8/19	Slig	1m4½f Hcap Auct 3-4yo yield		£15,946
	4/19	Clon	1m1½f Mdn 3-4yo yield		£10,822

Massive improver last season and ran away with a Group 3 by seven lengths to complete a four-timer within the space of eight weeks after starting her winning run off just 79; looked a strong stayer over 2m that day and trainer hopes she's a Gold Cup filly.

MY FIVE TO WATCH
Tom Collins, tipster

● Accountability ● Born With Pride
● Hamish ● King's Lynn ● Palace Pier

Kew Gardens (Ire)
5 b h Galileo - Chelsea Rose (Desert King)

Aidan O'Brien (Ir) | Derrick Smith & Sue Magnier & Michael Tabor

PLACINGS: 71241/32911317/2221- | RPR **122**

Starts	1st	2nd	3rd	4th	Win & Pl
17	6	5	2	1	£1,399,665
	10/19	Asct	1m7½/sf Cls1 Gp2 gd-sft		£255,195
	9/18	Donc	1m6½/sf Cls1 Gp1 3yo good		£421,355
	7/18	Lonc	1m4f Gp1 3yo good		£303,398
	6/18	Asct	1m6f Cls1 Gp2 3yo gd-fm		£113,420
	10/17	NmkR	1m2f Cls1 List 2yo good		£22,684
	8/17	Klny	1m Mdn 2yo soft		£7,897

Dual Group 1 winner as a three-year-old in 2018, including in the St Leger; took a long time to build on that last season, coming up just short over 1m4f and then pulling muscles in his back, but hit back with stunning win over Stradivarius on Champions Day; leading Gold Cup hope.

Khaadem (Ire)
4 br c Dark Angel - White Daffodil (Footstepsinthesand)

Charlie Hills | Hamdan Al Maktoum

PLACINGS: 311/172100- | RPR **119**

	Starts	1st	2nd	3rd	4th	Win & Pl
107	9	4	1	1	-	£225,371
	8/19	Gdwd	6f Cls2 91-107 Hcap gd-fm		£155,625
	5/19	Newb	6f Cls1 List 3yo good		£39,697
	9/18	Donc	6f Cls2 2yo gd-sft		£11,205
	8/18	NmkJ	6f Cls4 2yo good		£5,175

Has won all four races below Group level since his debut in 2018, most impressively when hacking up in the Stewards' Cup off 107 last season; twice well beaten at Group 1 level after that, though, and never better than seventh in three runs at the top level.

Khayzaraan
3 b f Kingman - Riqa (Dubawi)

Freddy Head (Fr) | Hamdan Al Maktoum

PLACINGS: 911- | RPR **97+**

Starts	1st	2nd	3rd	4th	Win & Pl
3	2	-	-	-	£27,477
	9/19	Chan	1m 2yo good		£15,315
	8/19	Deau	1m 2yo good		£12,162

Stunning winner of final two runs last season, storming home by nine lengths at Deauville and following up by four and a half at Chantilly; yet to be pitched into Group level (missed Prix Marcel Boussac with a minor problem) but no surprise if she proved a high-class miler.

King Of Change
4 b c Farhh - Salacia (Echo Of Light)

Richard Hannon | Ali Abdulla Saeed

PLACINGS: 22/1211- | RPR **122+**

Starts	1st	2nd	3rd	4th	Win & Pl
6	3	3	-	-	£766,138
	10/19	Asct	1m Cls1 Gp1 heavy		£623,810
	9/19	Sand	1m Cls1 List good		£22,684
	4/19	Nott	1m½/sf Cls5 3yo gd-fm		£3,881

Top-class miler who finished a stunning 66-1

second in last season's 2,000 Guineas on first run outside novice/maiden company and proved that was no fluke with a cosy win in the Queen Elizabeth II Stakes; still very lightly raced after just six runs.

King Of Comedy (Ire)

4 b c Kingman - Stage Presence (Selkirk)

John Gosden   Lady Bamford

PLACINGS: 12/112420-					RPR **121+**
Starts	1st	2nd	3rd	4th	Win & Pl
8	3	3	-	1	£228,533
5/19	Sand	1m Cls1 List 3yo gd-fm			£22,684
4/19	Yarm	1m Cls5 3yo gd-fm			£3,752
7/18	Sand	7f Cls4 2yo gd-fm			£6,469

Sharply progressive in first half of last season, finishing a neck second in the St James's Palace Stakes after a couple of wins in a lower grade; fair run when fourth in the Juddmonte International but twice disappointed back over a mile in the autumn.

King's Advice

6 ch h Frankel - Queen's Logic (Grand Lodge)

Mark Johnston   Saeed Jaber

PLACINGS: 16/10/11111161102-33					RPR **118**
Starts	1st	2nd	3rd	4th	Win & Pl
21	11	3	2	-	£222,186
108	8/19	Gdwd	1m6f Cls2 97-108 Hcap gd-fm		£62,250
101	7/19	NmkJ	1m6f Cls2 83-107 Hcap gd-fm		£74,700
98	5/19	Gdwd	1m6f Cls2 89-102 Hcap gd-fm		£15,753
95	4/19	Ripn	1m4f Cls2 87-106 Hcap gd-fm		£15,563
90	4/19	Thsk	1m4f Cls5 78-90 Hcap gd-fm		£9,704
83	4/19	Wolv	1m6f Cls5 79-92 Hcap stand		£7,439
77	3/19	Kemp	1m4f Cls4 70-79 Hcap std-slw		£6,469
71	3/19	Ling	1m4f Cls5 62-71 Hcap stand		£3,429
	5/18	Hopp	1m2f Hcap good		£6,195
	10/17	Duss	1m2½f Hcap sft-hvy		£5,128
	5/17	Dort	1m1f 3yo good		£2,564

Remarkable improver last season who won eight times in handicaps, scoring first from a mark of 71 in March and from 108 in August, most notably in big fields at Newmarket and Glorious Goodwood; disappointed in the Ebor and was well beaten in first two runs back in conditions races.

King's Command

3 b g Dubawi - O'Giselle (Octagonal)

Charlie Appleby   Godolphin

PLACINGS: 1831-					RPR **115**
Starts	1st	2nd	3rd	4th	Win & Pl
4	2	-	1	-	£49,319
10/19	StCl	7f Gp3 2yo v soft			£36,036
6/19	NmkJ	6f Cls4 2yo gd-sft			£5,175

Had become slightly disappointing last season but was gelded following a second defeat at Deauville and instantly reaped the benefits when running away with a Group 3 at Saint-Cloud from the front; form looks strong with Champagne Stakes runner-up Royal Crusade having finished second.

Kinross

3 b c Kingman - Ceilidh House (Selkirk)

Ralph Beckett   J H Richmond-Watson

PLACINGS: 15-					RPR **104**
Starts	1st	2nd	3rd	4th	Win & Pl
2	1	-	-	-	£10,555
10/19	NmkR	7f Cls4 2yo gd-sft			£5,175

Stunning eight-length debut winner at Newmarket last October, hacking up in a quick time; sent off just 13-8 for the Vertem Futurity Trophy after that but came up short in fifth; should learn from the experience and could still prove to be a Group 1 miler.

Kurious

4 b f Kuroshio - Easy To Imagine (Cozzene)

Henry Candy   Hot To Trot Racing

PLACINGS: 194/2011-					RPR **105**
Starts	1st	2nd	3rd	4th	Win & Pl
7	3	1	-	1	£72,245
7/19	Sand	5f Cls1 Gp3 gd-fm			£39,697
6/19	Sand	5f Cls1 List 3yo soft			£22,684
6/18	Sand	5f Cls5 2yo gd-fm			£4,528

Smart and progressive sprinter who won Group 3 and Listed races at Sandown last season, coping well enough with good to firm ground at the higher level despite being seen as better on soft; less effective when asked to settle over 6f and likely to stick to 5f.

Kynren (Ire)

6 b g Clodovil - Art Of Gold (Excellent Art)

David Barron   Elliott Brothers & Peacock & Partner

PLACINGS: 111/3203265/2253216-					RPR **112**
Starts	1st	2nd	3rd	4th	Win & Pl
18	4	5	4	-	£236,148
101	10/19	Asct	7f Cls2 92-109 Hcap soft		£112,050
85	9/17	Rdcr	1m Cls4 73-86 Hcap soft		£6,469
79	8/17	NmkL	7f Cls4 69-82 3yo Hcap soft		£5,175
	7/17	Carl	1m Cls5 Mdn 3-4yo gd-fm		£3,881

Remarkably consistent in top handicaps last season and gained a much-deserved victory in the Challenge Cup at Ascot; had finished second in the Lincoln and Victoria Cup before winning on his side when fifth in the Royal Hunt Cup; not handicapped out of further success.

Lampang (Ire)

3 b c Dandy Man - Black Mascara (Authorized)

Tim Easterby   King Power Racing Co Ltd

PLACINGS: 118-					RPR **95+**
Starts	1st	2nd	3rd	4th	Win & Pl
3	2	-	-	-	£10,350
9/19	Ripn	6f Cls5 2yo gd-fm			£3,881
8/19	Carl	6f Cls4 2yo gd-fm			£6,469

Hugely impressive winner of first two starts last season, notably when landing a novice stakes at Ripon by five lengths; sent off just even-money for a competitive Listed race at York after that but reportedly unsuited by testing conditions, though had won on good to soft at Ripon.

Lancaster House (Ire)

4 b c Galileo - Quiet Oasis (Oasis Dream)

Aidan O'Brien (Ir)   Michael Tabor, Derrick Smith & Sue Magnier

PLACINGS: 1117-					RPR **107+**
Starts	1st	2nd	3rd	4th	Win & Pl
4	3	-	-	-	£43,880
	9/19	List	1m1f List soft		£26,577
	8/19	Tipp	1m1f gd-yld		£8,253
	8/19	Gway	1m¹/₂f Mdn good		£9,051

Has won three out of four and had excuses when losing his unbeaten record at Leopardstown (found to be lame post-race); had only started racing last August but soon completed his hat-trick when hacking up in a Listed race, looking particularly effective on soft ground.

*Lancaster House (right):
highly likely this season to
add to his haul of three
wins from four starts*

Land Of Oz

4 ch c Australia - Madame Defarge (Motivator)

Sir Mark Prescott   John Brown & Megan Dennis

PLACINGS: 608/411113110-					RPR **99+**
Starts	1st	2nd	3rd	4th	Win & Pl
12	6	-	1	1	£77,965
87	9/19	NmkR	2m2f Cls2 76-100 Hcap gd-fm		£31,125
84	9/19	Kemp	2m Cls3 71-91 Hcap std-slw		£9,338
77	8/19	Sals	1m6f Cls4 64-77 3yo Hcap gd-sft		£8,927
70	8/19	Kemp	2m Cls4 69-82 Hcap std-slw		£6,469
64	7/19	Ayr	2m1¹/₂f Cls4 51-82 Hcap soft		£6,728
58	7/19	Yarm	1m6f Cls5 58-73 3yo Hcap gd-fm		£3,429

Typically rapid Sir Mark Prescott improver once sent handicapping and stepped up in trip last season, winning six times in little over two months including the Cesarewitch Trial; reportedly ran too freely when flopping in the real thing (has always been keen); likely to progress again.

Latrobe (Ire)

5 br h Camelot - Question Times (Shamardal)

Joseph O'Brien (Ir)   N C Williams & Mr & Mrs L J Williams

PLACINGS: 2/22117220/3442160-					RPR **114**
Starts	1st	2nd	3rd	4th	Win & Pl
16	3	6	1	2	£1,152,260
8/19	Leop	1m4f Gp3 gd-fm			£33,486
6/18	Curr	1m4f Gp1 3yo gd-fm			£756,637
6/18	Curr	1m4f Mdn gd-fm			£7,087

Hasn't built on surprise win in the 2018 Irish Derby, though has often been running over seemingly inadequate 1m2f; did better when stepped up in trip last season, winning a Group 3 at Leopardstown and a neck second in the Curragh Cup; badly drawn in the Melbourne Cup.

Lavender's Blue (Ire)

4 b f Sea The Stars - Beatrice Aurore (Danehill Dancer)

Amanda Perrett   Benny Andersson

PLACINGS: 12014-					RPR **109**
Starts	1st	2nd	3rd	4th	Win & Pl
5	2	1	-	1	£75,520
8/19	Sand	1m Cls1 Gp3 gd-fm			£39,697
4/19	NmkR	1m Cls4 Mdn 3yo gd-fm			£6,469

Initially campaigned as a middle-distance filly last season but flourished when dropped back to a mile after trailing home in the Oaks; most impressive when winning a Group 3 at Sandown and unlucky not to finish much closer when fourth in the Sun Chariot Stakes.

Liberty Beach

3 b f Cable Bay - Flirtinaskirt (Avonbridge)

John Quinn   Philip Wilkins

PLACINGS: 114112-   RPR **107+**

Starts	1st	2nd	3rd	4th	Win & Pl
6	4	1	-	1	£145,986

7/19	Gdwd	5f Cls1 Gp3 2yo good	£42,533
7/19	Sand	5f Cls1 List 2yo gd-fm	£17,013
6/19	Bevl	5f Cls2 2yo gd-fm	£24,900
5/19	Rdcr	5f Cls5 Auct 2yo gd-fm	£4,528

Exciting juvenile sprinter last season, winning four out of five over 5f, including the Molecomb Stakes at Goodwood, with sole defeat when best of those drawn low in the Queen Mary; second in the Lowther when stepped up to 6f but missed the Cheveley Park after a setback.

Limato (Ire)

8 b g Tagula - Come April (Singspiel)

Henry Candy   Paul G Jacobs

PLACINGS: 03241/0001119/41062-   RPR **119**

Starts	1st	2nd	3rd	4th	Win & Pl
31	13	6	1	3	£1,395,653

6/19	NmkJ	7f Cls1 Gp3 gd-fm	£34,026
10/18	NmkR	7f Cls1 Gp2 gd-fm	£68,052
9/18	York	6f Cls1 List gd-sft	£28,355
8/18	NmkJ	7f Cls1 List gd-fm	£22,684
10/17	NmkR	7f Cls1 Gp2 good	£68,052
10/16	Chan	7f Gp1 good	£126,044
7/16	NmkJ	6f Cls1 Gp1 gd-fm	£302,690
9/15	Donc	7f Cls1 Gp2 good	£56,710
4/15	Asct	6f Cls1 Gp3 3yo gd-fm	£45,368
10/14	Rdcr	6f Cls1 List 2yo good	£117,220
7/14	Newb	6f Cls1 List 2yo stand	£14,461
6/14	Kemp	6f Cls3 2yo stand	£6,225
6/14	Kemp	6f Cls5 Mdn 2yo stand	£2,588

Not quite the force of old but had another fine campaign last year and finished second when chasing a third win in the Challenge Stakes; particularly effective over that 7f trip, finishing first or second in seven out of nine career runs at 7f (both failures at Goodwood).

Living In The Past (Ire)

3 b f Bungle Inthejungle - Ayr Missile (Cadeaux Genereux)

Karl Burke   Clipper Logistics

PLACINGS: 313150-   RPR **109**

Starts	1st	2nd	3rd	4th	Win & Pl
6	2	-	2	-	£154,236

8/19	York	6f Cls1 Gp2 2yo good	£134,828
7/19	Bevl	5f Cls4 2yo gd-fm	£5,608

Comfortable all-the-way winner of last season's Lowther Stakes at York, bouncing back from a below-par effort at Ascot when unsuited by softer ground; below that level when faced with

more competition for the lead in the Cheveley Park and flopped at the Breeders' Cup.

Logician

4 ro c Frankel - Scuffle (Daylami)

John Gosden   K Abdullah

PLACINGS: 11111-   RPR **119+**

Starts	1st	2nd	3rd	4th	Win & Pl
5	5	-	-	-	£514,013

	9/19	Donc	1m6½f Cls1 Gp1 3yo gd-fm	£396,970
	8/19	York	1m4f Cls1 Gp2 3yo good	£96,407
90	7/19	Newb	1m4f Cls3 75-90 3yo Hcap gd-fm	£8,086
	6/19	NmkJ	1m2f Cls4 3yo gd-sft	£5,822
	5/19	Newb	1m2f Cls4 Mdn 3yo good	£6,728

Made his debut only last May but had won the St Leger less than four months later, easily completing a sensational five-timer; connections expect him to be best suited by a return to 1m4f; set to miss the first half of the season after illness but could be a big player in later Group 1 races.

Lope Y Fernandez (Ire)

3 b c Lope De Vega - Black Dahlia (Dansili)

Aidan O'Brien (Ir)   Derrick Smith, Sue Magnier & Michael Tabor

PLACINGS: 12316-   RPR **108**

Starts	1st	2nd	3rd	4th	Win & Pl
5	2	1	1	-	£86,186

8/19	Curr	6f Gp3 2yo gd-yld	£31,892
6/19	Curr	7f Mdn 2yo gd-yld	£9,712

Didn't live up to initial expectations last season (sent off just 5-4 when second in the Chesham) but looked better back at 6f when easily winning a strong Group 3 at the Curragh; slightly disappointing when only sixth in the Middle Park next time.

Lord Glitters (Fr)

7 gr g Whipper - Lady Glitters (Homme De Loi)

David O'Meara   Geoff & Sandra Turnbull

PLACINGS: 212/2223166/3015689-   RPR **120**

Starts	1st	2nd	3rd	4th	Win & Pl
26	7	8	2	1	£1,484,891

	6/19	Asct	1m Cls1 Gp1 good	£340,260
	8/18	York	1m1f Cls1 Gp3 gd-fm	£56,710
102	10/17	Asct	1m Cls2 98-110 Hcap soft	£155,625
	5/17	StCl	1m soft	£11,966
	4/17	Chan	1m stand	£11,966
	6/16	Le L	1m2f 3yo heavy	£9,926
	5/16	Chat	1m2f 3yo soft	£5,882

Veteran who made his Group 1 breakthrough in last season's Queen Anne Stakes, improving on his second in the 2018 race; suited by a strongly run straight mile and yet to reproduce that form elsewhere.

Lord North (Ire)

4 b g Dubawi - Najoum (Giant's Causeway)

John Gosden — Sheikh Zayed Bin Mohammed Racing

PLACINGS: 1/182121- — **RPR 114**

Starts	1st	2nd	3rd	4th	Win & Pl
7	4	2	-	-	£183,642

98	11/19	NmkR	1m2f Cls1 List heavy	£20,983
	9/19	NmkR	1m1f Cls2 83-107 Hcap good	£99,600
	4/19	Newc	1m Cls5 stand	£3,752
	10/18	Rdcr	1m Cls4 2yo soft	£7,116

Quickly made up into a high-class handicapper after being gelded last summer, winning the Cambridgeshire and nearly following up when second in the Balmoral; proved himself in a more tactical affair when winning a Listed race at Newmarket on his final run.

Madhmoon: smart performer powers home at Leopardstown for his sole win last season

Lord Of The Lodge (Ire)

3 b c Dandy Man - Archetypal (Cape Cross)

Karl Burke — Mrs Elaine M Burke

PLACINGS: 10612-1 — **RPR 109**

Starts	1st	2nd	3rd	4th	Win & Pl
6	3	1	-	-	£78,650

2/20	Newc	6f Cls2 3yo stand	£18,675
8/19	Hayd	6f Cls4 2yo gd-fm	£6,469
5/19	Ayr	6f Cls4 Mdn 2yo gd-fm	£4,787

Held in high regard and belatedly fulfilled that promise when faced with quicker ground last summer, notably when second in the Gimcrack Stakes; expected by connections to improve over further but knocked a joint when declared over 7f at Newmarket subsequently.

Love (Ire)

3 ch f Galileo - Pikaboo (Pivotal)

Aidan O'Brien (Ir)   Michael Tabor, Derrick Smith & Sue Magnier

PLACINGS: 4211513-					RPR **111**
Starts	1st	2nd	3rd	4th	Win & Pl
7	3	1	1	1	£313,407
	9/19 Curr	7f Gp1 2yo good			£205,405
	7/19 Leop	7f Gp3 2yo good			£31,892
	7/19 Leop	7f Mdn 2yo gd-fm			£9,318

Progressed throughout a busy campaign last season bar single disappointing run in the Debutante Stakes; bounced back to win the Moyglare and ran up to that level when third in a strong Fillies' Mile; seems sure to stay middle distances and looks a leading Oaks contender.

Madhmoon (Ire)

4 b c Dawn Approach - Aaraas (Haafhd)

Kevin Prendergast (Ir)   Hamdan Al Maktoum

PLACINGS: 11/242416-					RPR **117+**
Starts	1st	2nd	3rd	4th	Win & Pl
8	3	2	-	2	£572,666
	8/19 Leop	1m Gp3 good			£33,486
	9/18 Leop	1m Gp2 2yo gd-fm			£78,319
	8/18 Leop	1m Mdn 2yo good			£9,540

Won only once last season (in a moderate Group 3) but ran a couple of big races in the Classics, finishing fourth in the 2,000 Guineas and a half-length second in the Derby; shapes as if ideally suited by 1m2f but disappointed when sixth in the Irish Champion Stakes.

Magical (Ire)

5 b m Galileo - Halfway To Heaven (Pivotal)

Aidan O'Brien (Ir)   Derrick Smith & Sue Magnier & Michael Tabor

PLACINGS: 44/414012/111222151-					RPR **123**
Starts	1st	2nd	3rd	4th	Win & Pl
21	9	6		4	£3,366,313
	10/19 Asct	1m2f Cls1 Gp1 soft			£770,547
	9/19 Leop	1m2f Gp1 good			£641,892
	5/19 Curr	1m2½f Gp1 gd-fm			£212,613
	5/19 Curr	1m2f Gp2 gd-yld			£69,099
	4/19 Naas	1m2f Gp3 gd-yld			£34,550
	10/18 Asct	1m4f Cls1 Gp1 soft			£340,260
	7/18 Curr	1m1f Gp2 gd-fm			£60,044
	8/17 Curr	7f Gp2 2yo soft			£57,991
	8/17 Cork	1m Mdn 2yo gd-yld			£8,687

Four-time Group 1 winner who enjoyed her finest hour when winning last season's Champion Stakes at Ascot, escaping from Enable's shadow (second to that filly three times); was set to retire but connections reconsidering given how well she has wintered.

Maid In India (Ire)

6 br m Bated Breath - Indian Maiden (Indian Ridge)

Eric Alston   Con Harrington

PLACINGS: 1125/11752145/101-					RPR **110**
Starts	1st	2nd	3rd	4th	Win & Pl
15	7	2	-	1	£101,271
	9/19 Newb	5f Cls3 gd-fm			£34,026
	6/19 Hayd	5f Cls1 List heavy			£20,983
86	9/18 Pont	6f Cls2 77-93 Hcap soft			£18,675
80	5/18 Hayd	6f Cls4 66-80 Hcap good			£6,728
77	5/18 Thsk	5f Cls5 62-77 Hcap gd-fm			£5,434
65	8/17 Donc	6f Cls5 51-70 Hcap good			£3,235
	7/17 Donc	6f Cls5 Mdn gd-fm			£2,911

Has got better and better with age and took

her form to another level last season, managing Group 3 and Listed victories from just three races; did particularly well to beat Dakota Gold on final run at Newbury on good to firm given apparent preference for much softer.

Major Jumbo

6 gr g Zebedee - Gone Sailing (Mizzen Mast)

Kevin Ryan   TA Rahman

PLACINGS: /134233201/23239170-   RPR **113**

Starts	1st	2nd	3rd	4th	Win & Pl
32	7	8	8	2	£244,083
	8/19	Ches	6f Cls1 List gd-sft		£20,983
102	10/18	York	6f Cls2 94-105 Hcap soft		£62,250
94	4/18	NmkR	5f Cls3 81-95 Hcap gd-sft		£12,938
90	9/17	York	6f Cls3 77-97 3yo Hcap gd-sft		£9,704
82	2/17	Wolv	5f Cls4 70-87 3yo Hcap stand		£5,175
69	1/17	Newc	5f Cls5 61-76 3yo Hcap stand		£2,911
67	7/16	Thsk	5f Cls3 67-87 2yo Hcap gd-sft		£8,086

Smart sprinter who acts on quick ground (placed in last season's Palace House and Duke of York

Stakes on good to firm) but seems even better with some cut; made breakthrough handicap win in 2018 on soft and ran away with a Listed race last year on good to soft.

Make A Challenge (Ire)

5 b g Invincible Spirit - Crinoline (Street Cry)

Denis Gerard Hogan (Ir)   MG Hogan, Walter O'Connor & JJ Reilly

PLACINGS: **7834**/72151112115-   RPR **115+**

Starts	1st	2nd	3rd	4th	Win & Pl
15	6	2	1	1	£134,172
	10/19	Curr	6f List sft-hvy		£23,919
94	9/19	Curr	5f 76-101 Hcap soft		£26,577
88	8/19	Curr	6f 78-100 Hcap soft		£13,820
79	8/19	Gway	7f 63-79 Hcap good		£9,051
73	7/19	Gway	7f 71-80 Hcap good		£9,051
68	5/19	Fair	7f 50-74 Hcap gd-fm		£6,659

Hugely progressive as he was reinvented as a sprinter last season, winning five of his last seven races; started off at a mile but produced arguably

his best performance when running away with a 6f Listed race at the Curragh; not beaten far when fifth in the Champions Sprint.

Max Vega: impressive Zetland winner is a promising prospect

Master Of Reality (Ire)

5 b g Frankel - L'Ancresse (Darshaan)

Joseph O'Brien (Ir)   N C Williams, L J Williams Et Al

PLACINGS: 8117250/143352d-					RPR **119**
Starts	1st	2nd	3rd	4th	Win & Pl
13	3	1	2	2	£341,669

4/19	Navn	1m6f Gp3 yield	£33,514
5/18	StCl	1m4f 3yo good	£15,487
5/18	StCl	1m4f 3yo soft	£13,274

French recruit who was a revelation in first full season for Joseph O'Brien last year, winning at 33-1 first time out and finishing a length third at 66-1 in the Gold Cup; bounced back to that form when a head second in the Melbourne Cup (demoted to fourth); likely Cup horse again.

Max Vega (Ire)

3 ch c Lope De Vega - Paraphernalia (Dalakhani)

Ralph Beckett   The Pickford Hill Partnership

PLACINGS: 211-					RPR **108+**
Starts	1st	2nd	3rd	4th	Win & Pl
3	2	1	-	-	£39,998

10/19	NmkR	1m2f Cls1 Gp3 2yo soft	£34,026
9/19	Pont	1m Cls4 Auct 2yo gd-sft	£4,528

Won two out of three last season and relished a stiff test of stamina when running away with the Zetland Stakes by three lengths; sure to get further, although trainer has warned he doesn't see him as a Derby type; could be one for good staying races instead.

Mehdaayih

4 b f Frankel - Sayyedati Symphony (Gone West)

John Gosden   Emirates Park Pty Ltd

PLACINGS: 621/1171205-   RPR **115+**

Starts		1st	2nd	3rd	4th	Win & Pl
10		4	2	-	-	£286,274
	6/19	StCl	1m4f Gp2 3yo gd-sft			£66,757
	5/19	Ches	1m3½/sf Cls1 List 3yo gd-sft			£42,533
84	4/19	Chmd	1m2f Cls4 76-84 3yo Hcap stand			£5,531
	10/18	Yarm	1m Cls4 2yo gd-fm			£4,787

Developed into a top-class middle-distance filly in first half of last season, winning three times including a Group 2 at Saint-Cloud and the Cheshire Oaks; got no run in the Oaks and overhauled late in the Nassau; lost her way later but kept in training in pursuit of Group 1 win.

Military March

3 b c New Approach - Punctilious (Danehill)

Saeed bin Suroor   Godolphin

PLACINGS: 11-   RPR **115+**

Starts		1st	2nd	3rd	4th	Win & Pl
2		2	-	-	-	£39,201
	10/19	NmkR	1m Cls4 Gp3 2yo soft			£34,026
	7/19	NmkJ	7f Cls4 Mdn 2yo good			£5,175

Imposing colt who impressed in just two races last season, hosing up first time out before returning from a break on much softer ground to win the Group 3 Autumn Stakes (first two clear); should come into his own when stepped up to middle distances.

Millisle (Ire)

3 ch f Starspangledbanner - Green Castle (Indian Ridge)

Jessica Harrington (Ir)   Stonethorn Stud Farms Limited

PLACINGS: 12121-   RPR **116**

Starts		1st	2nd	3rd	4th	Win & Pl
5		3	2	-	-	£210,579
	9/19	NmkR	6f Cls1 Gp1 2yo good			£165,355
	8/19	Curr	5f List 2yo soft			£24,982
	7/19	Bell	5f Mdn 2yo good			£7,986

Beat Raffle Prize to win what looked a strong Cheveley Park Stakes last season, storming home to give some hope of staying a mile (had been seen as a sprinter); showed big improvement on previous second at Salisbury but reportedly upset by having a blood sample taken that day.

Miss O Connor (Ire)

5 b m Roderic O'Connor - Magadar (Lujain)

William Haggas   Lael Stable

PLACINGS: 1111-   RPR **108+**

Starts		1st	2nd	3rd	4th	Win & Pl
4		4	-	-	-	£74,248
	10/19	StCl	1m Gp3 heavy			£36,036
	8/19	Hayd	1m Cls1 List heavy			£26,654
	8/19	Nott	1m¹/sf Cls6 Auct 3-5yo soft			£3,235
	5/19	Gowr	1m Mdn yld-sft			£8,324

Unbeaten mare who completed a four-timer when winning a Group 3 at Saint-Cloud last autumn, building on an impressive Listed win at Haydock; gained both those victories on heavy ground and unproven on good ground; could be top-class given her conditions.

Miss Yoda (Ger)

3 ch f Sea The Stars - Monami (Sholokhov)

John Gosden   Westerberg

PLACINGS: 112-   RPR **100**

Starts		1st	2nd	3rd	4th	Win & Pl
3		2	1	-	-	£23,509
	9/19	Sand	1m Cls4 2yo good			£4,787
	8/19	Kemp	1m Cls4 Mdn 2yo std-slw			£5,822

Won first two starts last season (Sandown victory on second run under 6lb penalty worked out well) and coped well with a serious test of stamina in the Zetland Stakes, finishing second behind Max Vega; seems sure to get further and trainer is already eyeing the Ribblesdale.

Mogul

3 b c Galileo - Shastye (Danehill)

Aidan O'Brien (Ir)   Michael Tabor, Derrick Smith & Sue Magnier

PLACINGS: 2114-   RPR **109+**

Starts		1st	2nd	3rd	4th	Win & Pl
4		2	1	-	1	£102,606
	9/19	Leop	1m Gp2 2yo good			£79,730
	8/19	Curr	1m Mdn 2yo gd-yld			£9,318

Clear market choice among Aidan O'Brien's team for last season's Vertem Futurity Trophy but failed to live up to his billing when managing only fourth; had won at 1-2 in a soft Group 2 at Leopardstown prior to that; still an interesting middle-distance prospect.

Mohaather

4 b c Showcasing - Roodeye (Inchinor)

Marcus Tregoning   Hamdan Al Maktoum

PLACINGS: 211/15-   RPR **114**

Starts		1st	2nd	3rd	4th	Win & Pl
5		3	1	-	-	£97,777
	4/19	Newb	7f Cls1 Gp3 3yo gd-sft			£39,697
	10/18	Newb	7f Cls1 Gp3 2yo gd-sft			£22,684
	10/18	Nott	6f Cls5 2yo good			£3,881

Looked a serious 2,000 Guineas candidate when making it three wins out of four in last season's Greenham Stakes but then missed six months with a severe stone bruise; shaped with promise again when fifth on heavy ground in the QEII on his return.

Mohican Heights (Ire)

3 ch c Australia - Mohican Princess (Shirley Heights)

David Simcock   Qatar Racing Ltd & Sun Bloodstock

PLACINGS: 11-   RPR **100+**

Starts 2	1st 2	2nd -	3rd -	4th -	Win & Pl £26,724
8/19	Sals	1m Cls1 List 2yo good			£17,013
5/19	Leop	7f Mdn 2yo gd-yld			£9,712

Unbeaten colt who was bought for £520,000 after landing a Leopardstown maiden for Fozzy Stack last season and made a winning start for new connections in a modest Listed race at Salisbury; pedigree is full of stamina and looks a nice prospect for longer distances.

Molatham

3 ch c Night Of Thunder - Cantal (Pivotal)

Roger Varian   Hamdan Al Maktoum

PLACINGS: 2114-   RPR **104+**

Starts 4	1st 2	2nd 1	3rd	4th 1	Win & Pl £67,532
9/19	Donc	7f Cls1 List 2yo gd-fm			£17,013
8/19	York	7f Cls2 Mdn 2yo gd-fm			£43,575

Gained two notable victories last season, landing the most valuable maiden run in Britain at York and following up by beating subsequent runaway

Group 3 winner Wichita at Doncaster; below that form on much softer ground when fourth in the Autumn Stakes.

Monarch Of Egypt (USA)

3 b c American Pharoah - Up (Galileo)

Aidan O'Brien (Ire) P M Brant, Sue Magnier, M Tabor & Derrick Smith

PLACINGS: 12285-   RPR **113**

Starts 5	1st 1	2nd 2	3rd -	4th -	Win & Pl £101,812
4/19	Naas	5f 2yo gd-yld			£13,851

Failed to add to debut win last season but was highly tried and ran a couple of good races behind Siskin, notably when a close second in the Phoenix Stakes; twice disappointing at Newmarket in the autumn, including when stepped up to 7f in the Dewhurst.

Monica Sheriff

4 b f Lawman - Require (Montjeu)

William Haggas   Duke Of Devonshire

PLACINGS: 911111-   RPR **107+**

Starts 6	1st 5	2nd -	3rd -	4th -	Win & Pl £82,388
	10/19	StCl	1m6f Gp3 heavy		£36,036
87	9/19	Gdwd	1m6f Cls2 81-98 Hcap heavy		£28,013
83	8/19	Newc	1m4½f Cls4 64-83 Hcap std-slw		£5,208
	8/19	Ffos	1m4f Cls5 gd-sft		£3,429
	6/19	Hayd	1m3½f Cls3 heavy		£9,704

Hugely progressive last season, winning her last

Miss O Connor: four out of four last season and could go right to the top

five races; gained three of those wins on heavy ground, including a Group 3 at Saint-Cloud in comfortable fashion; kept away from quick ground since suffering sole defeat on good to firm and even a non-runner on good.

Moonlight Spirit (Ire)

4 b g Dubawi - Moonsail (Monsun)

Charlie Appleby   Godolphin

PLACINGS: 1/113412-   RPR **109**+

Starts		1st	2nd	3rd	4th	Win & Pl
7		4	1	1	1	£115,624
	9/19	Lonc	1m7f Gp3 3yo good			£36,036
86	4/19	Leic	1m4f Cls3 72-89 3yo Hcap gd-fm			£7,439
	3/19	Ling	1m2f Cls5 3yo stand			£2,911
	11/18	Newc	1m2f Cls4 Mdn 2yo stand			£6,728

Promising stayer who ran away with a Group 3 at Longchamp last autumn; beaten in both runs at a higher level but was a fair fourth in the Queen's Vase at Royal Ascot and pushed subsequent Group 1 winner Technician close on his final run back at Longchamp.

Morando (Fr)

7 gr g Kendargent - Moranda (Indian Rocket)

Andrew Balding   King Power Racing Co Ltd

PLACINGS: 7/1432/30521/184821-   RPR **119**

Starts		1st	2nd	3rd	4th	Win & Pl
20		7	3	2	3	£236,472
	10/19	Asct	1m4f Cls1 Gp3 soft			£34,026
	5/19	Ches	1m5¹/₂f Cls1 Gp3 soft			£56,710
	10/18	Newb	1m4f Cls1 Gp3 gd-sft			£23,463
	7/17	Wind	1m Cls1 List gd-sft			£20,983
96	9/16	Ayr	1m Cls2 87-101 Hcap gd-sft			£15,563
86	6/16	Ches	7¹/₂f Cls3 62-86 3yo Hcap good			£12,450
	5/16	Wind	1m Cls5 Mdn 3-4yo good			£2,911

Has developed into a high-class middle-distance performer since being stepped up in trip at the end of 2018; has form figures of 121 over 1m4f or beyond on soft ground, with two Group 3 wins last year by six lengths or more; disappointing in both runs at Group 1 level.

Mount Everest (Ire)

4 b c Galileo - Six Perfections (Celtic Swing)

Aidan O'Brien (Ir)   Flaxman Stables, Sue Magnier, M Tabor, D Smith

PLACINGS: 6212/44160-   RPR **112**+

Starts		1st	2nd	3rd	4th	Win & Pl
9		2	2	-	2	£91,986
	10/19	Leop	1m2f List sft-hvy			£23,919
	8/18	Curr	1m Mdn 2yo good			£9,540

Once seen as a potential Derby horse (stable first string when just pipped by Japan in the 2018 Beresford) but missed much of last season with injury; ran five times during a busy autumn,

including a Listed win at Leopardstown and a fast-finishing sixth in the Breeders' Cup Turf.

Mums Tipple (Ire)

3 ch c Footstepsinthesand - Colomone Cross (Xaar)

Richard Hannon   Marian Lyons & Patricia Zanelli

PLACINGS: 117-   RPR **118**+

Starts		1st	2nd	3rd	4th	Win & Pl
3		2	-	-	-	£159,990
	8/19	York	6f Cls2 2yo good			£147,540
	7/19	Asct	6f Cls2 Mdn 2yo gd-fm			£12,450

Produced one of the most spectacular performances of last season when running away with a valuable sales race at York by 11 lengths; flopped on his only run in Group company in the Middle Park but reportedly returned lame and might be worth another chance.

Mustashry

7 b/br g Tamayuz - Safwa (Green Desert)

Sir Michael Stoute   Hamdan Al Maktoum

PLACINGS: 24/0117/12110/31751-   RPR **122**

Starts		1st	2nd	3rd	4th	Win & Pl
21		9	3	1	2	£589,409
	10/19	NmkR	7f Cls2 Gp2 gd-sft			£68,052
	5/19	Newb	1m Cls1 Gp1 good			£198,485
	9/18	NmkR	1m Cls1 Gp2 gd-fm			£56,710
	9/18	Donc	7f Cls1 Gp2 good			£61,417
	7/18	Sand	1m2f Cls1 List gd-fm			£22,684
	8/17	York	1m1f Cls1 Gp3 good			£51,039
105	8/17	Chmd	1m Cls2 93-105 Hcap stand			£32,345
95	7/16	Asct	1m Cls2 80-98 3yo Hcap gd-fm			£28,013
	5/16	Thsk	1m Cls5 Mdn good			£3,235

Has got better with age and made his Group 1 breakthrough last season in the Lockinge Stakes; perhaps flattered by that win but still proved himself a high-class and versatile performer when dropping back to 7f to add the Challenge Stakes having won over as far as 1m2f in 2018.

Mutamaasik

4 ch g Dubawi - Muhawalah (Nayef)

Roger Varian   Hamdan Al Maktoum

PLACINGS: 21111-   RPR **107**

Starts		1st	2nd	3rd	4th	Win & Pl
5		4	1	-	-	£30,418
97	9/19	Donc	7f Cls2 81-97 3yo Hcap gd-fm			£12,450
87	8/19	NmkJ	7f Cls4 70-87 3yo Hcap good			£5,822
	8/19	Chmd	7f Cls4 stand			£6,469
	6/19	Wolv	7f Cls5 stand			£3,752

Tremendously progressive last season, winning last four races; coped with a 10lb rise and quicker ground when signing off with a game victory at Doncaster (just four runners); raised just 3lb for that and could have another handicap in him before sights are raised.

Mythical (Fr)

3 b c Camelot - Inchmina (Cape Cross)

Aidan O'Brien (Ir)   Sue Magnier, Michael Tabor & Derrick Smith

PLACINGS: 6143-					RPR **103+**

Starts	1st	2nd	3rd	4th	Win & Pl
4	1	-	1	1	£37,917
	9/19	Gowr	1m Mdn 2yo soft		£8,785

Looked a top prospect when running away with a Gowran Park maiden last September but didn't quite build on that when only fourth (2-1 favourite) in the Zetland Stakes next time; did a bit better when third in a Group 1 at Saint-Cloud; should stay well.

Nayef Road (Ire)

4 ch c Galileo - Rose Bonheur (Danehill Dancer)

Mark Johnston   Mohamed Obaida

PLACINGS: 291173/165321537-					RPR **113**

Starts	1st	2nd	3rd	4th	Win & Pl
15	4	2	3	-	£279,657
	8/19	Gdwd	1m4f Cls1 Gp3 3yo good		£99,243
96	5/19	NmkR	1m2f Cls3 83-96 3yo Hcap good		£12,938
85	8/18	NmkJ	7f Cls4 80-92 2yo Hcap gd-fm		£9,704
	8/18	Hayd	7f Cls4 2yo gd-fm		£7,116

Solid performer in several middle-distance/staying Group races last season, including when third in the St Leger; had won one of the key trials in the Gordon Stakes as well as finishing second in the Bahrain Trophy and third in the Queen's Vase; should stay 2m.

New York Girl (Ire)

3 ch f New Approach - Annee Lumiere (Giant's Causeway)

Joseph O'Brien (Ir)   Healthy Wood Co Limited

PLACINGS: 41-					RPR **105**

Starts	1st	2nd	3rd	4th	Win & Pl
2	1	-	-	1	£36,487
	9/19	Curr	7f Gp3 2yo heavy		£35,878

Did remarkably well to win the Group 3 Park Stakes at the Curragh on just her second run last season having learned a lot from her debut fourth; finished strongly on heavy ground and should improve over further (dam was Listed-placed over 1m2½f).

Old Persian

5 b h Dubawi - Indian Petal (Singspiel)

Charlie Appleby   Godolphin

PLACINGS: 3117/1211615/117310-					RPR **122**

Starts	1st	2nd	3rd	4th	Win & Pl
17	9	1	2	-	£3,409,618
	9/19	Wood	1m4f Gd1 good		£103,448
	3/19	Meyd	1m4f Gp1 good		£2,834,646
	3/19	Meyd	1m4f Gp2 good		£141,732
	8/18	York	1m4f Cls1 Gp2 3yo gd-fm		£96,407
	6/18	Asct	1m4f Cls1 Gp2 3yo gd-fm		£127,598
	5/18	NmkR	1m2f Cls1 List 3yo gd-fm		£22,684
94	4/18	NmkR	1m2f Cls3 79-94 3yo Hcap good		£12,938
	10/17	NmkR	1m Cls4 2yo good		£4,528
	9/17	Chmd	1m Cls4 2yo stand		£7,439

Built on a strong three-year-old campaign when winning last year's Dubai Sheema Classic but failed to show the same form when back

Old Persian: globetrotter can continue to be a force at 1m4f

159

in Europe; made the most of a soft opening in Canada when odds-on to win a Grade 1 and disappointed again at the Breeders' Cup.

On The Warpath
5 ch g Declaration Of War - Elusive Pearl (Medaglia D'Oro)
Charlie Appleby   Godolphin

PLACINGS: 4211/52/23121-   RPR **115**

Starts	1st	2nd	3rd	4th	Win & Pl
11	4	4	1	1	£163,187
102	5/19	NmkR	6f Cls2 88-109 Hcap good		£31,125
97	2/19	Meyd	7f 96-104 Hcap good		£82,677
	12/17	Sthl	7f Cls5 2yo stand		£2,911
	11/17	Sthl	7f Cls5 2yo stand		£2,911

Missed much of last season but was going from strength to strength before layoff, taking a massive step forward when running away with a valuable handicap at Newmarket's Guineas meeting on his first run over 6f; could be a Pattern sprinter.

One Master
6 b m Fastnet Rock - Enticing (Pivotal)
William Haggas   Lael Stable

PLACINGS: 311/4341158/432512-   RPR **117**

Starts	1st	2nd	3rd	4th	Win & Pl
16	5	2	3	3	£721,828
	10/19	Lonc	7f Gp1 v soft		£180,171
	10/18	Lonc	7f Gp1 good		£176,982
	8/18	Tipp	7¹/₂f Gp3 gd-yld		£33,938
	10/17	Asct	7f Cls1 List gd-sft		£22,684
	9/17	Yarm	6f Cls5 Mdn soft		£3,558

Top-class mare who has won the last two runnings of the Prix de la Foret at Longchamp; also proved her class at a mile when second in the Falmouth Stakes and third in the Queen Anne last season before dropping in trip to come second in the Champions Sprint.

Outbox
5 b g Frankel - Emirates Queen (Street Cry)
Simon Crisford   Sheikh Mohammed Obaid Al Maktoum

PLACINGS: 111/26233-   RPR **111**

Starts	1st	2nd	3rd	4th	Win & Pl
8	3	2	2	-	£77,136
	10/18	Newb	1m5¹/₂f Cls2 2yo gd-sft		£32,345
	9/18	Leic	1m4f Cls4 good		£5,175
	9/18	Ffos	1m4f Cls5 gd-fm		£3,817

Won all three runs as a three-year-old in 2018 but just failed to get on the scoreboard

last season, finishing second by a head and a neck; form tailed off after second near miss at Goodwood but trainer retains every faith he can develop into a high-class stayer.

Oxted
4 b g Mayson - Charlotte Rosina (Choisir)
Roger Teal   S Piper, T Hirschfeld & D Fish

PLACINGS: 5/126421-   RPR **115**

Starts	1st	2nd	3rd	4th	Win & Pl
7	2	2			£67,581
105	9/19	Donc	5¹/₂f Cls2 90-106 Hcap gd-fm		£37,350
	4/19	Sals	7f Cls5 3yo gd-fm		£5,111

Lightly raced sprinter who won last year's Portland Handicap at Doncaster on just his seventh run; relished quick ground that day having twice disappointed on soft during the summer but largely progressive otherwise; likely to be aimed at Group races.

Pablo Escobarr (Ire)
4 b c Galileo - Bewitched (Dansili)
William Haggas   Hussain Alabbas Lootah

PLACINGS: 2421/22521-2   RPR **112**

Starts	1st	2nd	3rd	4th	Win & Pl
10	2	6	-	1	£107,155
	12/19	Kemp	1m4f Cls1 List std-slw		£25,520
	9/18	Gdwd	1m2f Cls3 Mdn 2yo gd-sft		£11,972

Improved when back from a wind operation late last year, chasing home Lord North at Newmarket and winning a Listed race at Kempton; had shown useful form early in the season (fifth in the King Edward VII Stakes) and could do better in 1m4f Group races.

Palace Pier
3 b c Kingman - Beach Frolic (Nayef)
John Gosden   Sheikh Hamdan Bin Mohammed Al Maktoum

PLACINGS: 11-   RPR **96+**

Starts	1st	2nd	3rd	4th	Win & Pl
2	2	-	-	-	£12,549
	9/19	Sand	7f Cls3 2yo good		£7,763
	8/19	Sand	7f Cls4 Mdn 2yo gd-fm		£4,787

Potential star miler who made a big impression in two wins over 7f at Sandown last season but missed bigger autumn targets after suffering a tibia injury; trainer still hopeful of getting him back for the Greenham with a view to a crack at the 2,000 Guineas.

Passion (Ire)
3 b f Galileo - Dialafara (Anabaa)
Aidan O'Brien (Ir)   Sue Magnier, Michael Tabor & Derrick Smith

PLACINGS: 517-   RPR **92**

Starts	1st	2nd	3rd	4th	Win & Pl
3	1	-	-	-	£9,097
	9/19	Cork	1m Mdn 2yo yield		£8,785

Impressive winner on her second run at Cork

MY **FIVE** TO WATCH

Simon Turner, RPRs

●Lismore ●Rebel Soldier Boy ●The Perfect Crown ●Throne Hall ●Ustath

CAVALOR®
WHEN THE RESULT COUNTS

> FOR PULMONARY SUPPORT AND ELASTICITY

www.cavalor.com | Consumer line 7/7 +44 (0)1352 746100

Pinatubo: hugely exciting colt is favourite for the 2,000 Guineas

last season and wouldn't have been beaten far in the May Hill Stakes but for being badly hampered at the furlong pole, eventually coming home seventh; should benefit from middle distances.

Peaceful (Ire)

3 b/br f Galileo - Missvinski (Stravinsky)

Aidan O'Brien (Ir)   Michael Tabor, Derrick Smith & Sue Magnier

PLACINGS: 912-   RPR **101 +**

Starts	1st	2nd	3rd	4th	Win & Pl
3	1	1	-	-	£14,436
	10/19	Thur	1m Mdn 2yo yld-sft		£7,986

Seven-length winner of a Thurles maiden second time out last season and ran well when stepped up to Listed grade after that, finishing a neck second to smart prospect Born With Pride;

stayed on strongly that day but not certain to get much beyond a mile on pedigree.

Persian King (Ire)

4 b c Kingman - Pretty Please (Dylan Thomas)

Andre Fabre (Fr)   Godolphin & Ballymore Thoroughbred Ltd

PLACINGS: 2111/112-   RPR **117**

Starts	1st	2nd	3rd	4th	Win & Pl
7	5	2	-	-	£724,040
	5/19	Lonc	1m Gp1 3yo heavy		£308,865
	4/19	Lonc	1m Gp3 3yo good		£36,036
	10/18	NmkR	1m Cls1 Gp3 2yo gd-fm		£34,026
	9/18	Chan	1m 2yo good		£19,469
	9/18	Chan	1m 2yo gd-sft		£11,947

Super colt who completed a five-timer when winning last season's French 2,000 Guineas before chasing home Sottsass when stepped up in trip for the Prix du Jockey Club; finished sore

after that race and missed the rest of the season; trainer considering options from 1m to 1m2f.

Pierre Lapin (Ire)

3 b c Cappella Sansevero - Beatrix Potter (Cadeaux Genereux)
Roger Varian   Sheikh Mohammed Obaid Al Maktoum

PLACINGS: 11-   RPR **112+**

Starts	1st	2nd	3rd	4th	Win & Pl
2	2	-	-	-	£49,001
9/19	Newb	6f Cls1 Gp2 2yo gd-fm			£42,533
5/19	Hayd	6f Cls4 2yo gd-fm			£6,469

Restricted to just two runs last season having not taken his debut run well but still managed to defy a long layoff to follow up in the Mill Reef Stakes, winning well despite racing keenly and looking green; regarded as a sprinter by his trainer, though worth a try over 7f.

Pinatubo (Ire)

3 b c Shamardal - Lava Flow (Dalakhani)
Charlie Appleby   Godolphin

PLACINGS: 111111-   RPR **128+**

Starts	1st	2nd	3rd	4th	Win & Pl
6	6	-	-	-	£714,691
10/19	NmkR	7f Cls1 Gp1 2yo soft			£302,690
9/19	Curr	7f Gp1 2yo good			£205,405
7/19	Gdwd	7f Cls1 Gp2 2yo good			£113,420
6/19	Asct	7f Cls1 List 2yo good			£51,039
5/19	Epsm	6f Cls2 2yo good			£37,350
5/19	Wolv	6f Cls4 2yo stand			£4,787

Brilliant unbeaten colt who produced the highest-rated two-year-old performance in 25 years when winning last season's National Stakes at the Curragh by nine lengths; followed up by adding the Dewhurst, proving ability on soft ground; red-hot 2,000 Guineas favourite.

Pocket Square
3 ch f Night Of Thunder - Shared Account (Dansili)

Roger Charlton   K Abdullah

PLACINGS: 311-   RPR **107+**

Starts	1st	2nd	3rd	4th	Win & Pl
3	2	-	-	-	£43,273
	10/19	Deau	1m Gp3 2yo heavy		£36,036
	9/19	Asct	1m Cls4 2yo gd-fm		£6,728

Progressed nicely in three runs last season, signing off with an impressive Group 3 victory at Deauville in October; proved her versatility that day by handling very heavy ground (Ascot win had come on good to firm); should stay at least 1m2f.

Positive
3 b c Dutch Art - Osipova (Makfi)

Clive Cox   A D Spence

PLACINGS: 1216-   RPR **109**

Starts	1st	2nd	3rd	4th	Win & Pl
4	2	1	-	-	£83,671
	8/19	Sand	7f Cls1 Gp3 2yo gd-fm		£28,355
	6/19	Sals	7f Cls4 Mdn 2yo gd-fm		£5,111

Beaten only by the mighty Pinatubo in first three races last season and did particularly well to win a very strong Solario Stakes over Kameko and Al Suhail; major disappointment when third favourite for the Dewhurst, appearing to hate the soft ground.

Powerful Breeze
3 b f Iffraaj - Power Of Light (Echo Of Light)

Hugo Palmer   Dr Ali Ridha

PLACINGS: 112-   RPR **114+**

Starts	1st	2nd	3rd	4th	Win & Pl
3	2	1	-	-	£166,884
	9/19	Donc	1m Cls1 Gp2 2yo gd-fm		£39,697
	8/19	NmkJ	7f Cls4 2yo gd-fm		£5,175

Exciting filly who won last season's May Hill Stakes at Doncaster and nearly followed up in the Fillies' Mile, just getting overhauled by Quadrilateral; had excuses that day (got loose in the paddock and was keen); misses first half of the season with a setback but remains exciting.

Prince Eiji
4 ch c Dubawi - Izzi Top (Pivotal)

Roger Varian   Sheikh Mohammed Obaid Al Maktoum

PLACINGS: 135/43-   RPR **108**

Starts	1st	2nd	3rd	4th	Win & Pl
5	1	-	2	1	£24,397
	9/18	Asct	7f Cls3 Mdn 2yo good		£7,763

Yet to come close to justifying 2.6 million guineas he cost as a yearling but has been very lightly raced and finished third at Group level for the second time on final run last season; better than the bare form of that Darley Stakes effort after missing nearly the whole year.

Promissory (Ire)
4 b f Dubawi - Seal Of Approval (Authorized)

John Gosden   Princess Haya Of Jordan

PLACINGS: 3123-   RPR **104**

Starts	1st	2nd	3rd	4th	Win & Pl
4	1	1	2	-	£34,173
	7/19	Donc	1m4f Cls4 gd-fm		£5,208

Lightly raced filly who was a hugely impressive five-length novice winner on just her second start last year; twice beaten at Group 3 level subsequently but sent off odds-on on the second occasion at Newmarket and can be forgiven that defeat (reportedly lost her action).

Qarasu (Ire)
4 br g Le Havre - Bella Qatara (Dansili)

Roger Charlton   Sheikh Mohammed bin Khalifa Al Thani

PLACINGS: 2/3151225-   RPR **109**

Starts	1st	2nd	3rd	4th	Win & Pl
8	2	3	1	-	£25,915
85	8/19	Newb	1m2f Cls4 73-85 Hcap soft		£5,208
	6/19	Wind	1m2f Cls5 soft		£3,752

Held in such high regard he was sent off favourite for last six runs last season, though he won just twice; most impressive when a four-length handicap winner at Newbury and ran well when second the next twice over 1m2f, both times looking a likely improver over further.

Quadrilateral
3 ch f Frankel - Nimble Thimble (Mizzen Mast)

Roger Charlton   K Abdullah

PLACINGS: 111-   RPR **115+**

Starts	1st	2nd	3rd	4th	Win & Pl
3	3	-	-	-	£336,564
	10/19	NmkR	1m Cls1 Gp1 2yo gd-sft		£321,829
	9/19	Newb	7f Cls2 2yo good		£10,271
	8/19	Newb	7f Cls4 Mdn 2yo gd-sft		£4,464

Shot to 1,000 Guineas favouritism with impressive nine-length win at Newbury last season and just about lived up to her billing with narrow win in the Fillies' Mile; set to return to Newmarket for the Guineas but could then step up in trip and looks sure to stay at least 1m2f.

Queen Daenerys (Ire)
3 b f Frankel - Song To Remember (Storm Cat)

Roger Varian   Sh Nasser bin Hamad Al Khalifa

PLACINGS: 216-   RPR **103+**

Starts	1st	2nd	3rd	4th	Win & Pl
3	1	1	-	-	£14,838
	9/19	NmkR	1m Cls4 2yo gd-fm		£5,175

Thrown in at the deep end in last season's Fillies' Mile and stayed on promisingly in sixth, looking sure to improve when stepped up to middle distances; had beaten a previous winner (pair clear) on a much quicker surface at Newmarket previously.

Queen Power (Ire)
4 ch f Shamardal - Princess Serena (Unbridled's Song)

Sir Michael Stoute   King Power Racing Co Ltd

PLACINGS: 1/2144-					RPR **103**
Starts	1st	2nd	3rd	4th	Win & Pl
5	2	1	-	2	£65,087
5/19	Newb	1m2f Cls1 List 3yo good			£39,697
10/18	NmkR	7f Cls3 Mdn 2yo gd-fm			£7,763

Claimed some big scalps, including three-time Group 1 winner Star Catcher, when winning a Listed race at Newbury last May; didn't quite build on that in just two runs subsequently, though still a fair fourth in the Ribblesdale Stakes; in good hands to progress again.

Quorto (Ire)
4 b c Dubawi - Volume (Mount Nelson)

Charlie Appleby   Godolphin

PLACINGS: 111/					RPR **122**
Starts	1st	2nd	3rd	4th	Win & Pl
3	3			-	£227,091
9/18	Curr	7f Gp1 2yo gd-yld			£176,549
7/18	NmkJ	7f Cls1 Gp2 2yo gd-fm			£45,368
6/18	NmkJ	6f Cls4 2yo gd-fm			£5,175

Outstanding unbeaten two-year-old in 2018, winning three times including a ready defeat of last year's Derby hero Anthony Van Dyck in the National Stakes; missed last season through injury but could yet make up for lost time in Group 1 races from 1m-1m2f.

Raakib Alhawa (Ire)
4 b c Kingman - Starlet (Sea The Stars)

David Simcock   Khalifa Dasmal

PLACINGS: 10/7515-					RPR **109**
Starts	1st	2nd	3rd	4th	Win & Pl
6	2		-	-	£33,901
8/19	Wind	1m3½f Cls1 List gd-fm			£20,983
9/18	Newb	1m Cls2 2yo gd-sft			£9,960

Proved a revelation when stepped up beyond a mile for the first time last season, easily winning a Listed race at Windsor on good to firm ground; might not have appreciated the return to soft when only fifth in a Group 3 at Ascot next time; still unexposed over middle distances.

Raffle Prize (Ire)
3 ch f Slade Power - Summer Fete (Pivotal)

Mark Johnston   Sheikh Hamdan Bin Mohammed Al Maktoum

PLACINGS: 211122-					RPR **114**
Starts	1st	2nd	3rd	4th	Win & Pl
6	3	3		-	£255,887
7/19	NmkJ	6f Cls1 Gp2 2yo gd-fm			£45,368
6/19	Asct	5f Cls1 Gp2 2yo gd-sft			£62,381
5/19	Ches	6f Cls2 Mdn 2yo good			£11,828

Top-class performer last season and unlucky not to bag a Group 1 to add to a pair of impressive Group 2 successes in the Queen Mary and Duchess of Cambridge Stakes; ran Earthlight close in the Prix Morny and might have done too much in front when second in the Cheveley Park.

Raffle Prize: Group 1 victory could be hers for the taking

Regal Reality

5 b g Intello - Regal Realm (Medicean)

Sir Michael Stoute   Cheveley Park Stud

PLACINGS: 1/6133/313458-   RPR **121**

Starts	1st	2nd	3rd	4th	Win & Pl
11	3	-	4	1	£245,487

5/19	Sand	1m2f Cls1 Gp3 gd-fm			£39,697
8/18	Gdwd	1m Cls1 Gp3 3yo gd-fm			£56,710
9/17	Yarm	7f Cls4 Mdn 2yo soft			£4,528

Good-looking, imposing horse who hasn't quite produced the form to match apparent potential, winning only two Group 3 races in the last two years and finishing no better than third in six attempts at a higher level; lost his way after last year's Eclipse third but has since been gelded.

Romanised (Ire)

5 b h Holy Roman Emperor - Romantic Venture (Indian Ridge)

Ken Condon (Ir)   Robert Ng

PLACINGS: 1762/61759/544112-   RPR **119**

Starts	1st	2nd	3rd	4th	Win & Pl
15	4	2	-	2	£975,747

8/19	Deau	1m Gp1 good			£514,775
7/19	Curr	7f Gp2 good			£63,784
5/18	Curr	1m Gp1 3yo gd-fm			£206,195
4/17	Navn	6f Mdn 2yo good			£8,687

In terrific form at the end of last year, belatedly proving shock win in the 2018 Irish 2,000 Guineas was no fluke; gained first win since then in a 7f Group 2 at the Curragh before adding the Prix Jacques le Marois and looking unlucky not to be awarded the Prix du Moulin.

Rose Of Kildare (Ire)

3 b f Make Believe - Cruck Realta (Sixties Icon)

Mark Johnston   Kingsley Park 14

PLACINGS: 241128513411-   RPR **104**

Starts	1st	2nd	3rd	4th	Win & Pl
12	5	2	1	2	£115,483

	10/19	NmkR	7f Cls1 Gp3 2yo gd-sft		£34,026
	9/19	Ayr	6f Cls1 Gp3 2yo good		£36,862
81	8/19	NmkJ	6f Cls2 67-87 2yo Hcap gd-fm		£16,178
	5/19	Haml	5f Cls4 Auct 2yo gd-sft		£5,434
	5/19	Rdcr	6f Cls4 Auct 2yo gd-fm		£5,822

Kept very busy last season and went from strength to strength, signing off with a pair of Group 3 victories; looked particularly good when stepped back up to 7f to win the Oh So Sharp Stakes under a penalty, albeit in what looked a modest race for the grade.

*Regal Reality:
Brigadier Gerard
Stakes winner has
been gelded since
his last appearance
on the track*

Roseman (Ire)

4 b c Kingman - Go Lovely Rose (Pivotal)

Roger Varian   Sheikh Mohammed Obaid Al Maktoum

PLACINGS: 31251-   RPR **117**

Starts	1st	2nd	3rd	4th	Win & Pl
5	2	1	1	-	£36,707
11/19	NmkR	1m Cls1 List heavy			£20,983
4/19	Nott	1m¹/₂f Cls5 3yo gd-sft			£3,881

Lightly raced colt who broke through at Listed level when storming to a wide-margin win at Newmarket last November; saw out a mile well on heavy ground and might be better over 1m2f on quicker (given too much to do when fifth at Royal Ascot on previous attempt at the trip).

Royal Crusade

3 b c Shamardal - Zibelina (Dansili)

Charlie Appleby   Godolphin

PLACINGS: 122-   RPR **111**

Starts	1st	2nd	3rd	4th	Win & Pl
3	1	2	-	-	£35,714
8/19	NmkJ	7f Cls4 2yo gd-fm			£5,175

Looked a top prospect when a neck second to Threat in the Champagne Stakes last season on just his second run having overcome greenness to comfortably make a winning debut at Newmarket; took a backwards step when well beaten by King's Command at Saint-Cloud.

Royal Dornoch (Ire)

3 b c Gleneagles - Bridal Dance (Danehill Dancer)

Aidan O'Brien (Ir)   Michael Tabor, Derrick Smith & Sue Magnier

PLACINGS: 0237151-   RPR **112**

Starts	1st	2nd	3rd	4th	Win & Pl
7	2	1	2	-	£105,791
9/19	NmkR	1m Cls1 Gp2 2yo good			£70,888
9/19	Gowr	7f Mdn 2yo yield			£8,785

Patchy record but much improved when stepped up to a mile to win the Royal Lodge, although probably flattered by bare form (runner-up Kameko still very green in front and third-placed Iberia beaten favourite next time); not guaranteed to get middle distances on pedigree.

Royal Line

6 ch h Dubawi - Melikah (Lammtarra)

John Gosden   Sheikha Al Jalila Racing

PLACINGS: 1137/311/4135-   RPR **115**

	Starts	1st	2nd	3rd	4th	Win & Pl
	11	5	-	3	1	£166,808
105	9/19	Kemp	1m4f Cls1 Gp3 std-slw			£39,697
105	11/18	Donc	1m4f Cls2 91-107 Hcap soft			£43,575
95	4/18	Epsm	1m4f Cls3 81-96 Hcap good			£15,563
88	9/17	Hayd	1m4f Cls3 80-94 Hcap heavy			£9,338
	9/17	Wind	1m3¹/₂f Cls5 Mdn 3yo gd-sft			£2,976

Has steadily climbed the ladder despite limited opportunities on his preferred soft ground in the last two seasons, gaining sole win last year in a Group 3 at Kempton before a fine third when up in trip for the Long Distance Cup; lightly raced for his age and remains capable of better.

Royal Lytham (second right): kicks off his career by winning a Navan maiden

Royal Lytham (Fr)

3 b c Gleneagles - Gotlandia (Anabaa)

Aidan O'Brien (Ir)   Michael Tabor, Derrick Smith & Sue Magnier

PLACINGS: 1713-					RPR **112**
Starts	1st	2nd	3rd	4th	Win & Pl
4	2	-	1	-	£78,849
7/19	NmkJ	6f Cls1 Gp2 2yo gd-fm			£45,368
6/19	Navn	5½f Mdn 2yo gd-yld			£9,157

Gutsy winner of the Group 2 July Stakes at Newmarket last season, although form proved only moderate for the grade; probably achieved a little more when a length third behind Siskin in the Phoenix; yet to race beyond 6f but always expected to stay further.

Safe Voyage (Ire)

7 b g Fast Company - Shishangaan (Mujadil)

John Quinn   Ross Harmon

PLACINGS: **1102414/110/1113343-**					RPR **117**
Starts	1st	2nd	3rd	4th	Win & Pl
23	9	1	3	3	£341,924
6/19	Hayd	7f Cls1 Gp3 heavy			£35,727
5/19	Hayd	7f Cls1 List gd-sft			£20,983
103 4/19	Hayd	7f Cls2 88-105 Hcap soft			£28,013
99 8/18	Gway	7f 82-102 Hcap yield			£52,212
88 4/18	Hayd	7f Cls2 88-105 Hcap soft			£28,013
84 6/17	Ayr	7f Cls4 71-84 Hcap good			£5,822
75 1/17	Newc	7f Cls4 69-79 Hcap stand			£4,852
75 1/17	Newc	7f Cls5 63-75 App Hcap stand			£2,911
67 7/16	Thsk	6f Cls5 51-70 App Hcap gd-sft			£2,911

Progressive again last season, making it five wins out of six since the start of 2018 with an early-season hat-trick at Haydock, all over 7f; went on to make the frame in four races at a higher level, most notably when a 40-1 third in the QEII; needs soft ground.

San Donato (Ire)

4 b c Lope De Vega - Boston Rocker (Acclamation)

Roger Varian   Sheikh Mohammed Obaid Al Maktoum

PLACINGS: 28111/3-					RPR **112**
Starts	1st	2nd	3rd	4th	Win & Pl
6	3	1	1	-	£92,034
10/18	Donc	6f Cls1 List 2yo gd-sft			£17,013
9/18	Kemp	6f Cls5 2yo std-slw			£3,881
9/18	Hayd	6f Cls4 2yo gd-sft			£6,469

Back in training after missing most of last season, running just once when a fine third behind Persian King in the French 2,000 Guineas; maintained upward curve after winning last three races as a two-year-old in 2018 and could be a leading miler.

Sands Of Mali (Fr)

5 b h Panis - Kadiania (Indian Rocket)

Richard Fahey   Phoenix Thoroughbred & Cool Silk P'Ship

PLACINGS: 71109/1120051/6300-					RPR **103**
Starts	1st	2nd	3rd	4th	Win & Pl
16	5	1	1	-	£726,220
10/18	Asct	6f Cls1 Gp1 soft			£358,691
5/18	Hayd	6f Cls1 Gp2 3yo good			£51,039
4/18	Chan	6f Gp3 3yo heavy			£35,398
8/17	York	6f Cls1 Gp2 2yo good			£127,598
8/17	Nott	6f Cls5 2yo soft			£3,235

Won the 2018 Champions Sprint at Ascot, underlining love of that track after Commonwealth Cup second in the summer; disappointing in just three runs last term but had ground go against him at Royal Ascot and lost a shoe when fading out of contention in the Champions Sprint.

Sangarius

4 b c Kingman - Trojan Queen (Empire Maker)

Sir Michael Stoute · K Abdullah

PLACINGS: 114/31- · RPR **114+**

Starts	1st	2nd	3rd	4th	Win & Pl
5	3	-	1	1	£104,331
	6/19	Asct	1m2f Cls1 Gp3 3yo soft		£51,039
	9/18	Donc	7f Cls1 List 2yo gd-sft		£17,013
	8/18	NmkJ	7f Cls4 2yo gd-fm		£5,175

Long held in high regard (fourth in the Dewhurst in 2018) and began to live up to his billing when stepped up to 1m2f at Royal Ascot last season, running away with the Hampton Court Stakes; missed the rest of the season but remains open to improvement and likely to have Group 1 races on his agenda.

Satono Japan (Jpn)

3 b c Deep Impact - Dubawi Heights (Dubawi)

Sir Michael Stoute · Satomi Horse Company Ltd

PLACINGS: 1- · RPR **80+** aw

Starts	1st	2nd	3rd	4th	Win & Pl
1	1	-	-	-	£3,881
	10/19	Kemp	7f Cls5 2yo std-slw		£3,881

Out of a dual US Grade 1 winner and fetched £1.37 million as a yearling; suggested that might be money well spent with a hugely impressive winning debut at Kempton, quickening up smartly over 7f; should thrive over a mile and perhaps slightly further.

Scentasia

4 b f Cape Cross - Sweet Rose (New Approach)

John Gosden · Sheikh Juma Dalmook Al Maktoum

PLACINGS: 34/32151011- · RPR **101+**

Starts	1st	2nd	3rd	4th	Win & Pl
10	4	1	2	1	£61,012
	11/19	Ling	1m2f Cls1 List stand		£21,266
	10/19	Ling	1m Cls1 List std-slw		£22,684
87	9/19	Yarm	1m Cls3 82-90 3yo Hcap gd-fm		£7,876
79	8/19	Yarm	1m Cls4 72-81 Hcap gd-fm		£5,208

Fair miler on turf last summer, winning a couple of handicaps at Yarmouth, but then took a massive step forward when winning two Listed races from 1m-1m2f on the all-weather at Lingfield; should thrive if translating that improvement back on to turf.

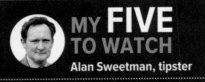
Sea Of Faith (Ire)

4 b f Sea The Stars - Jumooh (Monsun)

William Haggas · Sunderland Holding Inc

PLACINGS: 45131- · RPR **107**

Starts	1st	2nd	3rd	4th	Win & Pl
5	2	-	1	1	£28,639
95	8/19	Sals	1m4f Cls2 85-95 Hcap gd-sft		£18,675
	6/19	Donc	1m4f Cls5 Mdn soft		£3,752

Very green for much of last season, often starting slowly, but showed huge promise in defeat and took a giant step forward when winning a fillies' handicap at Salisbury by three lengths on her final run; already looks good enough to make a mark at Pattern level.

Search For A Song (Ire)

4 ch f Galileo - Polished Gem (Danehill)

Dermot Weld (Ir) · Moyglare Stud Farm

PLACINGS: 12411- · RPR **118**

Starts	1st	2nd	3rd	4th	Win & Pl
5	3	1	-	1	£381,716
	9/19	Curr	1m6f Gp1 gd-fm		£308,108
	8/19	York	1m4f Cls1 List good		£39,697
	5/19	Fair	1m2f Mdn gd-fm		£6,659

Sharply progressive in five runs last season; fine fourth in the Irish Oaks before winning a Listed race at York and took another big step forward when easily landing the Irish St Leger; possibly flattered by that win (given too much rope in front) but should have more to come.

Sergei Prokofiev (Can)

4 b c Scat Daddy - Orchard Beach (Tapit)

Aidan O'Brien (Ir) · Derrick Smith & Sue Magnier & Michael Tabor

PLACINGS: 21135718/1406- · RPR **107**

Starts	1st	2nd	3rd	4th	Win & Pl
12	4	1	1	1	£137,454
	3/19	Navn	5½f List good		£23,919
	10/18	NmkR	5f Cls1 Gp3 2yo gd-fm		£34,026
	5/18	Naas	5f List 2yo gd-fm		£33,938
	4/18	Navn	5f 2yo yld-sft		£10,903

Looked to have found his niche when dropped back to 5f in the Cornwallis Stakes in 2018, winning in spectacular fashion, but failed to build on a first-time-out win at Navan last year; wouldn't be the first sprinter to bounce back from a disappointing three-year-old campaign.

Sextant

5 b g Sea The Stars - Hypoteneuse (Sadler's Wells)

Sir Michael Stoute · The Queen

PLACINGS: 212/1411412- · RPR **111**

Starts	1st	2nd	3rd	4th	Win & Pl
10	5	3	-	2	£101,606
	9/19	Ches	1m4½f Cls1 List good		£22,117
98	7/19	Asct	1m4f Cls2 86-98 Hcap gd-fm		£18,675
97	6/19	Wind	1m3½f Cls2 88-97 Hcap gd-fm		£12,450
89	5/19	Asct	1m4f Cls3 87-97 Hcap gd-sft		£16,173
	8/18	Newb	1m4f Cls3 Mdn 3yo good		£9,704

Progressive middle-distance performer last season, winning three handicaps before landing

Moorcroft
Racehorse Welfare Centre

PROVIDING THE
VERY BEST
OF CARE
FOR OUR WONDERFUL
HORSES AWAITING A NEW
HOME AND A NEW LIFE

This centre in the south of England was set up to ensure that retired racehorses whatever age, can be re-trained to find another career in life. Much care and attention is given to each individual horse and when fully retrained new homes are found. The centre retains ownership for life and visits these horses every year to ensure that all is well.

This charity depends on generous donations from horse lovers. Many horses need a time for rehabilitation due to injury etc and start to enjoy an easier life after their racing careers. Visits by appointment are welcomed. Please ring Mary Frances, Manager, on 07929 666408 for more information or to arrange a visit.

Huntingrove Stud, Slinfold, West Sussex RH13 0RB
Tel: 07929 666408 | moorcroftracehorse@gmail.com | www.moorcroftracehorse.org.uk

a Listed race at Chester; couldn't land a blow in two runs at Group 3 level but still managed a distant second behind Morando at Ascot; lightly raced and open to improvement.

Shabaaby

5 br g Kyllachy - On The Brink (Mind Games)

Owen Burrows   Hamdan Al Maktoum

PLACINGS: 3114/347/1-					RPR **112**
Starts	1st	2nd	3rd	4th	Win & Pl
8	3	-	2	2	£44,438
5/19	Hayd	6f Cls2 gd-sft			£14,006
9/17	Donc	6f Cls2 2yo good			£11,205
8/17	NmkJ	6f Cls4 2yo soft			£4,528

Promising sprinter who took a big step forward when winning at Haydock last season on his first run after being gelded; missed the rest of the season but back in training this spring and open to plenty of improvement.

Sharja Bridge

6 b g Oasis Dream - Quetena (Acatenango)

Roger Varian   Sheikh Mohammed Obaid Al Maktoum

PLACINGS: 3212/28471/12096-					RPR **115**
Starts	1st	2nd	3rd	4th	Win & Pl
14	3	1	1	1	£219,941
3/19	Donc	1m Cls1 List good			£20,983
105 10/18	Asct	1m Cls2 98-110 Hcap good			£155,625
8/17	Nott	1m¹/₂f Cls5 Mdn gd-sft			£3,235

Largely progressive miler who thrived early last season, winning the Doncaster Mile and going close in the Sandown Mile; given a gelding operation after twice flopping at Group I level, although did little better when last of six at Haydock on his return.

Shekhem (Ire)

3 ch c Zoffany - Shelina (Dalakhani)

Dermot Weld (Ir)   Aga Khan

PLACINGS: 72212-					RPR **107**
Starts	1st	2nd	3rd	4th	Win & Pl
5	1	3	-	-	£34,168
9/19	List	7f Mdn 2yo soft			£9,318

Unlucky to bump into Mogul and Innisfree in maidens last season before getting off the mark in good style at Listowel; took a big step forward when again pushing Innisfree close in the Beresford Stakes, perhaps unlucky having raced too keenly early on.

Shine So Bright

4 gr c Oasis Dream - Alla Speranza (Sir Percy)

Andrew Balding   King Power Racing Co Ltd

PLACINGS: 15333/16145-					RPR **114**
Starts	1st	2nd	3rd	4th	Win & Pl
10	3	-	3	1	£233,764
8/19	York	7f Cls1 Gp2 gd-fm			£127,598
106 4/19	NmkR	7f Cls1 List 100-110 3yo Hcap gd-fm			£28,355
6/18	Nott	5f Cls5 Mdn 2yo good			£3,881

High-class 7f performer who pipped Laurens for a thrilling success in last season's City of York Stakes; didn't get home on only run over a mile in the 2,000 Guineas and reportedly unsuited by softer ground when signing off with a disappointing run in the Challenge Stakes.

Sir Dancealot (Ire)

6 b g Sir Prancealot - Majesty's Dancer (Danehill Dancer)

David Elsworth   C Benham, D Whitford, L Quinn & K Quinn

PLACINGS: 31714119550/7414510-					RPR **119**
Starts	1st	2nd	3rd	4th	Win & Pl
35	10	3	2	3	£733,499
9/19	Donc	7f Cls1 Gp2 gd-fm			£61,332
7/19	Gdwd	7f Cls1 Gp2 good			£176,935
8/18	Newb	7f Cls1 Gp2 good			£85,065
7/18	Gdwd	7f Cls1 Gp2 good			£176,935
6/18	NmkJ	7f Cls1 Gp3 gd-fm			£34,026
6/18	Haml	6f Cls2 good			£16,808
10/17	Donc	7f Cls3 gd-sft			£9,338
10/16	York	6f Cls1 List 2yo good			£28,355
9/16	Kemp	7f Cls4 2yo std-slw			£3,946
8/16	Kemp	7f Mdn Auct 2yo std-slw			£3,946

Top-class 7f performer who has won five Group races at the trip in the last two seasons, including a second successive Lennox Stakes at Goodwood last year; 0-9 at Group I level, mainly in sprints, and twice disappointing when stepped up to a mile last year.

Sir Dragonet (Ire)

4 b c Camelot - Sparrow (Oasis Dream)

Aidan O'Brien (Ir)   Sue Magnier, Michael Tabor & Derrick Smith

PLACINGS: 11544-					RPR **117**
Starts	1st	2nd	3rd	4th	Win & Pl
5	2	-	-	2	£146,764
5/19	Ches	1m4¹/₂f Cls1 Gp3 3yo gd-sft			£56,710
4/19	Tipp	1m4¹/₂f Mdn 3yo yld-sft			£6,659

Surprised even connections with early performances last season, needing to be supplemented for the Derby after eight-length win in the Chester Vase; perhaps not quite as effective on quicker ground when fifth in the Derby and fourth in the St Leger.

Siskin: won four times at two, but had to be withdrawn from the Middle Park Stakes for being unruly in the stalls

Sir Ron Priestley

4 ch c Australia - Reckoning (Danehill Dancer)

Mark Johnston   Paul Dean

PLACINGS: 24/1101112-					RPR **114**
Starts	1st	2nd	3rd	4th	Win & Pl
9	5	2	-	1	£333,408
8/19	Gdwd	1m6f Cls1 Gp3 3yo good			£56,710
98 7/19	Gdwd	1m4f Cls2 88-100 3yo Hcap good			£46,688
94 7/19	Hayd	1m6f Cls2 74-95 3yo Hcap gd-fm			£62,250
86 5/19	Hayd	1m4f Cls3 83-88 3yo Hcap gd-fm			£10,583
4/19	Ripn	1m4f Cls5 3yo good			£3,881

Capped a remarkable campaign last season by finishing second behind Logician in the St Leger; had won five of previous six races, including three handicaps and a 1m6f Group 3 at Goodwood; sole flop when unsuited by softer ground at Royal Ascot.

Siskin (USA)

3 b/br c First Defence - Bird Flown (Oasis Dream)

Ger Lyons (Ir)   K Abdullah

PLACINGS: 1111-					RPR **115**
Starts	1st	2nd	3rd	4th	Win & Pl
4	4	-	-	-	£263,486
8/19	Curr	6f Gp1 2yo soft			£154,054
6/19	Curr	6f Gp2 2yo good			£69,099
5/19	Curr	6f List 2yo gd-fm			£29,234
5/19	Naas	6f 2yo good			£11,099

Unbeaten in four races last season but blotted his copybook slightly when having to be withdrawn from the Middle Park for being unruly in the stalls; had looked best on a quicker surface, notably in the Railway Stakes, but still did just enough to land the Phoenix on soft.

173

Skalleti (Fr)

5 gr g Kendargent - Skallet (Muhaymin)

Jerome Reynier (Fr)　　　　　　　　Jean-Claude Seroul

PLACINGS: 81111111-　　　　　　　　RPR **113+**

Starts	1st	2nd	3rd	4th	Win & Pl
8	7	-	-	-	£315,315
11/19	Capa	1m2f Gp2 heavy			£105,405
10/19	Lonc	1m2f Gp2 v soft			£102,703
8/19	Deau	1m Gp3 good			£36,036
7/19	Vich	1m List soft			£23,423
6/19	Ponv	1m2f slow			£22,523
5/19	Lonc	1m soft			£12,613
3/19	Chan	1m stand			£12,613

Proved a revelation last year when winning his last seven races, including Group 2s at Longchamp and Capannelle (both on very soft/heavy ground); will have Group I races on his agenda this year, with the Prince of Wales's Stakes a possibility.

Skardu

4 ch c Shamardal - Diala (Iffraaj)

William Haggas　　　　　　　　Abdulla Al Khalifa

PLACINGS: 1/13444-　　　　　　　　RPR **114+**

Starts	1st	2nd	3rd	4th	Win & Pl
6	2	-	-	3	£143,707
4/19	NmkR	1m Cls1 Gp3 3yo gd-fm			£34,026
9/18	NmkR	7f Cls4 Mdn 2yo gd-fm			£6,469

Not far off the best three-year-old milers last season but arguably a bit disappointing after winning the Craven Stakes on just his second run and doing best of those on the far side when third in the 2,000 Guineas; beaten favourite in the Celebration Mile on final run.

Sottsass (Fr)

4 ch c Siyouni - Starlet's Sister (Galileo)

Jean-Claude Rouget (Fr)　　　　　　　　White Birch Farm

PLACINGS: 41/51113-　　　　　　　　RPR **123**

Starts	1st	2nd	3rd	4th	Win & Pl
7	4	-	1	1	£1,396,498
9/19	Lonc	1m4f Gp2 3yo good			£66,757
6/19	Chan	1m2½f Gp1 3yo good			£772,162
5/19	Chan	1m2f List 3yo soft			£24,775
10/18	Claf	1m 2yo soft			£11,947

Probably the leading three-year-old middle-distance colt in Europe last season; beat Persian King in the Prix du Jockey Club and returned from a break to follow up in the Prix Niel; best

of the three-year-olds when third in the Arc and likely to have that race top of his agenda again.

Southern Hills (Ire)

3 ch c Gleneagles - Remember You (Invincible Spirit)

Aidan O'Brien (Ir)　　Sue Magnier, Michael Tabor & Derrick Smith

PLACINGS: 521-　　　　　　　　RPR **101**

Starts	1st	2nd	3rd	4th	Win & Pl
3	1	1	-	-	£55,127
6/19	Asct	5f Cls1 List 2yo soft			£51,039

Progressed rapidly early last season and got off the mark when winning the Windsor Castle Stakes at Royal Ascot on his third run; could prove better still back on quicker ground; missed the rest of the year but still expected to make up into a leading three-year-old sprinter this year.

Sovereign (Ire)

4 ch c Galileo - Devoted To You (Danehill Dancer)

Aidan O'Brien (Ir)　　Sue Magnier, Michael Tabor & Derrick Smith

PLACINGS: 56143/2301-　　　　　　　　RPR **117**

Starts	1st	2nd	3rd	4th	Win & Pl
9	2	1	2	1	£807,347
6/19	Curr	1m4f Gp1 3yo good			£770,270
9/18	Gway	1m¹/₂f Mdn 2yo heavy			£9,540

Surprise winner of a remarkable Irish Derby, beating Anthony Van Dyck by six lengths having been given too much rope in front; form particularly questionable given five previous defeats at Group level but seems best suited by 1m4f and deserves another chance to prove himself.

Space Blues (Ire)

4 ch c Dubawi - Miss Lucifer (Noverre)

Charlie Appleby　　　　　　　　Godolphin

PLACINGS: 1/4211223-　　　　　　　　RPR **116**

Starts	1st	2nd	3rd	4th	Win & Pl
8	3	3	1	1	£187,469
5/19	Epsm	7f Cls1 List 3yo good			£28,355
5/19	York	7f Cls3 74-93 3yo Hcap gd-fm			£12,450
11/18	Nott	1m¹/₂f Cls5 Mdn 2yo gd-sft			£3,881

Got better and better last season as he was dropped in trip having initially disappointed beyond a mile; won twice over 7f before finishing second in the Jersey Stakes and Prix Jean Prat; could even have a future as a sprinter judging by length third in the Prix Maurice de Gheest.

Space Traveller

4 b c Bated Breath - Sky Crystal (Galileo)

Richard Fahey　　　　　　　　Clipper Logistics

PLACINGS: 117287/23716318-　　　　　　　　RPR **114+**

Starts	1st	2nd	3rd	4th	Win & Pl
14	4	2	2	-	£229,692
9/19	Leop	1m Gp2 good			£106,306
6/19	Asct	7f Cls1 Gp3 3yo good			£51,039
7/18	Haml	5f Cls4 2yo gd-fm			£5,434
7/18	Donc	6¹/₂f Cls5 2yo gd-fm			£3,752

Surprise winner of last season's Jersey Stakes

over 7f at Royal Ascot and proved that was no fluke with a Group 2 victory over a mile at Leopardstown; previously campaigned as a sprinter but clearly better over further and still fairly unexposed as a miler.

Speak In Colours

5 gr h Excelebration - Maglietta Fina (Verglas)

Joseph O'Brien (Ir)   Mrs C C Regalado-Gonzalez

PLACINGS: 311/230170/24144136-   RPR **113+**

Starts	1st	2nd	3rd	4th	Win & Pl
17	5	2	3	3	£265,187
	9/19	Curr	6f Gp3 soft		£31,892
	6/19	Curr	6f List good		£39,865
	8/18	Curr	6f Gp3 good		£31,327
	10/17	Donc	6f Cls1 List 2yo gd-sft		£17,013
	9/17	Asct	6f Cls4 Auct 2yo soft		£6,469

Smart sprinter who won Group 3 and Listed races over 6f at the Curragh last season; also proved effective over 7f with three good runs in top races, including when third in the Prix de la Foret (highest finish in six career runs at Group 1 level).

Star Catcher

4 b f Sea The Stars - Lynnwood Chase (Horse Chestnut)

John Gosden   A E Oppenheimer

PLACINGS: 6/131111-   RPR **115**

Starts	1st	2nd	3rd	4th	Win & Pl
7	5	-	1	-	£961,164
	10/19	Asct	1m3¹/₂f Cls1 Gp1 soft		£311,905
	9/19	Lonc	1m4f Gp1 good		£308,865
	7/19	Curr	1m4f Gp1 3yo good		£205,405
	6/19	Asct	1m4f Cls1 Gp2 3yo soft		£121,927
	4/19	Newb	1m2f Cls4 Mdn 3yo soft		£5,531

Established herself as the best middle-distance filly of her generation last season with a hat-trick of Group 1 wins; dominated the Irish Oaks and Prix Vermeille from the front before showing more battling qualities to come from behind to win at Ascot on Champions Day.

Stradivarius (Ire)

6 ch h Sea The Stars - Private Life (Bering)

John Gosden   B E Nielsen

PLACINGS: 121133/11111/111112-   RPR **123+**

Starts	1st	2nd	3rd	4th	Win & Pl
20	14	2	2	1	£2,555,638
	9/19	Donc	2m2f Cls1 Gp2 gd-fm		£56,710
	8/19	York	2m¹/₂f Cls1 Gp2 gd-fm		£127,598
	7/19	Gdwd	2m Cls1 Gp1 good		£283,550
	6/19	Asct	2m4f Cls1 Gp1 good		£283,550
	5/19	York	1m6f Cls1 Gp2 gd-fm		£93,572
	10/18	Asct	2m Cls1 Gp2 soft		£300,563
	8/18	York	2m¹/₂f Cls1 Gp2 gd-fm		£127,598
	7/18	Gdwd	2m Cls1 Gp1 good		£283,550
	6/18	Asct	2m4f Cls1 Gp1 gd-fm		£283,550
	5/18	York	1m6f Cls1 Gp2 gd-fm		£93,572
	8/17	Gdwd	2m Cls1 Gp1 good		£296,593
	6/17	Asct	1m6f Cls1 Gp2 3yo gd-fm		£91,445
78	4/17	Bevl	1m2f Cls4 64-80 3yo Hcap gd-fm		£5,041
	11/16	Newc	1m Cls5 Mdn 2yo stand		£3,235

Dominant stayer of the last two seasons, winning ten in a row before going down by a nose to Kew Gardens in the Long Distance Cup at Ascot last season; dual winner of the Gold Cup but perhaps best at Goodwood, where he has won the last three Goodwood Cups.

Suedois (Fr)

9 b g Le Havre - Cup Cake (Singspiel)

David O'Meara   George Turner & Clipper Logistics

PLACINGS: 4/70324/442333143-31   RPR **113**

Starts	1st	2nd	3rd	4th	Win & Pl
49	10	10	13	7	£1,494,518
110	1/20	Meyd	1m 90-110 Hcap good		£78,947
	8/19	Gdwd	7f Cls1 Gp3 good		£34,026
	10/17	Keen	1m Cls1 Gp1 firm		£487,805
	9/17	Leop	1m Gp2 good		£100,855
	8/15	Deau	6f Gp3 v soft		£31,008
	4/15	MsnL	6f List good		£20,155
	3/15	Chan	6¹/₂f stand		£19,380
	12/14	Deau	6¹/₂f 3yo stand		£12,083
	10/14	Chan	7f 3yo stand		£10,000
	2/14	Chan	6¹/₂f 3yo stand		£10,000

Grade 1 winner (2017 Shadwell Turf Mile at Keeneland) who wasn't quite the force of old last season but still ran to a consistently high level,

Star Catcher: Irish Oaks winner sure to be a formidable force at middle distances again

winning a Group 3 at Goodwood and getting placed three times in a higher grade; in winning form again at Meydan this spring.

Summer Romance (Ire)

3 gr f Kingman - Serena's Storm (Statue Of Liberty)

Charlie Appleby   Godolphin

PLACINGS: 1163-				RPR **107**+	
Starts	1st	2nd	3rd	4th	Win & Pl
4	2	-	1	-	£26,282
6/19	NmkJ	6f Cls1 List 2yo gd-fm			£17,013
6/19	Yarm	6f Cls5 Mdn 2yo soft			£3,752

Looked a top-class filly when bolting up by six lengths in a Listed race at Newmarket last June; failed to build on that when twice well beaten at a higher level subsequently (short-priced favourite both times) so something to prove now.

Summer Sands

3 b c Coach House - Koharu (Ishiguru)

Joseph O'Brien (Ir)   The Cool Silk Partnership

PLACINGS: 316531-				RPR **111**	
Starts	1st	2nd	3rd	4th	Win & Pl
6	2	-	-	-	£162,864
10/19	Rdcr	6f Cls1 List 2yo heavy			£99,243
6/19	Bevl	5f Cls2 2yo good			£24,900

Third in last season's Middle Park Stakes at 100-1, stepping up massively on defeats in the Windsor Castle and Gimcrack Stakes; possibly helped by racing against favoured near rail but went some way to backing up that form when winning Redcar's Two-Year-Old Trophy; has since joined Joseph O'Brien from Richard Fahey.

Tango: smart filly last season and it would be no surprise to see her make a mark in Group company this year

Sunday Sovereign

3 b c Equiano - Red Sovereign (Danzig Connection)

Roger Varian   King Power Racing Co Ltd

PLACINGS: 4118-				RPR **103**+	
Starts	1st	2nd	3rd	4th	Win & Pl
4	2	-	-	1	£22,544
6/19	Tipp	5f 2yo soft			£11,099
5/19	Curr	6f Mdn 2yo yield			£10,544

Looked hugely exciting for Paddy Twomey early last season, twice winning by wide margins, but disappointed when 13-8 favourite for the Norfolk Stakes at Royal Ascot; had been bought by King Power prior to that and subsequently sent to Roger Varian.

Tabdeed

5 ch g Havana Gold - Puzzled (Peintre Celebre)

Owen Burrows   Hamdan Al Maktoum

PLACINGS: 1/101/16-				RPR **109**+	
Starts	1st	2nd	3rd	4th	Win & Pl
6	4	-	-	-	£37,367
8/19	Donc	6f Cls3 gd-sft			£9,338
10/18	Asct	6f Cls2 85-100 3yo Hcap good			£18,675
5/18	Nott	6f Cls5 gd-fm			£3,881
8/17	Leic	6f Cls4 2yo good			£4,528

Fragile sprinter who has run just six times in three seasons of racing but has won four of those races, including an impressive return at Doncaster last season; disappointed on his only subsequent run at Ascot; has since been gelded; connections have Group 1 ambitions.

Tammani

3 b c Make Believe - Gentle On My Mind (Sadler's Wells)

William Haggas   Prince A A Faisal

PLACINGS: 813419-   RPR **106+**

Starts	1st	2nd	3rd	4th	Win & Pl
6	2	-		1	£41,765
	10/19 Deau	1m List 2yo heavy			£27,027
	7/19 Sand	7f Cls4 2yo good			£4,787

Patchy record in face of stiff tests last season but justified lofty ambitions with a four-length Listed win on heavy ground at Deauville (expected to enjoy testing conditions by connections); beaten favourite at that level earlier and only ninth in the Vertem Futurity Trophy on final run.

Tango (Ire)

3 b f No Nay Never - Idle Chatter (Galileo)

Aidan O'Brien (Ir)   Michael Tabor, Derrick Smith & Sue Magnier

PLACINGS: 219667418-   RPR **106**

Starts	1st	2nd	3rd	4th	Win & Pl
9	2	1	-	1	£67,542
	10/19 Curr	6f List 2yo sft-hvy			£29,234
	6/19 Navn	5½f Mdn 2yo gd-yld			£9,157

Progressive during a busy campaign last season; excellent fourth in the Cheveley Park Stakes and proved that was no fluke when running away with a Listed race at the Curragh by six lengths next time; disappointing on a much quicker surface at the Breeders' Cup.

Tarnawa (Ire)

4 ch f Shamardal - Tarana (Cape Cross)

Dermot Weld (Ir)   Aga Khan

PLACINGS: 322/1310119-   RPR **111+**

Starts	1st	2nd	3rd	4th	Win & Pl
10	4	2	2	-	£241,411
	9/19 Curr	1m2f Gp2 gd-fm			£132,883
	8/19 Cork	1m4f Gp3 yld-sft			£39,865
	5/19 Naas	1m2f Gp3 good			£42,568
	4/19 Leop	1m2f Mdn 3yo gd-yld			£8,879

Three-time Group winner last season, including a 1m2f Group 2 at the Curragh on Irish Champions Weekend; has also won over 1m4f but twice disappointed in Group 1 races over the longer trip, most recently when a tame ninth at Ascot on Champions Day.

Technician (Ire)

4 gr c Mastercraftsman - Arosa (Sadler's Wells)

Martyn Meade   Team Valor

PLACINGS: 3/125161611-   RPR **115+**

Starts	1st	2nd	3rd	4th	Win & Pl
10	5	1	1	-	£381,507
	10/19 Lonc	1m7½f Gp1 heavy			£180,171
	10/19 Lonc	1m7f Gp2 3yo v soft			£102,703
	8/19 Newb	1m5½f Cls1 Gp3 soft			£34,026
	6/19 Lonc	1m2f List 3yo soft			£24,775
	4/19 Leic	1m4f Cls3 3yo good			£9,704

Improved as he stepped up in trip last season and signed off with a breakthrough Group 1 win in the Prix Royal-Oak, making it three out of three at Longchamp; patchier form in England but did win the Geoffrey Freer Stakes at Newbury before a tame sixth in the St Leger.

Telecaster

4 b c New Approach - Shirocco Star (Shirocco)

Hughie Morrison
Castle Down Racing

PLACINGS: 21107-					RPR **117**
Starts	1st	2nd	3rd	4th	Win & Pl
5	2	1	-	-	£98,440

	5/19	York	1m2½f Cls1 Gp2 3yo gd-fm	£93,572
	4/19	Wind	1m2f Cls5 3yo good	£3,752

Won last season's Dante Stakes when outstaying Too Darn Hot but finished last when sent off just 5-1 for the Derby and did little better in the Eclipse; trainer feels those races came too soon for an immature colt and hopes he'll benefit from being given time.

Terebellum (Ire)

4 br f Sea The Stars - Marvada (Elusive City)

John Gosden
Princess Haya Of Jordan

PLACINGS: 1315-					RPR **113**
Starts	1st	2nd	3rd	4th	Win & Pl
4	2	-	1	-	£91,812

	8/19	Deau	1m2f Gp2 3yo soft	£66,757
	5/19	Gdwd	1m2f Cls4 Mdn 3yo good	£6,792

Held in very high regard at home and justified connections' faith by winning a Group 2 at Deauville on just her third run last season; beaten just over a length when fifth in the Prix de l'Opera next time; open to plenty of improvement after just four runs.

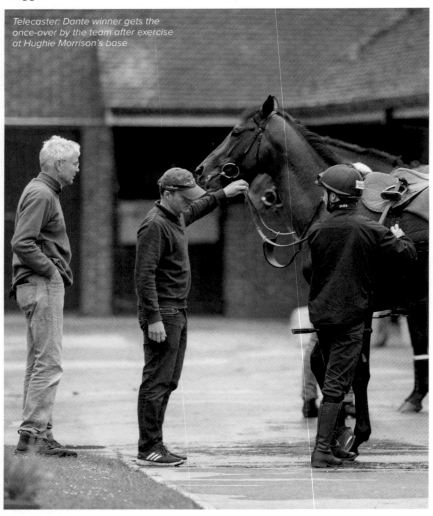

Telecaster: Dante winner gets the once-over by the team after exercise at Hughie Morrison's base

The Revenant

5 ch g Dubawi - Hazel Lavery (Excellent Art)

Francis-Henri Graffard (Fr)   Al Asayl France

PLACINGS: 13/1211/11112-   RPR **120**

Starts	1st	2nd	3rd	4th	Win & Pl
11	8	2	1	-	£475,223

10/19	Lonc	1m Gp2 v soft	£102,703
5/19	Badn	1m Gp2 good	£36,036
3/19	StCl	1m Gp3 good	£36,036
3/19	StCl	1m List heavy	£23,423
11/18	StCl	1m 3yo v soft	£15,487
10/18	Mars	1m 3yo soft	£9,735
9/18	Rcpp	1m¹/₂f 3-4yo gd-sft	£4,204
9/17	Hayd	1m Cls4 2yo gd-sft	£4,528

Prolific miler who won seven out of nine races in little over a year after moving to France as a three-year-old; gradually stepped up in grade and ran away with the Prix Daniel Wildenstein at Longchamp before finishing second on his Group I debut in the QEII; unproven on quick ground.

The Tin Man

8 b g Equiano - Persario (Bishop Of Cashel)

James Fanshawe   Fred Archer Racing

PLACINGS: 1/51835/14317/36720-   RPR **119**

Starts	1st	2nd	3rd	4th	Win & Pl
26	9	2	3	2	£1,257,257

9/18	Hayd	6f Cls1 Gp1 heavy	£184,421
5/18	Wind	6f Cls1 List gd-fm	£20,983
6/17	Asct	6f Cls1 Gp1 gd-fm	£340,260
10/16	Asct	6f Cls1 Gp1 good	£340,260
7/16	Newb	6f Cls1 Gp3 gd-fm	£34,026
5/16	Wind	6f Cls1 List good	£20,983
91	10/15	Asct	6f Cls2 84-103 3yo Hcap good	£18,675
79	7/15	Donc	6f Cls4 68-80 3yo Hcap gd-fm	£4,690
	6/15	Donc	6f Cls5 Mdn gd-fm	£2,911

Three-time Group I winner, with one top-level win in each season from 2016 to 2018; without a victory last season and twice beaten at short odds but came within half a length of keeping up his remarkable Group I record when second in the Sprint Cup.

Threat (Ire)

3 ch c Footstepsinthesand - Flare Of Firelight (Birdstone)

Richard Hannon   Cheveley Park Stud

PLACINGS: 122115-   RPR **115**

Starts	1st	2nd	3rd	4th	Win & Pl
6	3	2	-	-	£260,540

9/19	Donc	7f Cls1 Gp2 2yo gd-fm	£42,533
8/19	York	6f Cls1 Gp2 2yo gd-fm	£127,598
5/19	NmkR	5f Cls3 Mdn 2yo good	£7,763

Tough and consistent two-year-old last season; finally won a Group 2 when landing the Gimcrack after a couple of near misses and progressed again to follow up under a penalty in the Champagne Stakes; looked short of speed when back at 6f in the Middle Park.

Thunderous (Ire)

3 b c Night Of Thunder - Souviens Toi (Dalakhani)

Mark Johnston   Highclere T'Bred Racing - George Stubbs

PLACINGS: 111-   RPR **100**

Starts	1st	2nd	3rd	4th	Win & Pl
3	3	-	-	-	£31,352

8/19	Newb	7f Cls1 List 2yo soft	£22,684
7/19	Rdcr	7f Cls5 2yo gd-fm	£3,881
6/19	Donc	7f Cls4 2yo good	£4,787

Unbeaten in three runs last season, easily winning novices at Doncaster and Redcar before justifying favouritism in a Listed race at Newbury; only workmanlike that day but proved versatility on soft ground and expected to improve on a quicker surface; should stay further.

Top Rank (Ire)

4 gr c Dark Angel - Countess Ferrama (Authorized)

James Tate   Saeed Manana

PLACINGS: 1/11-   RPR **92**

Starts	1st	2nd	3rd	4th	Win & Pl
3	3	-	-	-	£17,660

83	9/19	NmkR	1m Cls3 83-93 Hcap good	£9,057
	4/19	Thsk	1m Cls5 3yo gd-fm	£4,528
	12/18	Ling	1m Cls5 Auct 2yo stand	£4,075

Unbeaten in three races, all well spaced out having been struck into when winning at Thirsk last April; completed the hat-trick after a 166-day layoff at Newmarket, winning impressively; could easily make a mark in top mile handicaps.

Tropbeau

3 b f Showcasing - Frangipanni (Dansili)

Andre Fabre (Fr)   Lady Bamford

PLACINGS: 61113-   RPR **111**

Starts	1st	2nd	3rd	4th	Win & Pl
5	3	-	1	-	£146,328

8/19	Deau	7f Gp2 2yo soft	£66,757
7/19	Deau	7f Gp3 2yo v soft	£36,036
7/19	Claf	7f 2yo gd-sft	£12,162

Won three times last season, including two Group races at Deauville, before a fine third in the Cheveley Park (might well have been second given a clear run and pulled clear of the rest); could return to Newmarket for the 1,000 Guineas, though looks more of a sprinter on pedigree.

Trueshan (Fr)

4 b g Planteur - Shao Line (General Holme)

Alan King   Barbury Lions

PLACINGS: 6/11211-   RPR **112**

Starts	1st	2nd	3rd	4th	Win & Pl
6	4	1	-	-	£132,542

	10/19	Newb	1m5¹/₂f Cls2 3yo heavy £32,345
93	10/19	NmkR	1m4f Cls2 79-100 3yo Hcap gd-sft £74,700
	8/19	Ffos	1m4f Cls5 good £3,429
	8/19	Wolv	1m4f Cls5 stand £3,429

Won four out of five last season, including a valuable three-year-old handicap at Newmarket; improved again when stepped back up in trip at Newbury, beating another progressive colt in Hamish (level weights); trainer quick to nominate the Ebor as a target.

Turjomaan (USA)

4 b/br c War Front - Almoutezah (Storm Cat)

Roger Varian   Hamdan Al Maktoum

PLACINGS: 1d1/12-   RPR **112**

Starts	1st	2nd	3rd	4th	Win & Pl
4	2	1	-	-	£30,039

	6/19	Newc	7f Cls5 std-slw £3,752
	10/18	Newc	7f Cls4 2yo stand £4,787

Restricted to just two runs last season but quickly proved himself a smart colt, finishing a close second to subsequent Celebration Mile winner Duke Of Hazzard on his Pattern debut at Goodwood; had been first past the post in all three 7f novices prior to that.

UAE Jewel

4 b c Dubawi - Gemstone (Galileo)

Roger Varian   Sheikh Mohammed Obaid Al Maktoum

PLACINGS: 114-   RPR **112+**

Starts	1st	2nd	3rd	4th	Win & Pl
3	2	-	-	1	£43,418

	5/19	NmkR	1m2f Cls1 List 3yo good £28,355
	4/19	NmkR	1m Cls3 Mdn 3yo gd-fm £9,704

Looked an exciting colt when winning first two starts early last season, including a Listed race at Newmarket, but ran only once more after a setback; had been due to step up in trip for the Prix du Jockey Club prior to that but instead kept to a mile on return when fourth in the Joel Stakes.

UAE Prince (Ire)

7 b g Sea The Stars - By Request (Giant's Causeway)

Roger Varian   Sheikh Mohammed Obaid Al Maktoum

PLACINGS: 316/15440/254/1-   RPR **109+**

Starts	1st	2nd	3rd	4th	Win & Pl
12	3	1	1	1	£57,541

99	5/19	York	1m2¹/₂f Cls2 86-100 Hcap gd-fm £18,675
93	4/17	Ripn	1m2f Cls3 78-96 Hcap gd-fm £7,246
	9/16	Leic	1m4f Cls5 Mdn gd-sft £3,881

One-time Derby hope who has taken an age to live up to his billing but finally looked to be heading in the right direction when winning first time out at York last season; missed the rest of the campaign through injury but back in training this spring.

Under The Stars (Ire)

3 b f Night Of Thunder - Jumeirah Palm Star (Invincible Spirit)

James Tate   Saeed Manana

PLACINGS: 114541-   RPR **108**

Starts	1st	2nd	3rd	4th	Win & Pl
6	3	-	-	2	£138,712

	10/19	NmkR	6f Cls2 Auct 2yo gd-sft £81,165
	7/19	Asct	6f Cls1 Gp3 2yo gd-sft £28,355
	7/19	Ripn	6f Cls5 Auct 2yo gd-fm £3,881

Won the Princess Margaret Stakes at Ascot on just her second run last season and continued to run well at a higher level, never beaten more than two lengths in competitive 6f-7f Group races; deservedly landed a valuable sales race at Newmarket on final start.

Vatican City (Ire)

3 ch c Galileo - You'resochrilling (Storm Cat)

Aidan O'Brien (Ir)   Sue Magnier, Michael Tabor & Derrick Smith

PLACINGS: 51-   RPR **88+aw**

Starts	1st	2nd	3rd	4th	Win & Pl
2	1	-	-	-	£7,986

	10/19	Dund	7f Mdn 2yo stand.. £7,986

Half-brother to five Group winners including 2,000 Guineas hero Gleneagles; not as precocious as that one last season but made a promising start in the autumn, winning well on his second run at Dundalk; looks a top-class prospect.

Ventura Rebel

3 b c Pastoral Pursuits - Finalize (Firebreak)

Richard Fahey   Abdullah Menahi

PLACINGS: 1124-   RPR **106+**

Starts	1st	2nd	3rd	4th	Win & Pl
4	2	1	-	1	£50,158

	5/19	Asct	5f Cls2 2yo gd-fm £9,057
	4/19	Thsk	5f Cls4 Mdn 2yo gd-fm £4,852

High-class two-year-old in first half of last season, running A'Ali to a neck in the Norfolk Stakes at Royal Ascot having won first two starts; didn't run again after a slightly disappointing fourth in the Super Sprint at Newbury when sent off just 5-4.

MY FIVE TO WATCH

Dave Orton, RPTV

●Darain ●Earthlight ●Highest Ground ●Snow Shower ●Victor Ludorum

Veracious

5 b m Frankel - Infallible (Pivotal)

Sir Michael Stoute   Cheveley Park Stud

PLACINGS: 31/3316/434124-					RPR **116**
Starts	1st	2nd	3rd	4th	Win & Pl
12	3	1	4	3	£428,018

	7/19	NmkJ	1m Cls1 Gp1 gd-fm	£113,420
	9/18	Sand	1m Cls1 Gp3 good	£39,697
	10/17	NmkR	7f Cls4 Mdn 2yo good	£6,469

Possibly flattered by Group 1 win in last season's Falmouth Stakes (allowed to dictate a steady gallop and just held on) but backed that up with fine efforts in the Sun Chariot Stakes and QEII; trainer was keen to keep her for 2020 and might well place her to more Group 1 success.

Victor Ludorum

3 b c Shamardal - Antiquities (Kaldounevees)

Andre Fabre (Fr)   Godolphin

PLACINGS: 111-					RPR **113+**
Starts	1st	2nd	3rd	4th	Win & Pl
3	3	-	-	-	£233,387

	10/19	Lonc	1m Gp1 2yo v soft	£205,910
	9/19	Chan	1m 2yo good	£15,315
	9/19	Lonc	1m 2yo good	£12,162

Very highly regarded and underlined his reputation by winning all three races in just five weeks last season, culminating in an impressive swoop to land a slowly run Prix Jean-Luc Lagardere at Longchamp; should stay 1m2f and expected to be aimed at the French Classics.

Visinari (Fr)

3 gr c Dark Angel - Visinada (Sinndar)

Mark Johnston   Rob Ferguson

PLACINGS: 1344-					RPR **106**
Starts	1st	2nd	3rd	4th	Win & Pl
4	1	-	1	2	£26,111

	6/19	NmkJ	6f Cls4 2yo gd-fm	£5,175

Stunning debut winner at Newmarket last season and sent off just 4-6 for a Group 2 back there next time when a close third but regressed in two runs over 7f subsequently; fine big colt who could easily get back on track having had time to fill his frame.

Waldkonig

3 b c Kingman - Waldlerche (Monsun)

John Gosden   Gestut Ammerland & Newsells Park Stud

PLACINGS: 1-					RPR **96+** aw
Starts	1st	2nd	3rd	4th	Win & Pl
1	1	-	-	-	£3,428

	12/19	Wolv	1m1/2f Cls5 2yo stand	£3,429

600,000gns half-brother to Waldgeist who overcame greenness to run out a nine-length winner on debut at Wolverhampton last December; seems sure to stay middle distances but also looks to have inherited plenty of speed from sire Kingman; could be a Derby horse.

Walkinthesand (Ire)

4 b c Footstepsinthesand - Masseera (Alzao)

Richard Hannon   Saeed Suhail

PLACINGS: 21/2251743-					RPR **114**
Starts	1st	2nd	3rd	4th	Win & Pl
9	2	3	1	1	£85,529

105	7/19	NmkJ	1m2f Cls2 88-105 3yo Hcap gd-fm	£49,800
	9/18	Sand	7f Cls3 2yo good	£8,715

Did really well to win under top weight in a big 1m2f handicap at Newmarket's July festival last season; twice just touched off in Listed races prior to that but disappointing when tried in Group company; type to improve again at four according to his trainer.

Wells Farhh Go (Ire)

5 b h Farhh - Mowazana (Galileo)

Tim Easterby   S A Heley & Partner

PLACINGS: 11/6614/1807-					RPR **113**
Starts	1st	2nd	3rd	4th	Win & Pl
10	4	-	-	1	£180,927

	6/19	NmkJ	1m4f Cls1 List gd-fm	£22,684
	7/18	NmkJ	1m5f Cls1 Gp3 3yo gd-fm	£85,065
	8/17	York	7f Cls1 Gp3 2yo gd-sft	£51,039
	7/17	York	7f Cls3 Auct 2yo good	£7,763

Still looks a work in progress but has shown glimpses of potential, winning Group 3 and Listed races in each of the last three seasons, including by four lengths at Newmarket; flopped three times subsequently, twice running much too freely.

West End Girl

3 b f Golden Horn - Free Rein (Dansili)

Mark Johnston   A D Spence & M B Spence

PLACINGS: 15189-					RPR **103**
Starts	1st	2nd	3rd	4th	Win & Pl
5	2	-	-	-	£36,277

	8/19	NmkJ	7f Cls1 Gp3 2yo gd-fm	£28,355
	7/19	Hayd	7f Cls4 2yo gd-fm	£7,116

Impressive winner of last season's Sweet Solera Stakes, comfortably making all to atone for a luckless fifth in a Listed race at Sandown on her second run; much better than she showed when down the field in the May Hill and Fillies' Mile subsequently.

Wichita (Ire)

3 b c No Nay Never - Lumiere Noire (Dashing Blade)

Aidan O'Brien (Ir)   Derrick Smith, Sue Magnier & Michael Tabor

PLACINGS: 1213-					RPR **116+**
Starts	1st	2nd	3rd	4th	Win & Pl
4	2	1	1	-	£101,554

	9/19	NmkR	7f Cls1 Gp3 2yo good	£28,355
	8/19	Curr	7f Mdn 2yo yield	£9,318

Hugely impressive seven-length winner of last season's Tattersalls Stakes at Newmarket, albeit against a moderate field; clear market pick of Aidan O'Brien's four Dewhurst runners but well beaten in third, perhaps struggling to cope with much softer ground.

Withhold

7 b g Champs Elysees - Coming Back (Fantastic Light)

Roger Charlton   Tony Bloom

PLACINGS: 42272121/31/18/1015-   RPR **116**

Starts	1st	2nd	3rd	4th	Win & Pl
16	6	4	1	1	£362,627

	9/19	NmkR	2m Cls1 List good	£22,684
107	7/19	Newb	2m¹/₂f Cls2 86-107 Hcap gd-sft	£62,250
99	6/18	Newc	2m¹/₂f Cls2 97-108 Hcap std-slw	£92,385
87	10/17	NmkR	2m2f Cls2 85-103 Hcap good	£155,625
80	10/16	Hayd	2m Cls4 72-84 Hcap good	£4,690
	8/16	Bath	1m5f Cls5 Mdn firm	£3,068

Lightly raced but prolific stayer who has won major handicaps in each of the last three seasons, most recently a £100,000 race at Newbury last year; six-length winner on first run in Listed grade at Newmarket but only fifth in the Long Distance Cup on Champions Day.

Wonderful Moon (Ger)

3 ch c Sea The Moon - Wonderful Filly (Lomitas)

Henk Grewe (Ger)   Stall Wasserfreunde

PLACINGS: 321-   RPR **115+**

Starts	1st	2nd	3rd	4th	Win & Pl
3	1	1	1	-	£57,297

	11/19	Kref	1m¹/₂f Gp3 2yo soft	£28,829

Last season's outstanding two-year-old in Germany; just beaten in a Group 3 on his penultimate run (stumbled badly leaving stalls) but made amends with a sensational 12-length victory in another Group 3 at Krefeld; strong favourite for the German Derby.

Yafta

5 gr h Dark Angel - Swiss Dream (Oasis Dream)

Richard Hannon   Hamdan Al Maktoum

PLACINGS: 42211/212217/230-   RPR **111+**

Starts	1st	2nd	3rd	4th	Win & Pl
14	4	6	1	1	£134,660

	7/18	Newb	6f Cls1 Gp3 gd-fm	£34,026
93	5/18	NmkR	6f Cls2 76-93 3yo Hcap gd-fm	£31,125
82	9/17	Chmd	6f Cls4 75-84 2yo Hcap stand	£7,116
	8/17	Bath	5¹/₂f Cls5 2yo good	£3,235

Developed into a Pattern sprinter in 2018, winning the Hackwood Stakes, and ran up to that level last season when just touched off in the Abernant Stakes and third in the Duke of York; missed the second half of the season after disappointing in the Diamond Jubilee.

Year Of The Tiger (Ire)

3 b c Galileo - Tiggy Wiggy (Kodiac)

Aidan O'Brien (Ir)   D Smith, Sue Magnier, M Tabor & Flaxman Stable

PLACINGS: 2717443-   RPR **105**

Starts	1st	2nd	3rd	4th	Win & Pl
7	1	1	1	2	£69,893

	7/19	Naas	7f Mdn 2yo good	£8,785

Missed much of last season after a disappointing seventh in the Superlative Stakes and got better and better when returning in the autumn,

finishing a good third in the Vertem Futurity Trophy on final run; might have needed the race when fourth in the Royal Lodge on previous attempt at a mile.

Zaaki

5 b g Leroidesanimaux - Kesara (Sadler's Wells)

Sir Michael Stoute   Ahmad Alotaibi

PLACINGS: 2545/133237/1127138-   RPR **117**

Starts	1st	2nd	3rd	4th	Win & Pl
17	4	3	4	1	£216,968

	8/19	York	1m1f Cls1 Gp3 gd-fm	£56,710
	6/19	Epsm	1m¹/₂f Cls1 Gp3 gd-fm	£51,039
	5/19	Asct	1m Cls1 List good	£20,983
	4/18	Thsk	1m Cls5 3yo gd-sft	£4,852

Developed into a smart miler last season after a gelding operation, beating Barney Roy at Ascot before winning a pair of Group 3 races; also beaten just a nose by Beat The Bank in the Summer Mile, though didn't get close in three other runs at Group 1 or 2 level.

Zabeel Prince (Ire)

7 ch g Lope De Vega - Princess Serena (Unbridled's Song)

Roger Varian   Sheikh Mohammed Obaid Al Maktoum

PLACINGS: 2/1110/102/11787-   RPR **120**

Starts	1st	2nd	3rd	4th	Win & Pl
13	6	2	-	-	£240,346

	5/19	Lonc	1m1f Gp1 gd-sft	£128,694
	4/19	NmkR	1m1f Cls1 Gp3 gd-fm	£34,026
	3/18	Donc	1m Cls1 List soft	£20,983
96	10/17	York	1m Cls2 82-96 Hcap good	£18,675
86	9/17	Yarm	1m Cls4 78-86 Hcap soft	£5,175
	6/17	Nott	1m¹/₂f Cls5 Mdn soft	£3,235

Very lightly raced for his age and finally realised some of his potential last season, winning the Prix d'Ispahan during an impressive start to the year; lost his way after that with three heavy defeats at the top level but could have benefited from subsequent break.

Zakouski

4 b g Shamardal - O'Giselle (Octagonal)

Charlie Appleby   Godolphin

PLACINGS: 1/5-11   RPR **113**

Starts	1st	2nd	3rd	4th	Win & Pl
4	3	-	-	-	£179,179

	2/20	Meyd	1m Gp2 good	£112,782
100	1/20	Meyd	1m 90-103 Hcap good	£60,902
	11/18	Kemp	7f Cls5 2yo std-slw	£3,881

Began last season as a leading 2,000 Guineas candidate but finished only fifth on his return in the Craven and didn't run again all year; got back on track in Dubai this spring after a gelding operation and remains an exciting prospect.

Form figures for the 250 key horses are correct up to and including February 21, 2020

KEY HORSES LISTED BY TRAINER

Eric Alston
Maid In India

Charlie Appleby
Al Hilalee
Al Suhail
Barney Roy
Cross Counter
Ghaiyyath
Glorious Journey
King's Command
Moonlight Spirit
Old Persian
On The Warpath
Pinatubo
Quorto
Royal Crusade
Space Blues
Summer Romance
Zakouski

Bruno Audouin
Holdthasigreen

Andrew Balding
Bangkok
Dashing Willoughby
Fox Chairman
Fox Tal
Happy Power
Kameko
Morando
Shine So Bright

David Barron
Kynren

Ralph Beckett
Feliciana De Vega
Hereby
Kinross
Max Vega

Michael Bell
Eagles By Day

Karl Burke
Living In The Past
Lord Of The Lodge

Owen Burrows
Shabaaby
Tabdeed

Henry Candy
Kurious
Limato

Jean-Pierre Carvalho
Alson

Roger Charlton
Headman
Pocket Square
Qarasu
Quadrilateral
Withhold

Paul Cole
Duke Of Hazzard

Ken Condon
Romanised

Clive Cox
Golden Horde
Positive

Simon Crisford
A'Ali
Century Dream
Jash
Outbox

Keith Dalgleish
Alright Sunshine

Tom Dascombe
Boomer

Michael Dods
Dakota Gold

Tim Easterby
Lampang
Wells Farhh Go

David Elsworth
Sir Dancealot

Andre Fabre
Earthlight
Persian King
Tropbeau
Victor Ludorum

Richard Fahey
Sands Of Mali
Space Traveller
Summer Sands
Ventura Rebel

James Fanshawe
The Tin Man

Aidan Fogarty
Forever In Dreams

John Gosden
Alrajaa
Ben Vrackie
Cape Palace
Crossed Baton
Dubai Warrior
Enable
Enbihaar
Enemy
Fanny Logan
First In Line
Forest Of Dean
King Of Comedy
Logician
Lord North
Mehdaayih
Miss Yoda
Palace Pier
Promissory
Royal Line
Scentasia
Star Catcher
Stradivarius
Terebellum
Waldkonig

Francis-Henri Graffard
The Revenant

Henk Grewe
Wonderful Moon

William Haggas
Addeybb
Born With Pride
Domino Darling

Faylaq
Hamish
Miss O Connor
Monica Sheriff
One Master
Pablo Escobarr
Sea Of Faith
Skardu
Tammani
Young Rascal

Richard Hannon
Al Madhar
Beat Le Bon
Billesdon Brook
Cloak Of Spirits
Dark Lady
King Of Change
Mums Tipple
Threat
Walkinthesand
Yafta

Jessica Harrington
Albigna
Alpine Star
Cayenne Pepper
Millisle

Freddy Head
Khayzaraan

Charlie Hills
Battaash
Equilateral
Khaadem

Denis Gerard Hogan
Make A Challenge

Eve Johnson Houghton
Accidental Agent

Richard Hughes
Brentford Hope

Mark Johnston
Communique
Elarqam
King's Advice
Nayef Road
Raffle Prize
Rose Of Kildare
Sir Ron Priestley
Thunderous
Visinari
West End Girl

Alan King
Trueshan

Ger Lyons
Buffer Zone
Siskin

Martyn Meade
Ebury
Technician

Ismail Mohammed
Good Effort

Hughie Morrison
Telecaster

Aidan O'Brien
Anthony Van Dyck

Arizona
Armory
Arthur's Kingdom
Broome
Circus Maximus
Delphinia
Etoile
Fleeting
Innisfree
Japan
Kew Gardens
Lancaster House
Lope Y Fernandez
Love
Magical
Mogul
Monarch Of Egypt
Mount Everest
Mythical
Passion
Peaceful
Royal Dornoch
Royal Lytham
Sergei Prokofiev
Sir Dragonet
Southern Hills
Sovereign
Tango
Vatican City
Wichita
Year Of The Tiger

Donnacha O'Brien
Fancy Blue

Joseph Patrick O'Brien
Alligator Alley
Buckhurst
Degraves
Latrobe
Master Of Reality
New York Girl
Speak In Colours

David O'Meara
Escobar
Lord Glitters
Suedois

Hugo Palmer
Powerful Breeze

Amanda Perrett
Lavender's Blue

Kevin Prendergast
Madhmoon

Sir Mark Prescott Bt
Land Of Oz

John Quinn
El Astronaute
Liberty Beach
Safe Voyage

Jerome Reynier
Skalleti

Jean-Claude Rouget
Sottsass

Kevin Ryan
Bielsa
Brando

Glass Slippers
Hello Youmzain
Juan Elcano
Major Jumbo

David Simcock
Bless Him
Desert Encounter
Mohican Heights
Raakib Alhawa

Bryan Smart
Alpha Delphini

Sir Michael Stoute
Davydenko
Dream Of Dreams
Highest Ground
Jubiloso
Mustashry
Queen Power
Regal Reality
Sangarius
Satono Japan
Sextant
Veracious
Zaaki

Saeed bin Suroor
Benbatl
Final Song
Military March

James Tate
Far Above
Hey Gaman
Top Rank
Under The Stars

Roger Teal
Oxted

Marcus Tregoning
Mohaather

Roger Varian
Cape Byron
Daahyeh
Defoe
Molatham
Mutamaasik
Pierre Lapin
Prince Eiji
Queen Daenerys
Roseman
San Donato
Sharja Bridge
Stylistique
Sunday Sovereign
Turjomaan
UAE Jewel
UAE Prince
Zabeel Prince

Ed Vaughan
Dame Malliot

Dermot Weld
Falcon Eight
Kastasa
Search For A Song
Shekhem
Tarnawa

RACING POST RATINGS: LAST SEASON'S LEADING TWO-YEAR-OLDS

KEY: Horse name, best RPR figure, finishing position when earning figure, (details of race where figure was earned)

Pinatubo (IRE) 128 1 (7f, Curr, Gd, Sep 15)
Mums Tipple (IRE) 118 1 (6f, York, Gd, Aug 22)
Arizona (IRE) 117 2 (7f, Newm, Sft, Oct 12)
Earthlight (IRE) 117 1 (6f, Newm, Gd, Sep 28)
Kameko (USA) 117 1 (1m 5y, Ncsw, SD, Nov 1)
Golden Horde (IRE) 116 2 (6f, Newm, Gd, Sep 28)
Millisle (IRE) 116 1 (6f, Newm, Gd, Sep 28)
Wichita (IRE) 116 1 (7f, Newm, Gd, Sep 26)
Military March 115 1 (1m, Newm, Sft, Oct 12)
Quadrilateral 115 1 (1m, Newm, GS, Oct 11)
Siskin (USA) 115 1 (6f, Curr, Sft, Aug 9)
Threat (IRE) 115 1 (7f 6y, Donc, GF, Sep 14)
Al Suhail 114 2 (1m, Newm, Sft, Oct 12)
Powerful Breeze 114 2 (1m, Newm, GS, Oct 11)
Monarch Of Egypt (USA) 113 2 (6f, Curr, Sft, Aug 9)
Raffle Prize (IRE) 113 1 (6f, Newj, GF, Jul 12)
Pierre Lapin (IRE) 112 1 (6f, Newb, GF, Sep 21)
Royal Dornoch (IRE) 112 1 (1m, Newm, Gd, Sep 28)
Royal Lytham (FR) 112 3 (6f, Curr, Sft, Aug 9)
A'Ali (IRE) 111 1 (5f 3y, Donc, GF, Sep 13)
Love (IRE) 111 3 (1m, Newm, GS, Oct 11)
Mystery Power (IRE) 111 1 (7f, Newj, GF, Jul 13)
Royal Crusade 111 2 (7f 6y, Donc, GF, Sep 14)
Summer Sands 111 3 (6f, Newm, Gd, Sep 28)
Tropbeau 111 3 (6f, Newm, Gd, Sep 28)
Daahyeh 110 1 (7f, Newm, Gd, Sep 27)
Innisfree (IRE) 110 2 (1m 5y, Ncsw, SD, Nov 1)
Cayenne Pepper (IRE) 109 1 (1m, Curr, Yld, Aug 30)
Juan Elcano 109 3 (7f 6y, Donc, GF, Sep 14)
King Neptune (USA) 109 4 (6f, Newm, Gd, Sep 28)
Living In The Past (IRE) 109 1 (6f, York, Gd, Aug 22)
Lord Of The Lodge (IRE) 109 2 (6f, York, GF, Aug 23)
Mogul 109 4 (1m 5y, Ncsw, SD, Nov 1)
Positive 109 1 (7f, Sand, GF, Aug 31)
Stylistique 109 2 (7f, Newm, Gd, Sep 27)
Year Of The Tiger (IRE) 109 3 (1m 5y, Ncsw, SD, Nov 1)
Alpine Star (IRE) 108 1 (7f, Curr, Yld, Aug 23)
Armory (IRE) 108 1 (7f, Curr, Yld, Aug 23)
Boomer 108 5 (1m, Newm, GS, Oct 11)
Cloak Of Spirits (IRE) 108 3 (7f, Newm, Gd, Sep 27)
Fort Myers (USA) 108 4 (7f 6y, Donc, GF, Sep 14)
Harpocrates (IRE) 108 2 (7f, York, Gd, Aug 21)
Iberia (IRE) 108 3 (1m, Newm, Gd, Sep 28)
Lope Y Fernandez (IRE) 108 1 (6f, Curr, Yld, Aug 30)
Max Vega (IRE) 108 1 (1m 2f, Newm, Sft, Oct 12)
Petite Mustique (IRE) 108 2 (7f, Curr, Yld, Aug 23)
Platinum Star (IRE) 108 1 (6f, Ripo, Gd, Aug 26)
Sir Boris (IRE) 108 1 (6f, Fair, Sft, Sep 23)
Under The Stars (IRE) 108 4 (7f, Newm, Gd, Sep 27)
Valdermoro (USA) 108 1 (7f, York, Gd, Aug 21)
Liberty Beach 107 2 (6f, York, Gd, Aug 22)
Shekhem (IRE) 107 2 (1m, Curr, Hvy, Sep 29)
So Wonderful (USA) 107 3 (7f, Curr, Gd, Sep 15)
Summer Romance (IRE) 107 1 (6f, Newj, GF, Jun 29)
Guildsman (FR) 106 3 (6f, Asco, Gd, Jun 18)
Rebel Tale (USA) 106 2 (7f, Curr, Yld, Aug 23)
Sinawann (IRE) 106 2 (1m, Leop, Gd, Sep 14)
Soul Search (IRE) 106 4 (7f, Curr, Gd, Sep 15)
Tango (IRE) 106 1 (6f, Curr, Hvy, Oct 13)
Ventura Rebel 106 2 (5f, Asco, Sft, Jun 20)
Visinari (FR) 106 3 (6f, Newj, GF, Jul 11)
Albigna (IRE) 105 1 (6f, Curr, Gd, Jun 28)
Dark Lady 105 1 (6f, Sali, Gd, Sep 5)
Justifier (IRE) 105 2 (7f, Dunw, SD, Oct 4)
Kimari (USA) 105 2 (5f, Asco, GS, Jun 19)
New York Girl (IRE) 105 1 (7f, Curr, Hvy, Sep 29)
Pistoletto (USA) 105 2 (5f, Newm, GS, Oct 11)
A New Dawn (IRE) 104 2 (7f, Curr, Hvy, Sep 29)
Air Force Jet 104 1 (5f, Nava, GF, Sep 7)
Alligator Alley 104 2 (5f, Good, Gd, Jul 31)
Alpen Rose (IRE) 104 3 (1m, Donc, GF, Sep 12)
Degraves (IRE) 104 1 (1m 1f, Leop, Hvy, Oct 26)
Dream Shot (IRE) 104 2 (5f, Dunw, SD, Oct 18)
Good Vibes 104 3 (6f, York, Gd, Aug 22)

Kinross 104 5 (1m 5y, Ncsw, SD, Nov 1)
Molatham 104 1 (7f 6y, Donc, GF, Sep 13)
Persia (IRE) 104 1 (1m 2f, Chmf, SD, Nov 2)
Precious Moments (IRE) 104 2 (6f, Curr, Gd, Jun 28)
Rose Of Kildare (IRE) 104 1 (7f, Newm, GS, Oct 11)
Temple Of Heaven 104 1 (6f, Ncsw, SD, Oct 22)
Wheels On Fire (FR) 104 3 (5f 3y, Donc, GF, Sep 13)
Agitare 103 1 (1m, Leop, Gd, Sep 14)
Al Dabaran 103 1 (7f, Asco, GS, Jul 27)
Final Song (IRE) 103 3 (6f, Newj, GF, Jul 12)
Geometrical (IRE) 103 3 (7f, Curr, Yld, Aug 23)
Know It All 103 3 (7f, Curr, Hvy, Sep 29)
Louisiana (IRE) 103 1 (1m, Thur, Sft, Oct 10)
Pyledriver 103 1 (1m 37y, Hayd, Sft, Sep 7)
Queen Daenerys (IRE) 103 6 (1m, Newm, GS, Oct 11)
Royal Commando (IRE) 103 4 (6f, Newb, GF, Sep 21)
Run Wild (GER) 103 4 (1m, Donc, GF, Sep 12)
Shadn 103 3 (6f, Newb, GF, Sep 21)
Sunday Sovereign 103 1 (5f, Tipp, Sft, Jun 4)
West End Girl 103 1 (7f, Newj, GF, Aug 10)
Aberama Gold 102 1 (6f, York, Sft, Oct 12)
Aroha (IRE) 102 2 (6f, Asco, GS, Jul 27)
Dr Simpson (FR) 102 1 (5f, Dunw, SD, Oct 18)
Kenzai Warrior (USA) 102 1 (7f, Newm, Hvy, Nov 2)
Roman Turbo (IRE) 102 4 (7f, Curr, Yld, Aug 23)
Stela Star (IRE) 102 1 (7f, Leop, Hvy, Oct 19)
Sun Power (FR) 102 2 (7f, Asco, GS, Jul 27)
Wejdan (FR) 102 5 (6f, York, Gd, Aug 22)
Zarzyni (IRE) 102 4 (6f, Curr, Yld, Aug 30)
Berkshire Rocco (FR) 101 3 (1m 2f, Newm, Sft, Oct 12)
Berlin Tango 101 3 (7f 6y, Donc, GF, Sep 13)
Born With Pride (IRE) 101 1 (1m, Newm, Hvy, Nov 2)
Nurse Barbara (IRE) 101 6 (6f, Newm, Gd, Sep 28)
Peaceful (IRE) 101 2 (1m, Newm, Hvy, Nov 2)
Repartee (IRE) 101 3 (6f, York, GF, Aug 23)
Ropey Guest 101 2 (7f, Newm, Hvy, Nov 2)
Southern Hills (IRE) 101 1 (5f, Asco, Sft, Jun 19)
Streamline 101 (6f, Kemw, SS, Sep 7)
Strive For Glory (USA) 101 1 (5f, Tipp, Sft, Jul 4)
Ventura Lightning (FR) 101 5 (6f, Curr, Yld, Aug 30)
Celtic Beauty (IRE) 100 2 (6f, Asco, GS, Jun 21)
Etoile (USA) 100 1 (6f, Naas, GF, May 19)
Fan Club Rules (IRE) 100 4 (5f, Good, Gd, Jul 31)
Fancy Blue (IRE) 100 1 (1m, Curr, Sft, Oct 13)
Golden Dragon (IRE) 100 5 (5f, Newm, GS, Oct 11)
Isabeau (IRE) 100 2 (5f, Curr, Sft, Aug 16)
Jouska 100 3 (5f, Newm, GS, Oct 11)
Malotru 100 5 (6f, Newb, GF, Sep 21)
Miss Yoda (GER) 100 2 (1m 2f, Newm, Sft, Oct 12)
Misty Grey (IRE) 100 2 (6f, Newb, GS, Jul 19)
Mohican Heights (IRE) 100 1 (1m, Sali, Gd, Aug 23)
Premier Power 100 1 (6f, Kemw, SS, Oct 10)
Separate 100 3 (7f, Newm, GS, Oct 11)
Show Me Show Me 100 3 (5f, Good, Gd, Jul 31)
Sound Of Cannons 100 5 (1m, Newm, Gd, Sep 28)
Thunderous 100 1 (7f, Newb, Sft, Aug 17)
Troubador 100 2 (6f, York, Gd, Aug 21)
Valeria Messalina (IRE) 100 2 (7f, Newm, GS, Oct 11)
Vitalogy 100 4 (7f, York, Gd, Aug 21)
Volatile Analyst (USA) 100 4 (6f, Good, Gd, Aug 1)
Ananya 99 5 (1m, Donc, GF, Sep 12)
Auxilia (IRE) 99 3 (1m, Curr, Sft, Oct 13)
Gold Maze 99 3 (1m, Curr, Hvy, Sep 29)
Graceful Magic 99 2 (6f, Ayr, Gd, Sep 21)
Highland Chief (IRE) 99 3 (7f, Asco, Gd, Jun 22)
Impressor (IRE) 99 3 (7f, Newm, Hvy, Nov 2)
Maxi Boy 99 3 (7f, Newj, GF, Jul 13)
Nope (IRE) 99 4 (7f, Newm, GS, Oct 11)
Peace Charter 99 3 (6f, Curr, Gd, Jun 28)
Real Force 99 4 (6f, Curr, Gd, Jun 29)
Soffika (IRE) 99 2 (7f, Newj, GF, Aug 10)
Symbolize (IRE) 99 5 (6f, Good, Gd, Aug 1)
Well Of Wisdom 99 3 (6f, Newb, Gd, May 18)
Cormorant (IRE) 98 2 (1m 2f, Chmf, SD, Nov 2)
Dune Of Pilat (FR) 98 1 (1m 13y, Souw, SD, Jan 28)
Glasvegas (IRE) 98 3 (5f, Asco, Sft, Jun 19)
Katiba (IRE) 98 3 (7f, Leop, Hvy, Oct 19)

Lazuli (IRE) 98 [1] (6f 2y, Donc, GF, Sep 11)
Monoski (USA) 98 [4] (7f, Curr, Gd, Sep 15)
Oh Purple Reign (IRE) 98 [2] (6f, Kemw, SS, Sep 7)
Persuasion (IRE) 98 [2] (7f, Newm, Gd, Sep 26)
Piece Of Paradise (IRE) 98 [1] (5f, Ayr, Gd, Sep 20)
Shehreen (IRE) 98 [4] (1m, Curr, Sft, Oct 13)
Tammani 98 [3] (1m 37y, Hayd, Sft, Sep 7)
Blissful (IRE) 97 [1] (7f, Leop, Gd, Sep 14)
Endless Joy 97 [3] (6f, Ayr, Gd, Sep 21)
Flaming Princess (IRE) 97 [4] (5f 3y, Donc, GF, Sep 13)
Hariboux 97 [2] (7f 6y, Donc, GF, Sep 11)
Huraiz (IRE) 97 [3] (6f, Kemw, SS, Sep 7)
Ickworth (IRE) 97 [1] (5f, Curr, Yld, May 6)
Kemble (IRE) 97 [4] (5f, Newm, GS, Oct 11)
Mrs Bouquet 97 [1] (5f, Good, Gd, Jul 31)
Orlaith (IRE) 97 [1] (5f 34y, Newb, GS, Aug 16)
Punita Arora (IRE) 97 [3] (7f, Dunw, SD, Oct 4)
Unforgetable (IRE) 97 [2] (7f 20y, Leop, Gd, Jul 25)
Walk In Marrakesh (IRE) 97 [1] (7f, Sand, Gd, Jul 25)
Al Aakif (IRE) 96 [1] (6f, York, GF, Jun 29)
Celestial Object (IRE) 96 [5] (1m, Curr, Sft, Oct 13)
Dubai Souq (IRE) 96 [1] (1m 2f 50y, Nott, GS, Oct 9)
Dubai Station 96 [3] (5f, Asco, Sft, Jun 20)
George Cornelius (IRE) 96 [1] (5f, Dunw, SD, Apr 14)
King Carney 96 [1] (1m 6y, Pont, Sft, Oct 21)
King's Caper 96 [1] (1m, Chmf, SD, Aug 31)
Lambeth Walk 96 [4] (6f, Newj, GF, Jul 12)
Light Blush (IRE) 96 [2] (7f, Sand, Gd, Jul 25)
Lil Grey (IRE) 96 [2] (6f 63y, Curr, Gd, Jul 20)
Mild Illusion (IRE) 96 [1] (6f, Newm, Sft, Nov 1)
Mount Fuji (IRE) 96 [5] (6f 63y, Curr, Gd, Jul 20)
Mythical (FR) 96 [4] (1m 2f, Newm, Sft, Oct 12)
Palace Pier 96 [1] (7f, Sand, Gd, Sep 18)
Rayong 96 [3] (5f 10y, Sand, GF, Jul 5)
Royal County Down (IRE) 96 [6] (1m, Leop, Gd, Sep 14)
Think Big (IRE) 96 [4] (5f, York, GF, Aug 24)
Tomfre 96 [1] (7f, Newm, Sft, Oct 12)
Waldkonig 96 [1] (1m 142y, Wolw, SD, Dec 7)
Above (FR) 95 [6] (7f, Dunw, SD, Oct 4)
Belle Anglaise 95 [5] (7f, Newm, GS, Oct 11)
Bomb Proof (IRE) 95 [1] (5f, York, GF, May 15)
Chasing Dreams 95 [1] (5f, Newm, GF, Apr 16)
Convict 95 [1] (1m 2f, Newm, Sft, Oct 23)
Flippa The Strippa (IRE) 95 [3] (5f, Good, Gd, Jul 31)
Kuwait Direction (IRE) 95 (6f, Asco, Gd, Jun 18)
Lampang (IRE) 95 [1] (6f, Ripo, GS, Sep 28)
Pronouncement (USA) 95 [3] (7f, Leop, Gd, Sep 14)
Rhea 95 [3] (7f, Sand, Gd, Jul 25)
Romsey 95 [4] (7f, Newj, GF, Aug 10)
Sky Commander (IRE) 95 [1] (7f, Kemw, SS, Dec 5)
Subjectivist 95 [2] (1m, Sali, Gd, Aug 23)
Ainsdale 94 [1] (5f 8y, Nott, Sft, Oct 30)
Al Raya 94 [2] (5f 34y, Newb, GS, Aug 16)
Alabama Whitman 94 [4] (6f, Asco, GS, Jun 21)
Art Power (IRE) 94 [1] (5f, York, Sft, Oct 11)
Between Hills (IRE) 94 [4] (6f 63y, Curr, Gd, Jul 20)
Boosala (IRE) 94 [1] (7f, York, Gd, Jul 16)
Cape Palace 94 [1] (7f 14y, Ncsw, SS, Aug 30)
Classy Moon (USA) 94 [6] (6f, Newj, GF, Jul 11)
Desert Safari (IRE) 94 [1] (6f, Kemw, SS, Sep 25)
Divine Spirit 94 [5] (6f, Newj, GF, Jul 12)
Dylan De Vega 94 [6] (5f, Ayr, Gd, Sep 20)
Franklin Street (IRE) 94 [4] (1m 1f, Leop, Hvy, Oct 26)
Full Authority (IRE) 94 [1] (5f 15y, Ches, Sft, May 9)
Helvic Dream (IRE) 94 [1] (7f 68y, Rosc, Hvy, Sep 2)
Illusionist (GER) 94 [5] (5f, Asco, Sft, Jun 19)
Lady Penelope (IRE) 94 [2] (5f, Ayr, Gd, Sep 20)
Magical Journey (IRE) 94 [2] (6f, Newm, Sft, Nov 1)
Makyon (IRE) 94 (6f, Asco, Gd, Jun 18)
Manigordo (USA) 94 [4] (6f 111y, Donc, GF, Sep 12)
Mighty Spirit (IRE) 94 [2] (5f, York, GF, May 17)
Morisco (IRE) 94 [5] (7f, York, Gd, Aug 21)
Ottoman Court 94 [1] (6f, Chmf, SD, Nov 8)
Raahy 94 [6] (5f, Good, Gd, Jul 31)
Secret Stash 94 [1] (7f 187y, Bell, Gd, Jul 3)
Stone Circle (IRE) 94 [1] (6f 63y, Curr, Gd, Sep 15)
Wyclif 94 [2] (1m 6y, Pont, Sft, Oct 21)
American Lady (IRE) 93 [4] (6f, Naas, GF, May 19)
Brentford Hope 93 [1] (1m 2f, Newm, Sft, Oct 23)
Brunelle (IRE) 93 [6] (6f, Curr, Yld, Aug 30)
Camachita (IRE) 93 [4] (7f, Leop, Hvy, Oct 19)

Cherokee Trail (USA) 93 [1] (7f, Newb, GF, Sep 21)
Grand Rock (IRE) 93 [3] (1m 6y, Pont, Sft, Oct 21)
Hamish Macbeth 93 [3] (6f 63y, Curr, Gd, Sep 15)
Hector Loza 93 [4] (7f, Sand, GF, Aug 31)
King Of The Throne (USA) 93 [6] (1m 5y, Ncsw, SD, Nov 1)
Man Of The Night (FR) 93 [2] (1m, Newb, Gd, Sep 20)
Prince Of Naples (IRE) 93 [7] (6f, Curr, Yld, Aug 30)
Riot (IRE) 93 [2] (7f, Sand, Gd, Jul 31)
Sesame Birah (IRE) 93 [2] (7f, Newb, Sft, Aug 17)
Spartan Fighter 93 [1] (5f, Ripo, GS, Jun 5)
The Perfect Crown (IRE) 93 [1] (7f, Chmf, SD, Nov 21)
Toronto (IRE) 93 [2] (7f 20y, Leop, Gd, Jul 25)
Tritonic 93 [1] (1m, Newb, Gd, Sep 20)
White Moonlight (USA) 93 [1] (1m, Newm, GS, Oct 5)
Amarillo Star (IRE) 92 [2] (6f, Ncsw, SD, Feb 19)
Electric Ladyland (IRE) 92 [1] (5f, Chmf, SD, Sep 24)
Endowed 92 [1] (6f, Kemw, SS, Aug 14)
Final Option 92 [5] (6f, Ayr, Gd, Sep 21)
Free Solo (IRE) 92 [1] (1m, Leop, Gd, Jul 25)
Governor Of Punjab (IRE) 92 [1] (7f, Good, Gd, Aug 1)
He's A Keeper (IRE) 92 [6] (1m 37y, Hayd, Sft, Sep 7)
Heaven Forfend 92 [6] (7f, Asco, Gd, Jun 22)
Iffraaz (IRE) 92 [3] (7f 6y, Donc, GF, Sep 11)
Jungle Cove (IRE) 92 [6] (7f, Curr, Yld, Aug 23)
King's Lynn 92 [1] (6f 111y, Donc, GF, Sep 12)
Lady Light 92 [3] (6f, Newm, Sft, Nov 1)
Light Angel 92 [2] (7f, Newj, GF, Jul 26)
Milltown Star 92 [2] (7f, Newm, Sft, Oct 12)
Pablo Diablo (IRE) 92 [1] (7f, Curr, Hvy, Sep 29)
Passion (IRE) 92 [7] (1m, Donc, Gd, Sep 12)
Praxeology (IRE) 92 [1] (5f 15y, Ches, Gd, Sep 14)
So Sharp 92 [7] (6f, Asco, GS, Jul 27)
Summeronsevenhills (USA) 92 [1] (1m 1f 104y, Wolw, SD, Dec 19)
Ultra Violet 92 [1] (6f, Newj, Gd, Jun 28)
Verboten (IRE) 92 [7] (5m 5y, Ncsw, SD, Nov 1)
Wild Thunder (IRE) 92 [2] (1m, Donc, Gd, Sep 14)
Arthur's Kingdom (IRE) 91 [1] (1m, Gowr, Hvy, Oct 14)
Assurance (IRE) 91 [9] (7f, Curr, Gd, Sep 15)
Bill Neigh 91 [2] (6f 17y, Ches, GS, Aug 4)
Chrysalism (IRE) 91 [5] (7f, Dunw, SD, Oct 4)
Dance Fever (IRE) 91 [1] (7f, Kemw, SS, Nov 6)
Edward Hopper (IRE) 91 [2] (7f, Gowr, Yld, Sep 4)
Even So (IRE) 91 [1] (1m, Gowr, Sft, Sep 26)
Gravity Force 91 [4] (7f, Newm, Hvy, Nov 2)
Homespin (IRE) 91 [1] (6f, Good, GF, Aug 2)
Howling Wolf (IRE) 91 [7] (1m, Leop, Gd, Sep 14)
Jm Jackson (IRE) 91 [2] (5f 10y, Sand, GF, May 23)
King Of Athens (USA) 91 [1] (7f 1y, Linw, SS, Oct 31)
Laser Show (IRE) 91 [2] (1m, Kemw, SS, Nov 19)
Last Opportunity (IRE) 91 [1] (6f, Leop, Gd, Aug 15)
Maystar (IRE) 91 [1] (6f 20y, Wolw, SD, Dec 7)
One Last Look (IRE) 91 [1] (7f 30y, Leop, Gd, Jun 20)
Path Of Thunder (IRE) 91 [1] (7f, Newj, GF, Jul 26)
Real Appeal (GER) 91 [4] (5f, Curr, Gd, Aug 16)
Silence Please (IRE) 91 [1] (7f, Cork, Gd, Sep 1)
Toro Strike (USA) 91 [3] (6f 111y, Donc, GF, Sep 12)
Ursulina 91 [6] (7f, Sand, Gd, Jul 25)
Wasaayef (IRE) 91 [2] (1m, Newm, GF, Sep 21)
Abstemious 90 [1] (6f, York, Sft, Jul 27)
Alpinista 90 [6] (7f, Good, Gd, Aug 24)
Boccaccio (IRE) 90 [1] (7f, Kemw, SS, Nov 27)
Brad The Brief 90 [1] (6f, Newm, Sft, Nov 1)
Corvair (IRE) 90 [1] (7f 36y, Wolw, SD, Jan 20)
Embolden (IRE) 90 [5] (7f, Newm, Hvy, Nov 2)
Firepower (FR) 90 [6] (6f, Newb, GF, Sep 21)
Gold Souk (IRE) 90 [2] (1m, Donc, Sft, Oct 25)
Hurstwood 90 [1] (6f, Pont, GF, Jul 1)
Kingbrook 90 [3] (1m, Donc, Gd, Sep 14)
Kondratiev Wave (IRE) 90 [1] (6f, Kemw, SS, Jan 20)
Lady Kermit (IRE) 90 [3] (5f, York, GF, May 17)
Latin Five (IRE) 90 [1] (6f, Curr, Gd, Jul 21)
Lemista (IRE) 90 [1] (1m, Gowr, Hvy, Oct 14)
Melodic Charm (IRE) 90 [4] (6f, Kemw, SS, Sep 7)
Mishriff (IRE) 90 [1] (1m 75y, Nott, Hvy, Nov 6)
Nasaiym (USA) 90 [8] (6f, York, Gd, Aug 22)
Never Alone 90 [1] (1m 142y, Wolw, SD, Feb 21)
One Voice (IRE) 90 [1] (7f 20y, Leop, Gd, Jul 25)
Pop Dancer (IRE) 90 [1] (5f 1y, Muss, Sft, Aug 9)
Raaeb (IRE) 90 [1] (6f, Kemw, SS, Oct 22)
Volkan Star (IRE) 90 [6] (1m 2f, Newm, Sft, Oct 12)
Bredenbury (IRE) 89 [3] (6f, Newj, GF, Aug 3)

Brook On Fifth (IRE) 89 [4] (1m, Curr, Yld, Aug 30)
Celtic Art (FR) 89 [2] (7f, York, GF, Aug 23)
Celtic High King (IRE) 89 [1] (1m, Leop, Sft, Oct 19)
Coase 89 [1] (5f 193y, Carl, Sft, May 30)
Cool Vixen (IRE) 89 [9] (6f, Curr, Yld, Aug 30)
Danielles Diamond (IRE) 89 [1] (5f, Naas, Gd, Sep 18)
Dontaskmeagain (USA) 89 [1] (7f 96y, Beve, Sft, Sep 24)
Emperor Of The Sun (IRE) 89 [3] (1m, List, Sft, Sep 9)
Emten (IRE) 89 [5] (5f 3y, Donc, GF, Sep 13)
Eshaasy 89 [5] (7f, Sand, GF, Aug 31)
Expressionist (IRE) 89 [5] (5f 10y, Sand, GF, Jul 5)
Fleeting Prince (IRE) 89 [3] (6f, Kemw, SS, Jan 20)
Game And Set 89 [1] (6f, Newb, GS, Aug 16)
Ha'penny Bridge (IRE) 89 [4] (7f, Leop, Gd, Sep 14)
Hot Touch 89 [5] (7f, Newm, Gd, Sep 27)
Indian Creak (IRE) 89 [4] (6f, Newm, GS, Oct 5)
Keep Busy (IRE) 89 [4] (6f, Newm, Sft, Nov 1)
Lucander (IRE) 89 [1] (7f 192y, York, Sft, Oct 12)
Mr Kiki (IRE) 89 [7] (6f, Newb, GF, Sep 21)
Phase After Phase (IRE) 89 [1] (5f, Bell, Gd, Aug 28)
Raheeq 89 [1] (5f 160y, Bath, Gd, Jun 26)
San Pedro (IRE) 89 [1] (7f, Leop, Hvy, Oct 26)
Splendidly 89 [1] (6f, Ncsw, SD, Dec 18)
Star Alexander 89 [1] (5f 10y, Bath, GS, Jun 15)
Starcat 89 [1] (1m, Kemw, SS, Dec 11)
Tell Me All 89 [1] (1m, Ayr, Gd, Sep 21)
United Front (USA) 89 [4] (6f, Newb, Gd, May 18)
Windracer (IRE) 89 [1] (7f, Curr, Yld, Jun 27)
World Title (IRE) 89 [1] (1m, Ripo, GS, Sep 28)
Al Madhar (FR) 88 [1] (7f, Newj, GF, Jul 12)
Back To Brussels (IRE) 88 [4] (6f, Curr, GF, May 24)
Bettys Hope 88 [1] (5f 34y, Newb, GS, Jul 20)
Breathalyze (FR) 88 [1] (7f 127y, Ches, Gd, Sep 13)
Companion 88 [2] (6f, Sali, Gd, Sep 13)
Dawn Rising (IRE) 88 [5] (1m 1f, Leop, Hvy, Oct 26)
Dream Kart (IRE) 88 [1] (5f 15y, Ches, GS, Aug 4)
Electrical Storm 88 [2] (5f, Newm, Gd, May 5)
Encipher 88 [1] (7f, Newb, GS, Jul 19)
For The Trees (IRE) 88 [1] (6f, Naas, Hvy, Oct 20)
Gallaside (FR) 88 [1] (1m 5y, Ncsw, SS, Sep 6)
Get Boosting 88 [2] (6f 20y, Wolw, SD, Dec 7)
Grove Ferry (IRE) 88 [1] (7f 3y, Epso, GF, Jul 11)
Hot Affair 88 [1] (5f, Ripo, Gd, Aug 27)
Huboor (IRE) 88 [1] (7f, Newm, Gd, Sep 28)

In The Present (USA) 88 [1] (7f, Dunw, SD, Dec 6)
Joker On Jack (USA) 88 [7] (6f, Newb, Gd, May 18)
Know No Limits (IRE) 88 [2] (7f 1y, Ches, Gd, Sep 13)
Last Surprise (IRE) 88 [2] (7f 36y, Wolw, SD, Oct 18)
Majestic Sands (IRE) 88 (6f, Asco, Gd, Jun 18)
Owney Madden 88 [1] (6f, York, Gd, Aug 21)
Progressive Rating 88 [1] (6f, Kemw, SS, Sep 16)
Queen Gamrah 88 [2] (1m 142y, Wolw, SD, Dec 26)
Raaeq (IRE) 88 [1] (7f, Newb, GF, Sep 21)
Red Epaulette (IRE) 88 [2] (5f, Naas, GF, May 19)
Rosadora (IRE) 88 [3] (6f 111y, Donc, GF, Sep 12)
Santiago (IRE) 88 [2] (7f, Galw, Gd, Aug 2)
Sunchart 88 [1] (1m 1f, Tipp, Hvy, Oct 6)
Surf Dancer (IRE) 88 [1] (7f, Chmf, SD, Aug 29)
Treble Treble (IRE) 88 [1] (6f, Hayd, GS, Jul 19)
Vatican City (IRE) 88 [1] (7f, Dunw, SD, Oct 30)
Zoheyr (IRE) 88 [2] (1m, Gowr, Hvy, Oct 14)
Acquitted (IRE) 87 [1] (1m, Newb, Hvy, Oct 25)
Afraid Of Nothing 87 [1] (7f 3y, Epso, Hvy, Sep 29)
Amaysmont 87 [1] (5f 193y, Carl, GS, Aug 21)
Aussie Showstopper (FR) 87 [6] (5f 10y, Sand, GF, Jul 5)
Cobra Eye 87 [6] (6f, York, Sft, Oct 12)
Cognac (IRE) 87 [2] (7f 127y, Ches, Gd, Sep 13)
Cool Sphere (USA) 87 [3] (5f, Dunw, SD, Oct 4)
Corrienthes 87 [1] (5f, Dunw, SD, Nov 1)
Dark Vader (IRE) 87 [1] (6f, Dunw, SD, Jan 17)
Discovery Island 87 [2] (1m, Newj, Gd, Aug 16)
Eastern World 87 [2] (1m, Kemw, SS, Dec 11)
English King (FR) 87 [1] (1m 2f 42y, Ncsw, SS, Nov 21)
Establish 87 [2] (7f, Newb, GF, Sep 21)
Eton College (IRE) 87 [2] (7f 6y, Catt, GF, Sep 21)
First View (IRE) 87 [1] (1m, Kemw, SS, Nov 5)
Freyja (IRE) 87 [1] (7f 96y, Beve, GF, Sep 18)
Full Verse (IRE) 87 [3] (5f, Asco, GF, May 1)
Heart Reef (FR) 87 [5] (1m, Newm, Hvy, Nov 2)
Hong Kong (USA) 87 [1] (6f, Naas, Hvy, Oct 20)
Johan 87 [1] (7f 33y, Muss, GS, Sep 29)
Knight Shield 87 [1] (6f, Newb, GF, Jul 25)
Kuramata (IRE) 87 [3] (1m, Kemw, SS, Dec 11)
Kurpany (FR) 87 [1] (5f, Tipp, Gd, Jun 23)
Lady Jane Wilde (IRE) 87 [6] (7f, Leop, Gd, Sep 14)
Layfayette (IRE) 87 [2] (7f, Naas, Hvy, Oct 20)
Love Locket (IRE) 87 [2] (7f, Naas, Hvy, Nov 3)

RACING POST RATINGS: LAST SEASON'S TOP PERFORMERS 3YO+

Battaash (IRE) 129 [1] (5f, York, GF, Aug 23)
Crystal Ocean 129 [2] (1m 3f 211y, Asco, GS, Jul 27)
Enable 128 [1] (1m 3f 188y, York, Gd, Aug 22)
Blue Point (IRE) 127 [1] (5f, Asco, Gd, Jun 18)
Waldgeist 126 [3] (1m 3f 211y, Asco, GS, Jul 27)
Japan 125 [3] (1m 2f 56y, York, Gd, Aug 21)
Ten Sovereigns (IRE) 125 [1] (6f, Newj, GF, Jul 13)
Benbatl 124 [1] (1m, Newm, Gd, Sep 27)
Magical (IRE) 123 [2] (1m 3f 188y, York, Gd, Aug 22)
Stradivarius (IRE) 123 [1] (2m, Good, Gd, Jul 30)
Addeybb (IRE) 122 [2] (1m 2f, Asco, Sft, Oct 19)
Defoe (IRE) 122 [1] (1m 4f 6y, Epso, Gd, May 31)
Elarqam 122 [3] (1m 2f 56y, York, Gd, Aug 21)
Kew Gardens (IRE) 122 [1] (1m 7f 127y, Asco, GS, Oct 19)
King Of Change 122 [1] (1m, Asco, Hvy, Oct 19)
Mustashry 122 [1] (7f, Newm, GS, Oct 11)
Advertise 121 [1] (6f, Asco, GS, Jun 21)
Dee Ex Bee 121 [2] (2m, Good, Gd, Jul 30)
Dream Of Dreams (IRE) 121 [2] (6f, Asco, GF, Jun 22)
Hello Youmzain (FR) 121 [1] (6f, Hayd, Sft, Sep 7)
King Of Comedy (IRE) 121 [4] (1m 2f 56y, York, Gd, Aug 21)
Magna Grecia (IRE) 121 [1] (1m, Newm, Gd, May 4)
Matterhorn (IRE) 121 [1] (1m 2f, Linw, SD, Apr 19)
Regal Reality 121 [3] (1m 1f 209y, Sand, GF, Jul 6)
Too Darn Hot 121 [1] (1m, Good, Gd, Jul 31)
Beat The Bank 120 [1] (7f 213y, Asco, GF, Jul 13)
Donjuan Triumphant (IRE) 120 [1] (6f, Asco, Hvy, Oct 19)
Lord Glitters (FR) 120 [1] (1m, Asco, Gd, Jun 18)
Nagano Gold 120 [2] (1m 3f 211y, Asco, Gd, Jun 22)

Phoenix Of Spain (IRE) 120 [1] (1m, Curr, GF, May 25)
The Revenant 120 [2] (1m, Asco, Hvy, Oct 19)
Zabeel Prince (IRE) 120 [1] (1m 1f, Newm, GF, Apr 18)
Anthony Van Dyck (IRE) 119 [3] (1m 2f, Leop, Gd, Sep 14)
Brando 119 [1] (6f 6y, Hami, Sft, Jun 6)
Circus Maximus (IRE) 119 [2] (1m, Good, Gd, Jul 31)
Cross Counter 119 [3] (2m, Good, Gd, Jul 30)
Desert Encounter (IRE) 119 [1] (1m 2f, Wind, GF, Aug 24)
Kachy 119 [1] (6f 1y, Linw, SD, Apr 19)
Khaadem (IRE) 119 [1] (6f, Good, GF, Aug 3)
Limato 119 [1] (7f, Newj, GF, Jun 29)
Logician 119 [1] (1m 6f 115y, Donc, GF, Sep 14)
Master Of Reality (IRE) 119 [3] (2m 3f 210y, Asco, Sft, Jun 20)
Morando (FR) 119 [1] (1m 3f 211y, Asco, Sft, Oct 5)
Romanised (IRE) 119 [1] (7f, Curr, Gd, Jul 20)
Sir Dancealot (IRE) 119 [1] (7f, Good, Gd, Jul 30)
The Tin Man 119 [2] (6f, Hayd, Sft, Sep 7)
Wissahickon (USA) 119 [1] (1m 2f, Linw, SD, Feb 2)
Bangkok (IRE) 118 [1] (1m 2f, Linw, SD, Feb 1)
Calyx 118 [1] (6f, Asco, GF, May 1)
Cape Byron 118 [1] (6f, Asco, Gd, Jun 22)
Enbihaar 118 [1] (1m 6f, Good, GF, Aug 3)
Invincible Army 118 [1] (6f, Ncsw, SS, Jun 29)
King's Advice 118 [1] (1m 6f, Good, GF, Aug 3)
Mirage Dancer 118 [3] (1m 3f 211y, Asco, Gd, Jun 22)
Search For A Song (IRE) 118 [1] (1m 6f, Curr, GF, Sep 15)
Soffia 118 [1] (5f, Curr, Gd, Jul 21)
Aspetar (FR) 117 [2] (1m 4f, Newb, GS, Apr 13)
Broome (IRE) 117 [1] (1m 2f, Leop, Sft, Apr 6)

Communique (IRE) 117 [1] (1m 4f, Newj, GF, Jul 11)
Deirdre (JPN) 117 [1] (1m 1f 197y, Good, Gd, Aug 1)
Fox Tal 117 [4] (1m 2f, Asco, Sft, Oct 19)
Gold Mount 117 [1] (1m 5f 188y, York, GS, Jun 15)
Headman 117 [5] (1m 2f, Leop, Gd, Sep 14)
Knight To Behold (IRE) 117 [2] (1m 1f 209y, Sand, GF, Apr 26)
Laurens (FR) 117 [2] (7f, York, GF, Aug 24)
Mabs Cross 117 [1] (5f, Newm, GF, May 4)
Madhmoon (IRE) 117 [2] (1m 4f 6y, Epso, GF, Jun 1)
Marmelo 117 [1] (1m 4f, Newb, GS, Apr 13)
Oh This Is Us (IRE) 117 [1] (1m 1y, Linw, SD, Feb 23)
Roseman (IRE) 117 [1] (1m, Newm, Hvy, Nov 2)
Safe Voyage (IRE) 117 [3] (1m, Asco, Hvy, Oct 19)
Sir Dragonet (IRE) 117 [1] (1m 4f 63y, Ches, GS, May 8)
Sovereign (IRE) 117 [1] (1m 4f, Curr, Gd, Jun 29)
Tabarrak (IRE) 117 [2] (7f, Asco, GF, Sep 7)
Telecaster 117 [1] (1m 2f 56y, York, GF, May 16)
Watch Me (FR) 117 [1] (7f 213y, Asco, Gd, Jun 21)
Weekender 117 [1] (1m 6f 44y, Sali, Gd, Sep 13)
Young Rascal (FR) 117 [1] (1m 3f 219y, Kemw, SS, Nov 4)
Zaaki 117 [1] (1m, Asco, GF, May 1)
Barney Roy 116 [2] (1m, Asco, GF, May 1)
Billesdon Brook 116 [1] (1m, Newm, GS, Oct 5)
Cardsharp 116 [1] (7f, York, GF, May 25)
Danceteria (FR) 116 [4] (1m 1f 209y, Sand, GF, Jul 6)
Dubai Warrior 116 [1] (1m 2f, Linw, SD, Feb 22)
First Eleven 116 [1] (1m 3f 188y, York, GF, May 15)
Forest Of Dean 116 [1] (1m 2f 56y, York, GF, Aug 24)
Happy Power (IRE) 116 [4] (1m, Good, Gd, Jul 31)
Hey Gaman 116 [2] (7f, Good, Gd, Jul 30)
Lah Ti Dar 116 [1] (1m 2f 56y, York, GF, May 16)
Laraaib (IRE) 116 [2] (1m 4f, Newb, Gd, May 18)
Mankib 116 [2] (6f 212y, Hayd, GS, May 11)
Mootasadir 116 [1] (1m 1f 219y, Kemw, SS, Mar 30)
Soldier's Call 116 [2] (5f, York, GF, Aug 23)
Veracious 116 [1] (1m, Newj, GF, Jul 12)
Vintager 116 [3] (1m 1f, Newm, GF, May 4)
Wadilsafa 116 [2] (7f 192y, York, Sft, Jun 14)
Waldpfad (GER) 116 [1] (6f, Newb, GS, Jul 20)
Withhold 116 [1] (2m 110y, Newb, GS, Jul 20)
Accidental Agent 115 [3] (1m, Newb, Gd, May 18)
Buckhurst (IRE) 115 [1] (1m 2f, Curr, Sft, Aug 16)
Constantinople (IRE) 115 [2] (1m 3f 188y, York, Gd, Aug 21)
Dakota Gold 115 [1] (5f, Asco, Sft, Oct 5)
Duke Of Hazzard (FR) 115 [1] (1m, Good, Gd, Aug 24)
Escobar (IRE) 115 [1] (1m, Asco, Hvy, Oct 19)
First In Line 115 [1] (1m 6f, Chmf, SD, Nov 2)
Flag Of Honour (IRE) 115 [2] (1m 2f, Naas, Yld, Apr 13)
Fleeting (IRE) 115 [2] (1m 4f, Curr, Gd, Jul 20)
Great Scot 115 [1] (1m 37y, Hayd, Sft, Sep 7)
Hermosa (IRE) 115 [1] (1m, Curr, GF, May 26)
Hunting Horn (IRE) 115 [6] (1m 1f 209y, Sand, GF, Jul 6)
I Can Fly 115 [3] (1m, Good, Gd, Jul 31)
Magic Wand (IRE) 115 [2] (1m 2f, Leop, Gd, Sep 14)
Make A Challenge (IRE) 115 [1] (6f, Curr, Hvy, Oct 13)
Mehdaayih 115 [2] (1m 1f 197y, Good, Gd, Aug 1)
Move Swiftly 115 [1] (1m, Asco, Sft, Jun 19)
Mr Lupton (IRE) 115 [1] (6f, Curr, GF, May 25)
On The Warpath 115 [1] (6f, Newm, Gd, May 5)
One Master 115 [2] (1m, Newj, GF, Jul 12)
Oxted 115 [1] (5f 143y, Donc, GF, Sep 14)
Rawdaa 115 [2] (1m 2f 56y, York, GF, May 16)
Red Verdon (USA) 115 [1] (1m 5f 188y, York, GF, Jul 13)
Royal Line 115 [3] (1m 7f 127y, Asco, GS, Oct 19)
Salouen (IRE) 115 [4] (1m 3f 211y, Asco, GS, Jul 27)
Sharja Bridge 115 [2] (1m, Sand, GF, Apr 29)
Southern France (IRE) 115 [1] (1m 6f, Curr, Sft, Aug 16)
Star Catcher 115 [1] (1m 3f 133y, Asco, Sft, Oct 19)
Alpha Delphini 114 [2] (5f, Hayd, GF, May 25)
Austrian School (IRE) 114 [1] (1m 5f 216y, Muss, Gd, Apr 20)
Auxerre (IRE) 114 [1] (1m, Donc, Gd, Mar 30)
Baghdad (FR) 114 [1] (1m 3f 211y, Asco, Gd, Jun 21)
Bin Battuta 114 [1] (1m 2f, Chmf, SD, Sep 28)
Danehill Kodiac (IRE) 114 [2] (1m 3f 218y, Good, GF, May 25)

Delphinia (IRE) 114 [2] (1m 3f 133y, Asco, Sft, Oct 19)
Falcon Eight (IRE) 114 [1] (2m 50y, Sand, GF, Jul 6)
Forest Ranger (IRE) 114 [2] (1m 1f, Newm, GF, Apr 18)
Glorious Journey 114 [1] (7f, Newb, Sft, Aug 17)
Gulliver 114 [1] (6f 16y, Souw, SD, Jan 28)
Hamish 114 [1] (1m 5f 188y, York, Sft, Oct 11)
Iridessa (IRE) 114 [1] (1m, Leop, Gd, Sep 14)
Judicial (IRE) 114 [1] (6f 1y, Linw, SD, Nov 16)
Latrobe (IRE) 114 [4] (1m 1f 212y, Asco, Sft, Jun 18)
Lord North (IRE) 114 [1] (1m, Asco, Hvy, Oct 19)
Mohaather 114 [1] (7f, Newb, GS, Apr 13)
Mohawk (IRE) 114 [1] (1m 1f, Leop, Gd, Jul 18)
Mubtasim (IRE) 114 [1] (7f, Newm, GF, Apr 18)
Mustajeer 114 [1] (1m 5f 188y, York, GF, Aug 24)
Pivoine (IRE) 114 [1] (1m 2f 56y, York, GF, Jul 13)
Raheen House (IRE) 114 [3] (1m 5f 188y, York, GF, Jul 13)
Raising Sand 114 [1] (7f, Asco, GS, Jul 27)
Raymond Tusk (IRE) 114 [4] (1m 5f 188y, York, GF, Aug 24)
Red Galileo 114 [2] (1m 5f 188y, York, GF, Aug 24)
Sangarius 114 [1] (1m 1f 212y, Asco, Sft, Jun 20)
Shine So Bright 114 [1] (7f, York, GF, Aug 24)
Sir Ron Priestley 114 [2] (1m 6f 115y, Donc, GF, Sep 14)
Skardu 114 [4] (7f 213y, Asco, Gd, Jun 18)
Space Traveller 114 [1] (1m, Leop, Gd, Sep 14)
Tis Marvellous 114 [1] (5f, Asco, GF, Jul 13)
Walkinthesand (IRE) 114 [1] (1m 2f, Newj, GF, Jul 12)
War Glory (IRE) 114 [1] (7f 1y, Linw, SS, Oct 31)
Afaak 113 [1] (1m, Asco, Sft, Jun 19)
Alrajaa 113 [1] (1m 1y, Linw, SD, Nov 16)
Anapurna 113 [1] (1m 4f 6y, Epso, Gd, May 31)
Barsanti (IRE) 113 [3] (1m 3f 218y, Good, GF, May 25)
Beat Le Bon (FR) 113 [1] (1m, Good, GF, Aug 2)
Ben Vrackie 113 [2] (1m 3f 211y, Asco, Gd, Jun 21)
Caspian Prince (IRE) 113 [9] (5f, Epso, GF, Jun 1)
Dashing Willoughby 113 [4] (1m 4f, Newj, GF, Jul 11)
Desert Fire (IRE) 113 [1] (1m 2f, Chmf, SD, Sep 4)
Desert Skyline (IRE) 113 [1] (1m 6f, Newj, GF, Jul 12)
Epaulement (IRE) 113 [1] (1m 3f 140y, Hayd, Sft, Sep 5)
Forever In Dreams (IRE) 113 [3] (6f, Asco, Hvy, Oct 19)
Fox Chairman (IRE) 113 [1] (1m 2f, Newb, Sft, Jul 20)
Gibbs Hill (GER) 113 [3] (1m 2f, Newb, GF, Sep 21)
Global Giant 113 [1] (1m 1f 104y, Wolw, SD, Jan 6)
Houtzen (AUS) 113 [2] (5f, Good, GF, Aug 2)
Il Paradiso (USA) 113 [2] (2m 56y, York, GF, Aug 23)
Indyco (FR) 113 [2] (1m 1y, Linw, SD, Apr 19)
Kastasa (IRE) 113 [1] (2m, Curr, Yld, Sep 28)
Le Brivido (FR) 113 [5] (1m, Asco, Gd, Jun 18)
Librisa Breeze 113 [2] (7f, Newb, Sft, Aug 17)
Loxley (IRE) 113 [2] (1m 4f, Newm, Gd, Sep 27)
Major Jumbo 113 [1] (6f 17y, Ches, GS, Aug 4)
Making Miracles 113 [1] (2m 2f 140y, Ches, Sft, May 10)
Masar (IRE) 113 [1] (1m 3f 211y, Asco, Gd, Jun 22)
Mekong 113 [4] (1m 7f 127y, Asco, GS, Oct 19)
Mojito (IRE) 113 [1] (1m, Sand, GF, Jul 6)
Nayef Road (IRE) 113 [3] (1m 6f 115y, Donc, GF, Sep 14)
Pablo Escobarr (IRE) 113 [1] (1m 3f 219y, Kemw, SS, Dec 4)
Snazzy Jazzy (IRE) 113 [1] (6f, Sali, Sft, Jun 16)
Space Blues (IRE) 113 [1] (7f, Asco, Gd, Jun 22)
Spanish Mission (USA) 113 [3] (1m 3f 218y, Good, Gd, Aug 1)
Speak In Colours 113 [4] (7f, Good, Gd, Jul 30)
Straight Right (FR) 113 [2] (7f 14y, Ncsw, SD, Jan 22)
Suedois (FR) 113 [1] (7f, Good, Gd, Aug 25)
Technician (IRE) 113 [1] (1m 5f 61y, Newb, Sft, Aug 17)
Turgenev 113 [2] (1m, Good, Gd, Aug 24)
Vale Of Kent (IRE) 113 [2] (7f 192y, York, Gd, Aug 22)
Wells Farhh Go (IRE) 113 [1] (1m 4f, Newj, GF, Jun 29)
Air Pilot 112 [1] (1m 1f 197y, Good, Hvy, Sep 25)
Amade (IRE) 112 [1] (2m, Chmf, SD, Mar 7)
Beshaayir 112 [1] (5f, Asco, GF, May 25)
Capri (IRE) 112 [6] (2m 3f 210y, Asco, Sft, Jun 20)
Cheval Grand (JPN) 112 [8] (1m 2f 56y, York, Gd, Aug 21)
Decrypt 112 [3] (1m, Curr, GF, May 25)
Downdraft (IRE) 112 [2] (1m 6f, Curr, Sft, Aug 16)
Equilateral 112 [2] (5f, Newm, GF, May 4)

Fairyland (IRE) 112 [1] (5f, Curr, Gd, Sep 15)
Fanny Logan (IRE) 112 [1] (1m 1f 201y, Sali, Sft, Aug 14)
Flight Risk (IRE) 112 [1] (7f, Cork, Gd, Aug 17)
Good Effort (IRE) 112 [1] (6f 1y, Linw, SD, Feb 1)
Indeed 112 [1] (1m, Newj, Gd, Jul 20)
Just Wonderful (USA) 112 [3] (1m, Leop, Gd, Sep 14)
Kelly's Dino (FR) 112 [1] (1m 4f, Newj, Gd, Aug 9)
Keystroke 112 [3] (6f, Asco, Sft, Oct 5)
Khuzaam (USA) 112 [2] (1m, Kemw, SS, Nov 20)
Kynren (IRE) 112 [1] (7f, Asco, Sft, Oct 5)
Larchmont Lad (IRE) 112 [3] (7f, Good, Gd, Aug 25)
Leo De Fury (IRE) 112 [2] (1m 2f, Curr, Sft, Aug 16)
Magnetic Charm 112 [2] (1m, Asco, Gd, Jun 21)
New Graduate (IRE) 112 [1] (1m, Ripo, Gd, Apr 27)
Pink Dogwood (IRE) 112 [2] (1m 4f 6y, Epso, Gd, May 31)
Set Piece 112 [1] (1m, Kemw, SS, Nov 20)
Setting Sail 112 [1] (1m 2f 17y, Epso, Gd, Aug 26)
Shabaaby 112 [1] (6f, Hayd, GS, May 11)
So Perfect (USA) 112 [2] (5f, Curr, Gd, Sep 15)
Sun Maiden 112 [3] (1m 3f 133y, Asco, Sft, Oct 19)
Tropics (USA) 112 [3] (5f, Chmf, SD, Aug 16)
True Self (IRE) 112 [6] (1m 5f 188y, York, GF, Aug 24)
Trueshan (FR) 112 [1] (1m 5f 61y, Newb, Hvy, Oct 25)
Turjomaan (USA) 112 [2] (1m, Good, GF, Aug 2)
UAE Jewel 112 [1] (1m 2f, Newm, Gd, May 4)
Via Serendipity 112 [1] (1m, Kemw, SS, Oct 10)
What's The Story 112 [1] (7f 192y, York, Gd, Aug 22)
Angel Alexander (IRE) 111 [1] (6f, Ayr, Gd, Sep 21)
Bye Bye Hong Kong (USA) 111 [1] (1m 31y, Wind, Gd, May 13)
Called To The Bar (IRE) 111 [8] (2m 3f 210y, Asco, Sft, Jun 20)
Copper Knight (IRE) 111 [2] (5f, Ncsw, SS, Jun 28)
Corinthia Knight (IRE) 111 [2] (5f 21y, Wolw, SD, Nov 26)
Court House (IRE) 111 [2] (1m 2f, Linw, SD, Feb 23)
Dame Malliot 111 [1] (1m 4f, Newj, Gd, Jul 20)
Danzeno 111 [3] (6f, York, Sft, Oct 12)
Dramatic Queen (USA) 111 [2] (1m 3f 175y, Hayd, GF, Jul 6)
Eagles By Day (IRE) 111 [3] (1m 3f 211y, Asco, GS, Jun 21)
El Astronaute (IRE) 111 [1] (5f, Curr, Yld, Jun 27)
Enjazaat 111 [1] (6f, Kemw, SS, Oct 9)
Extra Elusive 111 [2] (1m 2f 209y, Sand, GF, Jul 5)
Feliciana De Vega 111 [1] (1m 1f, Newm, Sft, Oct 12)
Flaming Spear (IRE) 111 [5] (7f, Good, Gd, Jul 30)
George Bowen (IRE) 111 [1] (6f, Kemw, SS, Mar 30)
Gustavus Weston (IRE) 111 [1] (6f, Curr, Sft, Aug 9)
Hathal (USA) 111 [1] (1m 142y, Wolw, SD, Feb 4)
Hazapour (IRE) 111 [1] (1m, Leop, Yld, May 12)
Jubiloso 111 [3] (7f 213y, Asco, Gd, Jun 21)
Kick On 111 [1] (1m, Sali, GS, Aug 15)
Lady Kaya (IRE) 111 [2] (1m, Newm, Gd, May 5)
Main Edition (IRE) 111 [1] (7f, Redc, Hvy, Oct 5)
Maqsad (FR) 111 [1] (1m 2f, Newm, Gd, May 5)
Mildenberger 111 [3] (1m 7f 218y, Kemw, SS, Jan 4)
Momkin (IRE) 111 [2] (1m, Newm, GF, Apr 17)
Mordin (IRE) 111 [1] (1m 37y, Hayd, Sft, Apr 27)
Mountain Angel (IRE) 111 [1] (1m 2f 17y, Epso, Gd, May 31)
Mountain Hunter (USA) 111 [1] (1m 4f, Newm, Gd, Sep 27)
Outbox 111 [2] (1m 6f, Good, GF, Aug 3)
Pondus 111 [2] (1m 2f 100y, Hayd, Hvy, Aug 10)
Prince Of Arran 111 [3] (1m 3f 219y, Kemw, SS, Sep 7)
Rock Eagle 111 [4] (1m 3f 218y, Good, GF, May 25)
Sextant 111 [1] (1m 4f 63y, Ches, Gd, Sep 14)
Stake Acclaim (IRE) 111 [1] (5f 34y, Newb, Sft, Apr 12)
Tarnawa (IRE) 111 [1] (1m 4f, Cork, Sft, Aug 17)
Twilight Payment (IRE) 111 [1] (1m 6f, Curr, Gd, Jun 28)
Willie John 111 [2] (1m 1f 197y, Good, GF, May 25)
Worth Waiting 111 [1] (1m 1f, Newm, Gd, May 5)
Yafta 111 [2] (6f, Newm, GF, Apr 17)
Above The Rest (IRE) 110 [1] (7f 14y, Ncsw, SD, Dec 14)
Anna Nerium 110 [1] (1m 113y, Epso, GF, Jun 1)
Best Solution (IRE) 110 [7] (1m 3f 219y, Kemw, SS, Sep 7)
Big Country (IRE) 110 [2] (1m 2f, Linw, SD, Feb 2)
Bless Him (IRE) 110 [1] (1m, Asco, Gd, Sep 6)
Buffer Zone 110 [1] (6f, Curr, Gd, Sep 15)
Byron Flyer 110 [2] (1m 4f 6y, Epso, GF, Jun 1)

Commander Cole 110 [2] (1m 2f, Chmf, SD, Sep 28)
Documenting 110 [2] (7f, Chmf, SD, Sep 21)
Emblazoned (IRE) 110 [2] (6f, Hayd, GS, May 11)
Faylaq 110 [1] (1m 2f 219y, Kemw, SS, Sep 25)
Flashcard (IRE) 110 [3] (1m, Sali, GS, Aug 15)
Funny Kid (USA) 110 [2] (2m 56y, Ncsw, SD, Dec 14)
Gifted Master (IRE) 110 [2] (7f 1y, Linw, SS, Oct 31)
Gifts Of Gold (IRE) 110 [2] (1m 2f 23y, Yarm, Fm, Aug 25)
Grey Britain 110 [1] (1m 7f 169y, Linw, SD, Feb 1)
Lucius Tiberius (IRE) 110 [2] (1m 3f 175y, Hayd, GF, Jul 6)
Maid In India (IRE) 110 [1] (5f 34y, Newb, GF, Sep 21)
Moyassar 110 [1] (6f, Newm, Gd, May 4)
Muthmir 110 [5] (5f, Epso, GF, Jun 1)
Qabala (USA) 110 [3] (1m, Newm, Gd, May 5)
Qaysar (FR) 110 [1] (1m, Donc, GF, Sep 14)
Raucous 110 [1] (6f 3y, Yarm, GF, Jul 10)
Red Tea 110 [1] (1m, Curr, Yld, May 6)
Sea The Lion (IRE) 110 [2] (1m 4f, Curr, Gd, Jun 27)
South Pacific 110 [6] (2m, Good, Gd, Jul 30)
Star Of Bengal 110 [1] (1m 2f, Chmf, SD, May 23)
Stratum 110 [1] (2m 2f, Newm, Sft, Oct 12)
Aircraft Carrier (IRE) 109 [1] (2m 120y, Wolw, SD, Jan 14)
Ambassadorial (USA) 109 [3] (1m, Chmf, SD, Aug 16)
Angel's Hideaway (IRE) 109 [4] (1m, Newm, Gd, May 5)
Another Batt (IRE) 109 [6] (1m, Donc, Gd, Mar 30)
Aquarium 109 [4] (1m 3f 218y, Good, GF, Aug 2)
Beringer 109 [2] (1m 1f, Newm, Gd, Sep 28)
Bielsa (IRE) 109 [3] (6f 2y, Donc, Hvy, Oct 25)
Bowerman 109 [1] (1m 5y, Ncsw, SD, Apr 29)
Chatez (IRE) 109 [1] (1m, Newb, GS, Apr 13)
Chief Ironside 109 [3] (1m 113y, Epso, GF, Jun 1)
Clon Coulis (IRE) 109 [2] (1m, Asco, Sft, Jun 19)
Count Calabash (IRE) 109 [1] (1m 3f 219y, Kemw, SS, Feb 16)
Crossed Baton 109 [1] (1m 2f, Linw, SD, Nov 16)
Crowned Eagle 109 [5] (1m 4f 10y, Ripo, Gd, Apr 27)
Doctor Sardonicus 109 [6] (5f 6y, Linw, SD, Mar 23)
El Misk 109 [1] (1m 3f 219y, Kemw, SS, Oct 30)
Elwazir 109 [2] (1m 2f 43y, Donc, GF, Sep 11)
Fabricate 109 [4] (1m 1f 209y, Sand, GF, Apr 26)
Final Venture 109 [2] (5f, Asco, Gd, Aug 10)
First Nation 109 [3] (1m 1f 209y, Sand, GF, Jul 5)
Fox Power (IRE) 109 [2] (1m 142y, Wolw, SD, Feb 3)
Guaranteed 109 [3] (1m 2f, Curr, Sft, Aug 16)
Habub (USA) 109 [5] (1m 1y, Linw, SD, Feb 22)
Imprimis (USA) 109 [6] (5f, Asco, Gd, Jun 18)
Key Victory (IRE) 109 [4] (1m, Sand, GF, Jul 6)
Keyser Soze (IRE) 109 [1] (7f 14y, Ncsw, SS, Feb 20)
Lake Volta (IRE) 109 [1] (6f, Good, GF, May 24)
Lavender's Blue (IRE) 109 [4] (1m, Newm, GS, Oct 5)
Leodis Dream (IRE) 109 [1] (5f, Chmf, SD, Sep 21)
Lim's Cruiser (AUS) 109 [6] (6f, Newj, GF, Jul 13)
Merhoob (IRE) 109 [2] (5f 6y, Linw, SD, Mar 23)
Micro Manage (IRE) 109 [1] (1m 4f, Curr, Yld, Jun 7)
Mitchum Swagger 109 [4] (1m 31y, Wind, Gd, May 13)
Mount Everest (IRE) 109 [2] (1m, Leop, Hvy, Oct 19)
Never No More (IRE) 109 [1] (7f, Leop, Sft, Apr 6)
Norway (IRE) 109 [1] (1m 4f, Leop, Gd, Sep 14)
Nyaleti (IRE) 109 [2] (1m 2f 42y, Ncsw, SS, Jun 28)
Ornate 109 [1] (5f, Beve, Gd, Jun 18)
Pincheck (IRE) 109 [1] (1m, Leop, Gd, Sep 14)
Proschema (IRE) 109 [3] (2m 56y, Ncsw, SS, Jun 29)
Qarasu (IRE) 109 [2] (1m 1f 197y, Good, Hvy, Sep 25)
Raakib Alhawa (IRE) 109 [1] (1m 3f 99y, Wind, GF, Aug 24)
Rainbow Dreamer 109 [1] (2m 120y, Wolw, SD, Jan 13)
Robin Of Navan (FR) 109 [3] (1m, Asco, GF, May 1)
Rocket Action 109 [1] (5f 21y, Wolw, SD, Nov 26)
Royal Intervention (IRE) 109 [1] (6f, York, GF, Jul 12)
Salute The Soldier (GER) 109 [1] (7f, Asco, GF, Sep 7)
Shaman (IRE) 109 [5] (7f 213y, Asco, Gd, Jun 14)
Spirit Of Appin (IRE) 109 [3] (1m 3f 219y, Kemw, SS, Nov 4)
Stargazer (IRE) 109 [1] (2m 56y, Ncsw, SD, Apr 1)
Tabdeed 109 [1] (1m 2y, Donc, GS, Aug 3)
Tarboosh 109 [1] (5f 1y, Muss, Sft, Oct 14)
The Grand Visir 109 [1] (2m 3f 210y, Asco, GS, Jun 18)

Thundering Blue (USA) **109** [3] (1m 1f 197y, Good, GF, May 25)
Twist 'n' Shake **109** [4] (7f 213y, Asco, Gd, Jun 21)
UAE Prince (IRE) **109** [1] (1m 2f 56y, York, GF, May 17)
Urban Icon **109** [2] (7f 3y, Epso, Gd, May 31)
Victory Wave (USA) **109** [1] (1m, Chmf, SD, Jun 6)
Vintage Brut **109** [4] (6f, Hayd, GS, May 11)
Waldstern **109** [4] (1m 3f, Newb, GF, Sep 21)
Watersmeet **109** [1] (1m 7f 169y, Linw, SD, Apr 19)
Who's Steph (IRE) **109** [1] (1m 1f 100y, Gowr, Yld, May 5)
Ancient Spirit (GER) **108** [2] (1m 2f, Leop, Hvy, Oct 19)
Antilles (USA) **108** [2] (1m, Chmf, SD, Apr 11)
Antonia De Vega (IRE) **108** [6] (1m 3f 133y, Asco, Sft, Oct 19)
Breton Rock (IRE) **108** [3] (7f 6y, Donc, GF, Sep 14)
Cenotaph (USA) **108** [2] (6f, Kemw, SS, Sep 4)
Century Dream (IRE) **108** [2] (1m, Newm, Hvy, Nov 2)
Cleonte (IRE) **108** [2] (2m 1f 197y, Donc, GF, Sep 13)
Cypress Creek (IRE) **108** [8] (1m 6f, Curr, GF, Sep 15)
Dark Vision (IRE) **108** [4] (1m 2f, Newj, GF, Jul 12)
Davydenko **108** [1] (1m 2f 43y, Donc, GF, Sep 12)
Elegiac **108** [2] (2m, Chmf, SD, Mar 7)
Festival Of Ages (USA) **108** [2] (2m 120y, Wolw, SD, Jan 14)
Floating Artist **108** [4] (1m 3f 218y, Good, Gd, Aug 1)
Garrus (IRE) **108** [1] (5f, York, GF, May 16)
Glendevon (USA) **108** [3] (1m 1y, Linw, SD, Apr 19)
Highgarden **108** [3] (1m 6f, Chmf, SD, Jun 19)
King Ottokar (FR) **108** [3] (1m 1f 212y, Asco, Sft, Jun 20)
Klassique **108** [5] (1m 3f 133y, Asco, Sft, Oct 19)
Lancelot Du Lac (ITY) **108** [4] (5f 21y, Wolw, SD, Feb 21)
Laugh A Minute **108** [4] (7f, Leic, GF, Apr 27)
Lord George (IRE) **108** [3] (1m 4f, Linw, SD, Jan 19)
Lucky Deal **108** [1] (2m 45y, Hayd, GF, May 25)
Magic Circle (IRE) **108** [9] (2m 3f 210y, Asco, Sft, Jun 20)
Makzeem **108** [1] (7f, Newb, GS, Jul 20)
Manuela De Vega (IRE) **108** [2] (1m 6f, Good, GF, Aug 3)
Marnie James **108** [3] (5f, York, GF, May 16)
Master The World (IRE) **108** [3] (1m 1f 219y, Kemw, SS, Mar 30)
Miss O Connor (IRE) **108** [1] (1m 37y, Hayd, Hvy, Aug 10)
Motafaawit (IRE) **108** [1] (7f, Asco, Sft, May 10)
Pactolus (IRE) **108** [2] (1m 1f 104y, Wolw, SD, Dec 26)
Pogo (IRE) **108** [1] (7f 192y, York, GF, Aug 23)
Prince Eiji **108** [3] (1m 1f, Newm, Sft, Oct 12)
Raise You (IRE) **108** [3] (1m 2f 100y, Hayd, Hvy, Aug 10)
Recon Mission (IRE) **108** [4] (5f, Asco, Gd, Aug 10)
Salateen **108** [1] (1m 1y, Linw, SS, Jan 5)
Sea Of Class (IRE) **108** [5] (1m 1f 212y, Asco, Sft, Jun 19)
Shades Of Blue (IRE) **108** [2] (6f, York, GF, Jul 12)
So Beloved **108** [2] (7f, York, GF, May 25)
Success Days (IRE) **108** [3] (1m 2f 70y, Ches, Sft, May 10)
Surfman **108** [3] (1m 2f 56y, York, GF, May 16)
Victory Bond **108** [1] (1m 2f, Linw, SD, Dec 4)
Who Dares Wins (IRE) **108** [1] (2m 56y, Ncsw, SS, Jun 29)
Alright Sunshine (IRE) **107** [1] (2m 1f 100y, Ayr, Gd, Sep 20)
Arecibo (FR) **107** [2] (5f, Asco, Sft, Oct 5)
Awesometank **107** [2] (1m 113y, Epso, GF, Jun 1)
Bayshore Freeway (IRE) **107** [1] (1m 6f, Chmf, SD, Jun 19)
Bedouin's Story **107** [2] (1m, Chmf, SD, Sep 12)
Blenheim Palace (IRE) **107** [3] (1m 4f, Leop, Gd, Sep 14)
Cape Of Good Hope (IRE) **107** [1] (1m 2f 17y, Epso, Gd, Apr 24)
Castle Lady (IRE) **107** [5] (7f 213y, Asco, Gd, Jun 21)
Coolagh Forest (IRE) **107** [1] (1m 2f 56y, York, Sft, Oct 12)
Corelli (USA) **107** [2] (1m 3f 188y, York, GF, Aug 23)
Dandhu **107** [1] (7f, Newb, GS, Apr 13)
Dazzling Dan (IRE) **107** [1] (6f, Newj, Gd, Aug 17)
Downforce (IRE) **107** [2] (6f, Curr, Sft, Sep 28)
Dubawi Fifty **107** [2] (2m 56y, Ncsw, SD, Jun 29)
Duneflower (IRE) **107** [1] (7f 213y, Asco, GF, Jul 26)
Glen Shiel **107** [3] (7f 14y, Ncsw, SD, Feb 19)
Gordon Lord Byron (IRE) **107** [2] (6f, Dunw, SD, Nov 1)
Here Comes When (IRE) **107** [4] (1m 1f 209y, Sand, GF, May 23)
I Am Superman (IRE) **107** [1] (7f, Naas, Gd, Jul 24)
Ispolini **107** [4] (1m 5f 188y, York, GF, May 17)
Jash (IRE) **107** [1] (7f, Newm, Gd, May 18)
Lancaster House (IRE) **107** [1] (1m 1f, List, Sft, Sep 9)
Land Of Legends (IRE) **107** [1] (7f, Good, GF, Aug 3)

Marie's Diamond (IRE) **107** [1] (1m 6y, Pont, Gd, Jul 28)
Mutamaasik **107** [1] (7f 6y, Donc, GF, Sep 12)
Numerian (IRE) **107** [2] (1m, Curr, GF, Sep 15)
Pallasator **107** [2] (2m 5f 143y, Asco, Gd, Jun 22)
Pretty Pollyanna **107** [4] (6f, Newj, GF, Jul 13)
Private Secretary **107** [3] (1m 3f 211y, Asco, GS, Jun 21)
Raa Atoll **107** [3] (1m 6f, Curr, Gd, Jun 28)
Rasima **107** [6] (1m 3f 219y, Kemw, SS, Sep 7)
Riven Light (IRE) **107** [6] (1m 1f 212y, Asco, Sft, Jun 18)
Roulston Scar (IRE) **107** [1] (6f, York, Gd, Sep 8)
Royal Birth **107** [1] (6f, Chmf, SD, Sep 28)
Scentasia **107** [1] (1m 2f, Linw, SD, Nov 16)
Sea Of Faith (IRE) **107** [1] (1m 4f 5y, Sali, GS, Aug 15)
Seniority **107** [3] (1m, Chmf, SD, Aug 23)
Sergei Prokofiev (CAN) **107** [1] (5f 164y, Nava, Gd, Mar 30)
Silent Attack **107** [2] (1m 1y, Linw, SD, Feb 8)
Silver Line (IRE) **107** [3] (1m, Sand, Gd, Sep 18)
Summerghand (IRE) **107** [2] (6f, Ripo, Sft, Aug 17)
The King (IRE) **107** [3] (1m 2f, Curr, Yld, May 6)
Woody Creek **107** [2] (6f, Curr, Sft, Aug 9)
Agrotera (IRE) **106** [1] (1m, Kemw, SS, Apr 20)
Air Raid **106** [1] (6f 6y, Hami, Sft, Jul 19)
Amazing Red (IRE) **106** [3] (1m 6f, Good, GF, May 25)
Another Touch **106** [1] (1m 5y, Ncsw, SS, Jan 8)
Arbalet (IRE) **106** [4] (1m 3ty, Wind, GF, Jun 29)
Arcanada (IRE) **106** [4] (7f 36y, Wolw, SD, Mar 9)
Arthur Kitt **106** [3] (1m 3f 179y, Leic, GS, Jun 10)
Azano **106** [2] (7f, Newm, Gd, May 18)
Blown By Wind **106** [1] (7f 33y, Muss, Sft, Oct 14)
Breden (IRE) **106** [1] (1m, Newb, Gd, May 18)
Broad Street **106** [3] (1m 4f, Leop, GF, Aug 8)
Cap Francais **106** [2] (1m 2f 17y, Epso, Gd, Apr 24)
Certain Lad **106** [1] (1m 2f, Ayr, Gd, Sep 21)
Charles Kingsley **106** [2] (1m 6f 115y, Donc, GF, Sep 13)
Dan's Dream **106** [2] (6f, Curr, Yld, Jun 7)
Deja (FR) **106** [1] (1m 3f 219y, Kemw, SS, Jul 3)
Di Fede (IRE) **106** [1] (7f, Asco, Sft, Oct 5)
Eightsome Reel **106** [4] (1m 1f 212y, Asco, Sft, Jun 20)
Encore D'or **106** [3] (5f, Chmf, SD, Jun 8)
Fanaar (IRE) **106** [3] (7f 192y, York, GF, Aug 23)
Fayez (IRE) **106** [1] (1m 1f 197y, Good, Gd, Jul 30)
Fifth Position (IRE) **106** [5] (1m 1f 209y, Sand, GF, Jul 5)
First Contact (IRE) **106** [6] (1m 1f, Newm, GF, Apr 18)
Four White Socks **106** [1] (1m 1f 100y, Gowr, Sft, Sep 26)
Fox Champion (IRE) **106** [7] (7f 213y, Asco, Gd, Jun 19)
Francis Xavier (IRE) **106** [1] (1m 4f 98y, Ncsw, SS, Nov 21)
Fujaira Prince (IRE) **106** [3] (1m 3f 211y, Asco, Gd, Jun 21)
Goring (GER) **106** [1] (7f 1y, Linw, SD, Apr 19)
Hameem **106** [1] (1m 3f 219y, Kemw, SS, Aug 5)
Harmony Spirit (IRE) **106** [1] (6f, Asco, Gd, Aug 10)
Hey Jonesy (IRE) **106** [2] (6f 212y, Hayd, GS, Jul 19)
Hidden Message (USA) **106** [1] (1m, Sand, GF, Jul 6)
Humanitarian (USA) **106** [7] (1m 4f 6y, Epso, GF, Jun 1)
Iconic Choice **106** [7] (1m, Newm, Gd, May 5)
Imaging **106** [2] (7f 100y, Tipp, Hvy, Oct 6)
Intuitive (IRE) **106** [1] (7f, Kemw, SS, Oct 9)
Inverleigh (IRE) **106** [1] (5f 164y, Nava, Yld, Apr 28)
Jahbath **106** [1] (1m 13y, Souw, SD, Jan 24)
Johnny Drama (IRE) **106** [2] (1m 2f 56y, York, GF, Aug 24)
Kaeso **106** [2] (7f, Asco, GS, Jul 27)
Khafoo Shememi (IRE) **106** [3] (1m 6y, Pont, Gd, Jul 28)
Kuwait Currency (USA) **106** [3] (1m 1y, Linw, SD, Dec 31)
Le Don De Vie **106** [1] (1m 1f 197y, Good, Gd, Aug 25)
Low Sun **106** [4] (2m 2f 140y, Ches, Sft, May 10)
Marshall Jennings (IRE) **106** [3] (1m, Curr, Gd, Jun 29)
Massif Central (IRE) **106** [2] (1m 2f 150y, Dunw, SD, Oct 11)
Monica Sheriff **106** [1] (1m 6f, Good, Hvy, Sep 25)
Nazeef **106** [1] (1m, Newm, GF, Sep 21)
Perfection **106** [1] (6f, Pont, Gd, Aug 18)
Persian Moon (IRE) **106** [2] (1m 3f 211y, Asco, GF, Sep 7)
Petrus (IRE) **106** [3] (1m, Sand, GF, Jul 6)
Pocket Dynamo (USA) **106** [2] (5f 8y, Nott, GF, Apr 10)

INDEX OF HORSES

INDEX OF HORSES

Want the
BIGGEST
offers?

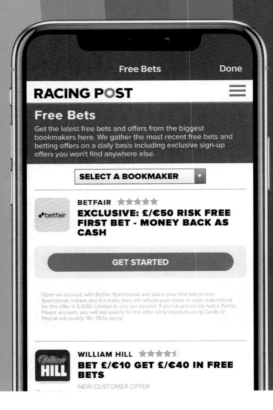

racingpost.com/freebets